Journeys with a Brother

Other Books by Bartholomew

"I Come As a Brother": *A Remembrance of Illusions*

From the Heart of a Gentle Brother

Planetary Brother

Reflections of an Elder Brother: *Awakening from the Dream*

All of the above books may be ordered directly from:

White Dove International
P.O. Box 1000
Taos, NM 87571

or by calling Hay House, Inc., at **(800) 654-5126**

❋ ❋

Informal tapes of 600 recorded sessions with Bartholomew, as well as information on talks by Mary-Margaret Moore, may be ordered from:

Mary-Margaret Moore
P.O. Box 1414
Ranchos de Taos, NM 87557

❋ ❋

Please visit the Hay House Website at: **www.hayhouse.com**

Journeys with a Brother

Japan to India

Bartholomew

Hay House, Inc.
Carlsbad, CA

Published and distributed in the United States by:
Hay House, Inc., P.O. Box 5100, Carlsbad, CA 92018-5100 • (800) 654-5126 • (800) 650-5115 (fax)

Edited by: Joy Franklin and Mary-Margaret Moore • *Designed by:* Renée G. Noël
Hay House editorial: Jill Kramer

Library of Congress Cataloging-in-Publication Data

Bartholomew (Spirit)
        Journeys with a brother : Japan to India / Bartholomew.
            p.   cm.
        Originally published: Taos, N.M. : High Mesa Foundation, 1995.
        ISBN 1-56170-389-3
        1. Spirit writings. I. Bstan-'dzin-rgya-mtsho, Dalai Lama XIV,
1935– II. Title.
BF 1301.B3574   1999
133.9'3–dc21

                                     99-34632
                                     CIP

Originally published by High Mesa Press, January 1995

ISBN 1-56170-389-3

02 01 00 99   4 3 2 1
First Printing, Hay House Edition, September 1999

Printed in Canada

This book is dedicated to
Seekers and Finders
everywhere.

❋ ❋

With the deepest appreciation and
gratitude for Bartholomew's
loving tenacity.

❋ ❋

Contents

Caught Between a Preface and an Acknowledgment

As editor of the Bartholomew books, it has always been my delightful assignment to choose what particular material to use and what form it should take. The journey described in this book happened seven years ago but remains vividly present to this day. It was a journey that often demanded that we change our previous notions of reality, and challenged us to uncover the personal lessons embedded in our experiences. It was perhaps the most demanding physically, and at the same time the most deeply rewarding, of all our adventures. The events as we lived them were such an intimate reflection of Bartholomew's teachings that I felt a narrative would be the best form for this book to take. I hope it will give the reader an opportunity to relate to his or her own wisdom in a new, more personal way.

I would like to express my gratitude to those intrepid explorers who accompanied us and who were willing to reveal their fears as well as their triumphs so the reader could share all our experiences. The first-person impressions are my contribution to the story, and the spiritual wisdom and light-hearted humor come from Bartholomew.

My appreciation to Justin Moore, who kept the tapes and equipment functioning; to Phyllis Johnson for her uncanny ability to translate our editorial scribbles into something more understandable; and to Mary-Margaret Moore, for the graciousness, patience, and good humor with which she met my constant requests for more information, more editing, and more interviews.

And my deepest gratitude to Bartholomew, who has transformed the idea of a journey home into the possibility of freedom in this lifetime.

— Joy Franklin, editor

Introduction

This book is about a tour that a group of Americans and Australians took with Bartholomew to Japan and India. It brings to life the wondrous and frightening experiences that were a part of each of many such tours we took together during the 18 years we spent working worldwide with Bartholomew.

While on these trips, we saw many amazing things, visited many exotic and beautiful places, and met many fascinating people. But the most important part of each tour was, for me, what went on in our "inner world." Each time we traveled on the surface of the planet, we were changed in the deep, unseen inner core of our Being. We were changed in dramatic and inspiring ways, and those changes never left. In Christian terms, this could perhaps be called "the quickening of the spirit."

The trip to Japan and India played a great part in that "quickening" process for me. I had studied Zen Buddhism for years before my work with Bartholomew, and still find it to be one of the clearest mirrors for Truth on the Earth plane. To actually experience some of that clarity in the Zen gardens and temples of Kyoto was a high point. When we found ourselves atop a mountain in a shrine that had been the focus of pilgrims for centuries, none of us needed to "try" to feel the power of the site. The power was absolutely present, as close as breath, as warm as the sunlight. We cried, we laughed, we became Silence Itself. Wonder of wonders.

Then, in the high Himalayan mountains, again the overwhelming Presence of Silence. No need to "find it" or "tune in to it." All that was needed was the willingness to fall out of the mental chatter of mind and fall into the open arms of the Silent Moment, filled with vast peace. No matter how difficult the external world was—and we had moments of extreme discomfort, both emotionally and physically—we always felt the ever-present option to fall once again into that ever-waiting Space. Suspended high above the clouds, looking down onto the world below, you could sense the possibility of letting go of one's old world and awakening into an awareness that was ancient beyond ancient, yet pristinely new every moment. I look back on those solitary walks along the valley rim as some of the most grace-filled moments in my life.

For me, one of the many great gifts from India to the world lies in its being the birthplace of one of the most awakened beings of this or any century. I am referring to Ramana Maharshi, the Sage who brought us the direct approach to the Self, to God—the approach of being willing to discover Who we *really* are—not who we have been taught we are, but Who, in our experience *right now*, we are. When we ask, "Who am I?" and do not answer with thoughts we have been trained to believe but simply see directly in this moment what is really there inside, we find something (or nothing) far different from what our minds have postulated.

Ramana clarifies this approach beautifully in the following dialogue with a visitor to his ashram:

Q: How shall I reach the Self?

A: There is no reaching the Self. If Self were to be reached, it would mean that the Self is not here and now and that it is yet to be obtained. What is got afresh will also be lost. So it will be impermanent. What is not permanent is not worth striving for. So I say the Self is not reached. You are the Self; you are already that.

The fact is, you are ignorant of your blissful state. Ignorance supervenes and draws a veil over the pure Self, which is bliss. Attempts are directed only to remove this veil of ignorance that is merely wrong knowledge. The wrong knowledge is the false identification of the Self with the body and the mind. This false identification must go, and then the Self alone remains.

Therefore, realization is for everyone; realization makes no difference between the aspirants. This very doubt, whether you can realize, the notion of "I-have-not-realized" are themselves the obstacles. Be free from these obstacles, also.

Q: How long does it take to reach *mukti* (liberation)?

A: Mukti is not to be gained in the future. It is there forever, here and now.[1]

One of Bartholomew's greatest gifts is that our work together has made seemingly difficult truths so very simple. Again and again, people say, "Bartholomew helps me see things simply, directly," and that has been my experience as well. I have gradually realized, for example, the meaning of Ramana's approach of directly asking, "Who am I?" I began with it being just a great idea, and now it is a Truth. I have also learned the meaning of the Zen approach of "just sitting, no big deal." These awarenesses have come directly from my spending more hours with Bartholomew, as we work together, not trying, just relaxing, flowing.[2] When the words are spoken to clarify a point for someone, my understanding is also clarified. When Love is fully present for someone in pain and confusion, my sense of what Love really is becomes stronger. And what I have truly discovered is that each of us, right now, in this moment, has the ability to be fully aware of our True Self, our God-Self. Nothing extra is needed, nothing taken away. Just this moment and our willingness to acknowledge that the essence of Who we are is constantly present—and that awareness never leaves. How could it? Where would it go? It has finally occurred to me how very funny it is to say, "I have to find out who I really am." Where will I go to find it? Who will show it to me? What a joke—and what an incredible relief to finally know that I am who I am—now and always. Thank you, Bartholomew, whoever or whatever you are.

So I close this introduction with vast amounts of gratitude for all that has been experienced. I am grateful to those stalwart ones who traveled with us on our journey, to our Tibetan cooks who became friends, and I am most deeply grateful to His Holiness, the 14th Dalai Lama, for his willingness to permit us to join him in this amazing adventure. And, as always, I am eternally grateful to Bartholomew.

Mary-Margaret

Mary-Margaret Moore

part 1

March–July 1992

Chapter 1

Going . . .

The screen door slammed as Mary-Margaret Moore entered the office of High Mesa Press and announced, "Australia's out. So is New Zealand." She dropped her bag and an armload of papers onto the couch and kicked off her boots.

"We just received the quote, and the extra airfare from New Zealand to India is way too expensive," she said. "We've already been to Bali, and I don't think visiting temples in Thailand in the summer will have very much appeal." Mary-Margaret is a tall, attractive woman with long, honey-colored hair and lively blue eyes. She moves with strength and grace, the result of many years spent swimming in the waters of her native Hawaii.

I turned from typing my third letter in two hours, happy at the interruption and eager to hear how the tour to India was shaping up. "What other countries are in that area?" I asked.

"Singapore, Taiwan, New Guinea . . . I don't know," she muttered. "Do you have an atlas?"

I gazed out the window while mentally conducting a quick inventory of the office. It was early March, and winter had given way to a beautiful spring morning on the mesa. The recent rains had scrubbed the sky clean and left a smell of fresh sagebrush and juniper in the air. The rising sun cast soft shadows over the valley, and the town of Taos was just waking up. It was still hard to believe that in five months we would be in the Himalayas, where we hoped to attend a Kalachakra initiation[3] with His Holiness the Dalai Lama.[4] We had been planning this tour for a year and a half, and now it was becoming a reality . . . if we could find someplace to stop en route. I returned my attention to the problem at hand. A map, an atlas, a globe? There must be something around here that would work.

"Ha!" I exclaimed, pushing my chair away from the desk. "The puzzle."

"The puzzle!" echoed Mary-Margaret.

"Yes, it was meant for the school, and I know just where it is."

Soon we had the Middle East in hot pink, the Far East in sky blue, and Micronesia in buttery yellow spread out on the desk between us.

"Where's India?" I asked. "What's more, where's Delhi?"

"There, above and to the right of Africa," Mary-Margaret answered, pointing to a very large country on our hot-pink puzzle.

"It doesn't look promising," I said, looking at the surrounding countries. "Unless . . ." I slid the blue map over, ". . . we could go to China—or Japan," I added quietly, pointing.

We looked at each other. Mary-Margaret knew of my desire to visit Japan and of my disappointment at the failure of a tour scheduled to go there seven years ago. She smiled.

"Japan might work. We stop in Singapore on our way to India, and I think we also stop in Tokyo," she said, her blue eyes beginning to sparkle, "and Japan is certainly a country of spiritual power."

"But Japan is awfully hot in the summer, too!" I protested, not daring to hope.

"Yes, but it will be hot *everywhere* over there in July," she answered. With a characteristic toss of her head that sent her long hair flying, she turned and looked seriously at me. "It's too expensive to pay for an organized tour. You will have to help me get it together. We'll need to find places cheap enough to stay in." She laughed. "And inexpensive places to eat. And some way to get around. And we don't have a lot of time to set this up," she added. Looking at me quizzically, she asked, "Can do?"

I sighed. Was I going to let these small details stand in the way of going to the one place I had longed to see for so many years?

"You mean it?"

"You bet!"

I did not hesitate. "My pleasure," I replied.

"You're on," she agreed, breaking up the puzzle and helping me put away the pieces.

Chapter 2

Going . . .

Four weeks later, progress had been made. A decision was reached to locate ourselves in one major city to avoid the expense of traveling from place to place. Since we were arriving in Tokyo and leaving from Osaka, the city had to be accessible to both. Furthermore, it had to be close to interesting sites so we would have the option of taking day trips.

We chose Kyoto, one-time capital of Japan and an important center of culture and religion. Mary-Margaret was drawn to its Zen traditions, and I was excited by the opportunity to visit the temples I had studied in my art history classes long ago.

We would travel by train. It was the most efficient and economical means of transportation in the country. From the information I gathered, we chose a hotel in Kyoto that was air-conditioned (very important), had its own restaurant (for the less adventurous diners), had enough Western-style rooms to hold us all, was centrally located, had a fax (which we put to work immediately), and best of all, fit our budget. I spent a lot of time reading about regional delicacies, where to eat, and what to expect in the way of prices.

During this planning stage, I swung between moments of intense excitement and overwhelming anxiety. I would be bursting with confidence, then filled with fear. Could we do it? Could Mary-Margaret, her husband, Justin, and I take 17 other people to a country so totally different from ours? Would we have any fun?

The screen door slammed. I turned as Mary-Margaret entered the office, her arms full. "We've heard from Chai!" she exclaimed. Chai and her partner Russell were the two Australian friends who were helping organize our trip to India. Chai had met and meditated with His Holiness, the Dalai Lama, many times in Dharamsala, and was doing her best to arrange for us to attend a Kalachakra initiation with him while we were there.

"Good news," Mary-Margaret continued. "The best. It looks as though we'll be able to attend the Kalachakra initiation with His Holiness." She opened her bag and extracted a large soft-cover book.

"What exactly is a Kalachakra initiation?" I asked.

"It's a ceremony both powerful and complicated, at least to the Western mind," she replied as she sat down and pulled out her glasses. "I've been doing some research, and here's what I found." She began to read.

"Buddhas are Enlightened Beings who, having overcome all misery and ignorance themselves, teach others methods for doing the same. As all beings have different temperaments and capacities, Buddhas teach many varying paths leading to Liberation from suffering as well as to the full Enlightenment of Buddhahood.[5]

"The Kalachakra initiation was such a method given to the world by Shakyamuni Buddha after his Enlightenment. Buddha manifested himself in the form of the Kalachakra meditational deity and gave the full initiation and discourse, introducing this new teaching to his people."

Mary-Margaret looked up. "The aim, as I understand it, is to become fully aware of our True Nature as Emptiness. In fact, it's an initiation through visualization," she said. "And that which is visualized and related to is the form of the Kalachakra deity. Since it is impossible for everyone to physically see the sand mandala of the deity, the master, in our case the Dalai Lama, takes you with his words, via your imagination, through the Kalachakra mandala. A large, intricately detailed mandala of colored sand is created at every initiation. It is 'dis-created' at the end of each ceremony by being immersed in moving water. Here it will be the Sutlej River."

"It's still amazing to think we'll be there to participate in it," I responded.

Mary-Margaret got up and rummaged through her stack of papers, selecting several sheets. "Here's the letter from Chai," she said, as she settled herself on the couch, and began reading Chai's words.

"The Dalai Lama will be arriving in Kalpa directly from Europe, so the official dates of the teachings have not yet been confirmed. This is apparently not uncommon. He teaches for at least three days before giving the Kalachakra initiation. His teachings are dynamic and demanding, true Bartholomew style; you'll love it. It makes no difference if you're a Buddhist or not, because the heart of the teachings has to do with the states of mind/consciousness. He teaches how to respond to life with clarity rather than to react from ignorance. He may spend a day on Emptiness, and another on how all sentient beings and all matter are intimately connected. I'm just guessing from past experience, yet I'm sure it will be exciting; it always is. I am not going to tell you all the details, because in my telling, I will give you only my limited experience and really diminish the power of it all. But the basic outline goes like this:

"Kalachakra Tantra is a Female Tantra—that is, emphasizing wisdom, as opposed to Male Tantra that emphasizes the method aspect. His Holiness empowers himself as Kalachakra, blesses and purifies and empowers the Initiates; thus, everyone there becomes Kalachakra. This, of course, takes much time and many mantras. It's necessary to completely drop all sense of ordinariness in order to really *be* Kalachakra. This shouldn't be difficult high up in the Himalayas with all those monks and nuns and Tibetan devotees. The Tibetans are light and joyful, and just when it's all getting a bit spacey—bang, crash, and boom of gongs, cymbals, and trumpets and loud laughter and plenty of tea right in the middle of it all, and one can wonder if this is an Initiation or a mad hatter's tea party." Mary-Margaret laughed.

"Sounds like it was made for us," I agreed with a smile.

She rustled the papers. "Listen to this," she said.

"Many Tibetans, Bhutanese, Ladakhis, mountain people from Lahaul Spiti and Kinnaur, and Tibetan nomads will be arriving from June onwards. They will be setting up stalls, restaurants, and accommodations, and trading and celebrating being together. Any Tibetan celebration is full of fun, and one where His Holiness, the Dalai Lama, attends is the greatest fun!"

"Where is Chai now?" I asked.

Mary-Margaret looked up. "In Delhi. And she also tells us how we're getting from Delhi to Kalpa." After more shuffling of papers, she went back to reading.

"On arrival at Delhi Airport, you will be collected by air-conditioned bus and taken to an air-conditioned, first-class hotel in the center of New Delhi. It has large twin rooms with bathroom and includes a luggage room, two restaurants—one with live Indian music—and fine Indian cuisine. We'll leave Delhi the following morning at 7:30 and fly to Shimla, an old English resort town, charming and not affected by the monsoons. We will spend the night there and leave the next day by minibus for Narkanda (9,000 feet). The drive is enchanting, and Narkanda has remarkable views of the inner Himalayas. Then we go through Sarahan, which is on the Old Hindustan Tibet road. It is the gateway to the Kinnaur region, and Kalpa. Kalpa is close to the Tibetan border and a very sacred place with Mount Kinnaur Kailash 20,000 feet high on its right, and another almost as high on the left. It sits above the Sutlej River. We will be staying in big army tents while we are there. Up until last September, Westerners could not go to this area. It's very exciting going into unknown territory, but also impossible to arrange without having been there, so Russell and I are heading off to Kalpa when the snow has eased off to confirm the accommodations, and to find out all the interesting history and local stories to ensure that our time there will be as exciting as can be.

"After the initiation, Russell and I are going to return via Lahaul, Spiti, and over the Rotung Pass and come out at Manali, if anyone cares to join us. By the way, bring lightweight, long raincoats and maybe a pair of gum boots and a fold-up umbrella, and then you'll be prepared for anything. Also bring a cozy sleeping bag and a good pair of walking boots. We will drink mineral water only and eat cooked food and fruit. That's all for now. We'll keep in touch. Love, Chaitanya and Russell."

"Gum boots?" I inquired.

Mary-Margaret folded the fax and her glasses. "Rain boots? Mud boots? Something to keep our feet dry. It's going to be wet until we get into the mountains," she answered.

"Hot in Delhi and cold in Kalpa; we'll have it all," I concluded.

"Yes, and hopefully we'll have more information from Chai," replied Mary-Margaret. "I've been trying to get a fax through to her for the last 48 hours with no luck, so I'm sending this via her friend Paul Tipper in Australia."

March 23, 1992

To: Chaitanya
P.O. Dharamsala
INDIA

Thank you for your recent long and informative fax. We now have twenty (20) of us, as everyone signed up again as soon as they heard the new information. I will be taking the Americans to Japan for a week before coming to Delhi. I don't think the Australians will be interested, but I will invite them and leave it up to them. Some of us will be staying on with you in Kalpa and hiking, etc. I would LOVE to be one, but Bartholomew is due to speak in Albuquerque that weekend.

Would you please fax me any information you have on what shots, immunizations, etc., you Australians took before going to India? The World Health Organization [WHO] is full of "suggestions," but many of us prefer not to go through all that. Which ones are really necessary? Which ones did you take? The WHO suggests malaria, typhoid, cholera, tetanus, polio, measles/mumps, rubella, and meningitis. Good grief!!!! What did your group do last summer?

More questions: Do we need to bring iodine crystals for purifying water, or can we always buy bottled? Can women wear pants and jeans? Are there any special things we need to know about dressing? How cold will it be in the Himalayas?

Will it be better for all of us to bring sleeping bags for Kalpa? We can use them to sit on if necessary. My worry is that it will be too cold for comfortable sleeping in the tents, and that the bags would take care of that. What do you say? Do you know what kind of bedding we will be able to expect, or should we just assume the bags would be best? Do we need the sleeping mats because the cots will be uncomfortable, or to sit on at the teachings? Or both?

As far as I know, I am the only one who has taken initiation in Buddhism, but many of us have been studying Zen for many years, as well as the Buddhist teachings of Thich Nhat Hanh, a Vietnamese monk who is known to His Holiness, as he has written various things on this monk's outstanding work. All of us have regular meditation practices, in addition to reading teachings of the Realized Ones. It would be a tremendous honor to have a session with His Holiness. We are very, very grateful to you, dearest Chai, for your efforts on our behalf. We shall see if our karma is good enough to allow us that honor! As we say here, "It is in the hands of the gods!"

All for now, dear one. Again, so many millions of thanks to you and Russell for all you are doing for us. It will be a trip of a lifetime, I am sure. I will quote some of your letter in the information that I send out . . . it was great, just like you!

Important! Just found out that there are definitely some people who want to take you up on your kind offer to continue on, although they need to leave Delhi on August 25. Could you send, today, please, a return fax giving us just a brief idea of what you two have in mind?

In love and gratitude,

Mary-Margaret

I never did have any luck reaching Chai in Dharamsala, so Paul and his fax machine turned out to be indispensable in tracking Chai all over the world. He remained a key contact person up until the time we left and was part of the Australian group we joined with in Delhi. The flurry of faxes continued, as plans would be finalized only to change again as transportation, accommodations, and scheduling continued to rearrange themselves almost weekly.

The faxes were interspersed from time to time with informative letters to the Americans.

April 30, 1992
From Mary-Margaret Moore to the Tour members

Dear Ones,

At long last I have some firm data for us! We will be leaving Los Angeles airport (LAX) for Tokyo on July 27, back to LAX on either August 19 or August 26 for extension people.

JAPAN: Here we'll be traveling by train. Japan's rail system is among the best in the world but has some of the smallest overhead storage. You can put a suitcase under your seat, but this space is slightly smaller than an under-the-seat space on an airplane. So we realize that we have an interesting challenge here. These are some solutions.

Make sure all your luggage is what is classified as "soft" luggage. We suggest 2 midsized carry-on bags plus a backpack. We suggest the backpack because it leaves both your hands free to negotiate your luggage, as we need to get on and off these trains quickly. In fact, the famous bullet train stops for only 120 seconds, so you and your luggage have to get either on or off in that amount of time. (Don't panic! We have a plan.) For safety's sake, please make your luggage look as boring as possible, although we do not really anticipate trouble in that area.

Your flight arrives at Narita Airport at approximately 5:30 P.M. Tuesday evening. We are arranging to spend the night at a hotel only five minutes from the airport. The hotel will provide transportation for us and our luggage. We do this in recognition of the degree of exhaustion you are likely to be feeling after your flight. On Wednesday morning, we return to the airport to send our excess baggage on to Kyoto. Then we catch a subway to Tokyo where we connect with the bullet train, which will whisk us to Kyoto in less than three hours.

WEATHER: There is no question that the weather in Japan in July sucks! We need to be ready for it. Our hotel rooms are air-conditioned, and we hope to be traveling to cooler places for day trips. It could be rainy and muggy (high 93, low 72), so don't forget a collapsible umbrella and lightweight raingear. Sleeveless blouses and walking shorts are fine. Let's stay away from short shorts and brief tops, as we will be visiting many sacred places both in Japan and India. Bring tennis shoes as well as sandals for walking on gravelly temple paths.

FOOD: One of the greatest delights of our time in Japan will undoubtedly be the food. Since this is a subject dear to Joy's heart, she has researched the possibilities in depth and will provide us with packets containing information on what to order, how to order, what it will cost, etc. For planning purposes, $25 a day for food is possible, if we are careful. We'll become very creative in this category. There is absolutely no worry about the quality of food or water supply, or cleanliness of any kind, in Japan.

INDIA: We arrive in New Delhi at 9:30 at night, departing early the next morning for Shimla. It is my present understanding that we will be traveling by bus. It will definitely be by private transportation. (Do we hear a sigh of relief? Can you envision us with all our luggage on an Indian train?)

INOCULATIONS: Chai suggests the following shots: Cholera (this is a two-shot series, first one about June 22, second around July 20. It's considered 50% effective and should last 5 months); tetanus-diphtheria booster (good for 8 to 10 years); typhoid (different books say different things—one says good for 3 years immunity, another says 5 years—you or your doctor can decide); gamma globulin is, in our opinion, a must (it protects against hepatitis, should be taken about one week prior to departure, and lasts for about 4 months). Chai says don't worry about malaria.

WEATHER: It will be hot and sticky in Delhi, so the clothes and raingear from Japan should suffice. For the Himalayas we need long-sleeve warm winter jackets and a flashlight with new batteries—very important. Hiking boots, warm socks, thermal or silk underwear, a sun hat, warm woolen hat, and warm scarf are essential. Sunscreen, sunglasses, and insect repellent are also recommended. Temperatures will range from warm to very cold at this high elevation, so the layered look seems to be the way to go. We will be able to leave any items from Japan that we don't need in our hotel in New Delhi.

FOOD: It is absolutely essential that you bring at least one nonleaking water container. Chai assures me that we can buy all the purified water we need wherever we are. We will be her third group tour to India and none of her participants have gotten ill from the food yet. She knows precisely what we should eat and where we should eat it. We will dine very well in India, probably for a maximum of $15 a day.

WE ALL NEED TO BRING A SLEEPING BAG. One good for keeping warm at 20 to 25 degrees should be adequate. We are aware what a hassle all this gear will be for you to carry around, so we have come up with what we hope is a good solution to this problem. When you meet up with Joy in Los Angeles, she will have four huge duffel bags for everyone to put their sleeping bags and extra gear in. We hope to ship these directly to Kyoto for you, then on to Delhi. You won't see them after Los Angeles until you need them in India, so don't put in anything you'll need beforehand.

I guess that's all for now, if you can believe it. You'll be receiving one last communication from us and it will contain SOME VERY IMPORTANT INFORMATION ON HOW TO GET YOUR VISA FOR TRAVELING IN INDIA. This we cannot do for you, sorry to say. And we are even sorrier to tell you, in view of all the requests that have been made for passport photos, that—oh boy, do I hate to type these next few words—<u>you</u>

need to get additional black-and-white or color passport photos for the restricted-area permit in India. I cannot tell you how sorry I am that this comes once again into our lives, but it is necessary so that we can enter the incredible world of the Himalayas and the lives of those amazing people who live there. So until next time, Sayonara . . . Japanese good-bye, and in love as always.

Mary-Margaret

The office door opened, and a chill, rainy wind blew in, followed by a dripping Mary-Margaret. She shook her long, wet hair, brushed the water from her jacket with one hand, and balanced her books and papers in the other, while kicking off her muddy boots and exclaiming, "Yuck, what a mess your road is! I barely got up the hill!"

I shoved the mail on my desk to one side to make room for her papers, and glanced out the window. It was indeed nasty, cold, wet, and windy, with rain that was depressing in its persistence. "It's hard to believe that in less than three months, we will all be sweating and wishing for this kind of weather. What's new?" I asked.

"Another, and I hope the *last* letter for the tour group. After all the difficulties we had filling out and getting the extra photos for the restricted-area permits, I thought I'd come and type a letter explaining how to get our visas for India. By the way, here's something I got in the mail that might interest you."

She gently laid a manila envelope in front of me and turned to sit at the computer. I opened it to find a small book printed in Japanese and the following letter.

May 11, 1992
Ms. Mary-Margaret Moore
Taos, New Mexico 87571

Dear Ms. Moore,
On behalf of Ms. Yuko Takaki of Mahoroba Art Co., Ltd, a Japanese publisher of metaphysical books, I am writing this letter to request your permission to translate Bartholomew's *"I Come As a Brother"* into the Japanese language for publication in Japan.

Mahoroba Art publishing company is a small publisher located just outside of Tokyo, dedicated to increasing Awareness among the Japanese people through publication of metaphysical books. Ms. Takaki is also a writer and last year published her own book on creating abundance.

I am a Seattle-based English/Japanese translator with 20 years' experience. I was born and raised in Japan and graduated from a top women's college in Tokyo. In 1971, I came to the U.S. for graduate studies and received a master's degree in linguistics from Georgetown University. Having lived in the U.S. for 17 years, I am bilingual and familiar with both cultures.

I am really excited about what I have been learning and have a strong yearning to share this knowledge and understanding with the Japanese people. I regard the work of translation as "channeling," not in the sense of "plumbing" by becoming a tool to replace an English word with a Japanese word, but by receiving a message in one language, and then digesting and expressing it in another language. The translator is a co-creator of the translated book, and her understanding of the material is crucial. My passion for and understanding of the Bartholomew material will be an asset in the translation.

The Japanese people have only a limited selection of channeled information and other metaphysical materials. No Seth books or Michael books are available in Japanese. No *Course in Miracles* or Ramtha books. And, most importantly, no Bartholomew!!!

I find Bartholomew very loving, practical, and familiar with human emotions, which makes his examples easy to understand. His meditations and exercises are wonderful. Ms. Takaki also regards the Bartholomew books highly. She is anxious to publish a Japanese translation. Ms. Takaki and I believe strongly that the Japanese people will benefit from reading the Bartholomew books. His familiarity with Buddhism and Eastern philosophy will appeal to many in Japan.

If you are agreeable to having us translate and publish *"I Come As a Brother,"* or wish more information on us or our plan, please let me know. I am waiting for your reply expectantly.

Sincerely yours,

Yoko H. Huey

"Good grief!" I exclaimed, feeling a tingle of excitement. "First the books are translated into German and now Japanese. Is it a coincidence that we're going to Japan in a few months?" I leaned back in my chair, turning the small, tastefully designed book over in my hands. "Interesting. Of all the places in the world, the two countries we've gone to war with are the ones that have approached us to translate the Bartholomew material."

The chattering of the computer keyboard stopped. Swiveling her chair around, Mary-Margaret pushed herself over to the facing desk and leaned forward on her elbows. "Perhaps these are places where the Bartholomew energy can make a difference," she said quietly. "Countries that we have historically been enemies with can now be our friends. Healing can take place. It's a great opportunity and a great challenge."

"Well, I am 100 percent in favor of having the book come out in Japanese," I responded. "Besides, you know how I appreciate the synchronicity of events like these and like to take complete advantage of them. I'll get a letter off right away. Even better," I said with a smile, "I'll call."

With a nod, Mary-Margaret returned to her typing, and I went to brew some tea. Spooning a large gob of honey and a small splash of milk into my cup, I returned with the tea and a glass of water. I could still feel the tingles of anticipation the letter from Yoko Huey had produced. I could also feel my mind forming desires around possibilities I could only imagine. "But that is then, and now is now," I told myself sternly.

Mary-Margaret finished typing and was printing out her latest communication. Looking it over, we both agreed it would be a vast relief to have permits, visas, and the seemingly unending requests for more passport photos over and done with.

I had to laugh as I read the following complicated instructions:

May 15, 1992

Well, here I am again, for chapter number 87 of the ongoing discourse of this tour!

The main purpose for this letter is to give you all the information you are going to need on how to send for your visa for India (Japan does not require them).

Let's start with PART A of your application form: We have filled in some of the information for you. Question #18: Please just leave this one as we have already done it. Don't add Kalpa, Manali, etc. #19: First group departs August 18, second group August 25, 1992 (please don't forget to put in the year. My experience is that bureaucrats enjoy making things difficult).

1. Remember, you must use block letters for all of this or type it out. Enclosed is the letter from your travel agent that must be included (see section C under requirements for Tourist Visa under general guidelines). Under section G of these guidelines, you do NOT qualify for the one-month tourist visa, as it is good for one month beginning with the date it is issued. You are applying for a six-month visa, even though you will be there only 2 or 3 weeks. The fee will have to be $25. We have found that it is MUCH easier to send the additional $3 for them to return your passport registered mail rather than waiting for regular mail. So a check for $28 cashier's check, money order, or traveler's cheque (made out to Consulate General of India) should do it. Please do this soon, because if something does go wrong and you lose your passport, you will have plenty of time to get another one.

2. Horror of horrors, our wondrous postal service has been known to lose things entrusted to it, like your precious passport. In order to lessen the amount of panic this can cause you, please copy the photo page and signature page (pages 1 and 2) of your passport before sending it to the Consulate General. That way, if anything does happen, you can easily get another one. If you have not gotten your passport and visa back within two weeks of sending it, please call the Consulate General's office and inquire.

3. Justin and I will be in Europe until May 20, so if you get desperate, call Joy. (Don't tell her I said so.)

That's it for now, and much love to all of you goes with this from . . .

Mary-Margaret

Mary-Margaret left, her work finished. I turned to the phone with a rare sense of pleasure and dialed Yoko Huey's number.

"You won't believe this!" I called Mary-Margaret right after speaking to her.

"Yes, I will," she said calmly. "What is it?"

I hesitated for a brief moment, struck by the miracle I was about to reveal. "She's going to be in Japan the same time we are," I breathed. "Not only that," I burst out, "but she arrives in Tokyo the same day we do *and* is also overnighting in Narita *and* will be in the Kyoto area *and* would like to meet us there," I finished triumphantly, lapsing into silence, still stunned by this information.

The tour to Japan I had organized years ago had been interesting, exciting, and easy, but had never happened. Now here I was again, this time calling, faxing, writing, and worrying the tour into existence. We'd been having major difficulties planning overnight visits to places other than Kyoto. We couldn't get through to make the necessary reservations, even though our agent, who spoke some Japanese, had tried calling directly. Time was rapidly running out, and we were prepared to fall back on an alternative plan as soon as we figured out what that might be. Yoko's timely letter was a gift from the gods. I was pulled from my reverie by the sound of Mary-Margaret's voice.

"That's great!" She gave a deep sigh of relief. "It means we're on the right track. I've been worried because things haven't quite come together, but now it sounds as though help is on the way. Thank you, Yoko Huey and Mahoroba Art."

❧ ✳ ☙

Chapter 3

Gone . . .

The phone rang in the office, only a moment prior to my reaching it. It was 7:30 A.M., too early for business. I stood by the desk and waited, hand poised above the receiver. The phone rang again. "Yes?" I answered.

"I just got word that our reservations for the Travelers Inn have been confirmed. That takes care of accommodations in Kyoto. Good morning," came the bright sound of Mary-Margaret's satisfied voice.

"Good morning," I responded automatically. "What about a place to stay near the airport?"

"I think we've also solved that problem. The hotel is expensive, but they do take three people to a room, and that will cut down significantly on the cost."

"That's a relief," I said as I sat down, propping my feet on the edge of the desk. "I think it would be very disorienting to leave the States, end up in Narita after an all-day flight, then have to make our way to Tokyo to spend the night, *and* find the train station in the morning." I paused, thinking it over. "It wouldn't be my favorite thing to do."

"Don't worry, it's all taken care of," Mary-Margaret responded with a laugh. "Any news about our rail passes?" she inquired.

"Good news and bad news. We have to pick up the actual rail passes at the Japan Rail Center in Japan. There is supposed to be one somewhere underneath the airport," I answered, drawing small, fat planes sniffing out rail passes on a pad with my free hand.

"I was afraid of that," Mary-Margaret sighed. "It's a good thing Justin and I are flying in a day early. We can arrange for group transportation from the airport to the hotel, and while we're at it, we'll find the Japan Rail Center. What's the good news?"

"The vouchers for the passes came by UPS yesterday afternoon." I explained.

"Good, but you'll have to bring them with you," she replied. "With all the moving around we'll be doing for the workshops in Australia, I really don't want to run the risk of losing them while we're there."

"Okay. Could you also make reservations for the train from Narita to Tokyo when you pick up the rail passes?" I continued. "We need to avoid the morning rush hour but still get there in time to catch the bullet train to arrive in Kyoto at a reasonable hour. I'm a little worried about locating the correct train platform in Tokyo. Yoko said the station was very large and we should leave extra time to get lost. I think once we negotiate the passage from the station to the hotel in Kyoto, we'll have enough confidence to tackle the local trains, buses, and taxis."

I leaned further back in my chair as Mary-Margaret agreed, and mentally reviewed the tactics we had decided on to ensure the smooth transfer of people and luggage from Narita to Tokyo, from Tokyo to Kyoto, and from the train station to the Inn. I had studied the train and bus schedules until they finally dissolved into a blur of unintelligible English and inscrutable glyphs.

"And Chai says she thinks George will be able to see the Dalai Lama's personal physician while we are in Kalpa. Not only that, but she's 95 percent certain we can have a short, private audience with His Holiness," Mary-Margaret concluded triumphantly.

There was the sound of rustling paper from the other end of the phone. "Ah!" she exclaimed. "What about the excess baggage problems?"

"We can send them separately for an additional charge," I responded.

"How much?"

My feet hit the floor sharply as I leaned forward. "Thirty dollars a bag!"

"Well, we can certainly ship the 'Bart' bags, and anyone who wishes can pay the extra charge for their own excess luggage," Mary-Margaret said soothingly.

Luggage had become a major problem, since storage space was at a premium in Japan and we needed so many extra things for India. We solved the problem by the acquisition of four oversized black duffel bags on which I had stenciled "Bart 1" through "Bart 4," and into which we planned to stuff the sleeping bags and whatever other miscellaneous items would fit. The size and quantity of the duffel bags had us both worried about violating the first rule of travel: Never, never, *ever* get separated from your luggage.

"I hope we can count on Japanese efficiency to get our bags to us," I said.

"So do I," came Mary-Margaret's fervent reply. "This whole trip is full of questions and we're running out of time to find the answers. I've got to get everything together soon because next weekend is the monthly meeting in Albuquerque."

"And you leave on Monday for Australia," I said, startled by the close proximity of her departure.

"Yes, so I'll talk to you later," she said briskly. "Bye."

"Yeah, bye," I echoed, looking down at the dead phone in my hand.

✳ ✳

July thundered in like an express train, sweeping Mary-Margaret and Justin off the mesa and on toward Australia. *Oh no,* I thought as I waved good-bye. *I still have to find out if the taxis in Japan charge by the person or the cab, arrange for the Kyoto-Osaka Airport limo, discover if our Japan Rail passes are good for the city buses in Kyoto, and unearth someone to print the name and address of our hotel as well as its bus stop in Japanese 20 times!* The list seemed endless and the difficulties overwhelming.

At times my psyche would expand with exuberant anticipation at the prospect of our adventure, and at other times it would collapse in fear around the unknown. I amassed great quantities of helpful literature to decrease the tension I was causing myself, ending up with so much that I assembled individual packets to pass out when we all met in Los Angeles. They would contain the ever-present but finally familiar train schedule, city maps, and pamphlets of Kyoto and Nara, instructions on how to use the local buses, and booklets on everything from where to find a public bathroom to how to order an inexpensive meal.

Sublime moments would occur when all tension was swept away by a feeling of absolute trust. Events were taking shape with such positive appropriateness that I felt it was more than coincidence. At those times I would walk on the mesa, under a vast sky, totally surrounded by mountains, alive and aware, breathing in the pungent scent of sagebrush. Then the opening would snap shut, and I would walk the mesa unseeing, barely breathing at all in my anxiety. All in all, it was a time of intensity, when I felt I was participating in my life, not being dragged through it. Whereas the usual rise and fall of ordinary events left me numb and dumb, irritated at myself for simply drifting with them, every response in this frantic period before departure was in focus, sharper, more immediate.

I had sudden feelings of expectation, that something *good* was about to happen, that change would come, that good changes were already here. Yoko's next call was one of them.

Luckily, Mary-Margaret had left a schedule of her Australian tour that included phone and fax numbers. Our last-minute communication started up again almost immediately with the following euphoric fax.

July 13, 1992
To: Paul Tipper

Dear Paul,

I have some very important information for Mary-Margaret and Justin that I'm hoping you can somehow get to them. Please let me know either way. I just spoke with Yoko Huey, the Japanese translator of the first Bartholomew book. She had contacted our publisher in Japan, who upon hearing we were going to be in her country for a week, has offered to have a friend act as our guide for the first three days of our visit to Kyoto, while she herself would be our guide for the rest of the time.

In addition, Yoko would join us on the 2nd and just happens to be arriving on the magic date, 28 July. She will be coming in at 5:15 P.M. via Japan Airlines and is staying overnight at the Narita Nikko. The way things are going, I'll probably be standing next to her at customs. This is a wonderful opportunity, and we could certainly use the help. We would be their guests, and they in turn would attend the morning Bartholomew meetings.

Ms. Takaki will be calling one of us at the Narita View Hotel to arrange the time for us to meet in Kyoto. I'm so excited by all this I could spit. Please strongly suggest to Mary-Margaret that we humbly and gratefully accept their kind offer. I already have!

In anticipation,
JF

A response came back almost instantly.

July 14, 1992
From: Mary-Margaret Moore

Hello again; Chai just called to tell me of your fax about Japan which she read to me. What a wonderful, marvelous thing that all is! Of course we would love to do all of it, and boy, am I grateful! I have been wondering about the guide end of things, and of course this takes care of so much of that!!!!! Amazing. I trust your decisions as much as my own especially when dealing with Japan!

Here in Byron Bay until Friday noon. Please send a fax, just to keep me smiling!!

MM

Yoko called again three days later. I hung up the phone, swiveled my chair around to the computer, and quickly pounded out the next episode in our serial communication.

July 17, 1992
To: Paul Tipper
For: Mary-Margaret and Justin Moore

Good morning, Moores. This, I think, will be the last communication before I see you. We leave in nine days. The time has been going by extraordinarily fast. Just got the second series of India shots and spent a miserable night. Better today.

I heard from Yoko Huey again last night, who in turn had gotten another fax from Yuko Takaki. Yuko will now meet us in Kyoto at our hotel on the 29th. She and a friend will be staying there with us until the weekend. The hotel is full up over the weekend, so she and Yoko will find another place nearby. They have it all worked out.

They had visions of trying to stuff 20 of us on a public bus and whisking us around to temples all day long. Ms. Takaki thought it was just about impossible and looked into a charter bus for us. She found one for hire at $1,500 for the week, and I told Yoko that I thought it was too expensive, but would pass the information on to you. She will await your immediate reply before faxing Ms. Takaki again. We also agreed that the day trips should happen during the week when there wouldn't be so much traffic. I am passing all this along so I won't forget it in the last-minute rush.

Also, don't let's forget to make all seat reservations at Japan Rail before we leave the airport. I have everyone's tickets and will pass them

out in L.A. The last of the final letters, information, and baggage tags are going out today. That's it for now. Much, much love from all.
JF

The fax machine was silent for another three days as Mary-Margaret and Justin drifted somewhere out of range between Australia and New Zealand. By this time, my own departure was only a week away. I felt like a nervous astronaut moving toward a final countdown, and I carried a wrinkled checklist in my back pocket that grew longer as the time grew shorter.

On July 20, I received this fax from Mary-Margaret.

Hello again . . . just got your fax . . . here goes!!!!!!!

I know this will be a drag, but could you please bring my baggy tan walking shorts???? I forgot them!!!! They should be in the right-hand dresser drawer. If not, then (God help you) they will be somewhere in the closet (ugh) or next to the bed in the night-stand. If you can't get those, then it will have to be my grey ones . . .

Now, about the bus. I have been very, very worried about our train plans since talking to people who have been to Japan, as they say that we will have a lot of trouble getting close to many of the best sites without a bus or car. They also said that the trains were totally crowded and impossible. So I would like to take them up on their offer. I think that I will have much greater freedom if there is a bus and someone else is in charge, and I don't have to worry or even be there all the time.

Please see if we can return the rail passes and get our money back. Even if we can't, still get the bus. See if it can start from our hotel at Narita. If not we'll have to "train it" to Kyoto—and keep the rail passes. For me, it is an answer to a prayer. I have been really very worried.

Please send me a fax about all this. I'll be here through the weekend. In love to all of you very dear ones,
Mary-Margaret and Justin.

An hour later I sent this fax to Mary-Margaret.

July 20, 1992
To: Mary-Margaret and Justin Moore

Urgent! I have just spoken with Yoko, and the first thing we need to clear up is the fact that the bus rental cost is not for a week, it is for two days. I think the bus costs about $750/day. Next, I want you to know that I would gladly give up my rail pass, my sandals, and all responsibilities to be able to sit back in air-conditioned comfort in a bus while someone else figures out how to get where we're going.

The bus we're talking about renting is strictly for Kyoto . . . to replace the local buses we would be using to get around. I have already called to see if we could possibly get a refund on the JRP, but he doesn't hold out much hope.

I am calling Yoko back in a few minutes to talk about this some more before she faxes Japan. Needless to say, the faster we make a decision, the greater the chance we have of getting the bus. It turns out Ms. Takaki's friend is the one who is making the arrangements. I'll do the best I can running on intuition. Sometimes I wish I were psychic. Please get back to me ASAP.

xoxo, Joy

While waiting for her final response, I packed, unpacked, and repacked, trying to stuff everything I wanted to take into a soft 22x14x8-inch black bag. It had to be small enough to fit under an airplane seat but large enough to hold both cool clothes for Japan and warm clothes for India. I crammed, jammed, wrestled, folded, and all but stapled my things together in an effort to get them into a bag that seemed to shrink every time I came near it.

Carolyn Lake, my future roommate in India, would also be on the extension trip after the tour. Since we would be camping, we needed to bring extra supplies. These included a lightweight tent, inflatable mattresses, hiking boots, rain gear, two sleeping bags, and very warm clothing, since we would be above timberline most of the time. All this and more was carefully stowed in a surplus army bag that Carolyn would have when she met us in Singapore. Standing upright, the bag came almost to her armpit.

Carolyn, who is five feet four inches tall, was born and raised in rural Colorado, and luckily does not question her ability to haul a four-foot, 60-pound duffel bag halfway around the world.

Two days later I received the final farewell fax from Mary-Margaret.

July 23, 1992
From: Mary-Margaret Moore

Greetings from rainy, lovely, and fascinating New Zealand! People are wonderful, the land very different from Australia (hot vs. cold), but so special in its own way. Glad we came!

So—I vote for the one day on the bus—it will be so great to know where we are going for at least one day! I'm sure we'll all love traveling in air-conditioned splendor. Perhaps we can ask Yuko what temples are within easy drive—maybe ones high up some cool mountain, with rushing streams and tinkling temple bells, amid whispering pines. (I sound like a Japanese travel book.)

This is my last epistle to you, so I hope I haven't forgotten any questions. It will be so good to see all of you at Narita. Justin and I are getting excited, as are the Australians we just left.

So, onward through the fog! Have you lost any of your enthusiasm for being a travel coordinator? (Tee hee!)

Arigato gozaimasu. (It means thank you. I'm just showing off!)

With love to all,

Mary-Margaret

The sun rose, the birds sang, and the day of departure arrived. The last fax chattered out of the machine as I drank my morning coffee. It was from Yoko, and after reading it, I decided to simply take the information with me. Ms. Takaki had reserved a bus for us and saved us 20,000 yen doing it. She was hoping to catch the same train for Kyoto as we were.

I checked everything one last time, then, throwing my bags in back, I jammed my hat down to my sunglasses, grabbed my bundle of information packets, and squeezed myself and my backpack into Carolyn's car for the three-hour ride to Albuquerque.

At the airport I spotted Larry and Roberta Knox immediately. They had driven down from Santa Fe early and were eager to get started. Both were dressed casually chic. Larry, ruggedly built, with dark hair and blue eyes, had a laconic sense of humor that he put to good use in tense situations. Roberta, attractive, energetic, and bursting with good humor, was off immediately, dark curls bouncing, in search of tea and cookies.

I turned as George Westmoreland approached and presented himself for inspection. He was dressed all in black, and he carried his cameras strapped like bandoliers across his large chest. A huge grin lit up his dark face. He looked more like a rock star than the psychologist he was.

Emmy Cheney rushed up and hugged him. A small slender woman, she was interesting, independent, and easy to be around. We would be roommates in Japan. For now, we headed up the escalator and through the security checkpoint toward our departure gate. The plane was right on time.

At Los Angeles, our small group made its way across the airport to the international terminal. There, I immediately ran across Jim and Ellen Williams, just in from Atlanta, Georgia. We had been friends for many years, and I was happy to see them. Ellen was a combination writer, teacher, and impassioned seeker, far more hardy than her soft Southern appearance indicated. Jim greeted me with a sweet smile of welcome on his bearded face. If any possibility of excitement or exploration presented itself, Jim was always ready to go.

I unlocked and unzipped one Bart bag, and removed the others, glancing up just in time to avoid being run over by a heavily loaded baggage cart being pushed by an excited pair of women. Greta Tisdale, most recently from Pennsylvania, was having an enthusiastic reunion with Linda Moore, most recently from Washington state. We had all traveled together before. Greta, tall and thin, wide-eyed behind her round glasses, was our outrider. She often disappeared, following some inner impulse to get out and get going. Linda, smaller and quicker, with bright blue eyes, carried her backpack on her chest and was prepared for anything. They stood head to head, list to list, making sure everything they needed was checked off.

Larry and Jim took charge of rounding up and stuffing the empty Bart bags with the growing pile of mats, collapsible chairs, sleeping bags, extra water bottles, shoes, and other assorted odds and ends. I handed out as many information packets as I could get rid of, and went in search of the Singapore Air group check-in counter. There I found Darcy Thole, Sharon Swenson, and Laurel Sand awaiting me.

Darcy and Sharon had come in from Santa Cruz, California, loaded down with luggage and high-tech camping gear for the extension. Darcy was lounging on her one-legged stool to take the weight off her right leg, which she had injured skiing many years ago. She was in animated conversation with Laurel, whom she had just met but who sounded like a long-lost friend. Sharon was carefully double-checking their neat stack of luggage as I approached. Both Santa Cruz women were tall, blonde, and blue-eyed. Sharon was quieter, very well organized, and given to sudden unexpected bursts of outrageous humor. Darcy was her partner, an energetic explorer who would go anywhere, do anything, and enjoy every moment no matter what was happening.

25

An airline official suddenly materialized behind the counter. More information packets changed hands, and I linked arms with Laurel and went back to get the others. I hadn't seen her in more than a year and wanted a chance to say hello. Although restrained in manner, she laughed easily and often, and I was happy to see her.

We gathered up the rest of the group and returned just as a small crowd of people approached, slightly out of breath, carts piled high with collective luggage. The exuberance grew as we were joined by Eleanor Vogel from California, Lee Balch from Michigan, Barbara Van Camp from New Jersey, and Patricia Morely from Rhode Island. What a varied group of people! We all shared a love of Bartholomew and an urge to see new places and experience new things. This trip was destined to have it all.

We started the check-in procedure, exchanging tickets for boarding passes, and mountains of luggage for baggage checks. In the midst of this process, I heard my name called and turned to see Judith Small waving. She was living outside San Francisco and had driven down to L.A. the night before. Judith was petite and fashionable. She had blonde, curly hair and was Mary-Margaret's close friend. Their relationship went back to the days in California when they had raised their children together, long before the Bartholomew energy had made itself known. Since then, Judith had been a constant source of support and encouragement when many of Mary-Margaret's other friends found her job with Bartholomew difficult to believe. She had joined the tour at the last minute and hugged me in greeting. I looked around. We were all here. Everything that could be done had been done. This was it! We were finally on our way.

꒰ �֎ ꒱

PART II

Japan

July–August 1992

Chapter 4

Getting There

Suspended in that limbo of before where and after when, we were caught in that extraordinary state of time/space travel we so nonchalantly hurl ourselves through whenever we step into an airplane—that state of foggy boredom that sets in after you have rushed to find your seat and stow the luggage and now have nothing to do for eight, twelve, or fifteen hours.

I was restless, unable to settle down, so I walked up and down the aisles, drank juice, and chatted with members of the group. I sat on the armrest of the seat opposite George to find out how he was feeling. He had been diagnosed in April as having cancer of the salivary gland and decided to go with us because he intuitively felt the trip would be important to him. We talked about the week he had spent at the Maharishi Ayurvedic Health Center in New York, when he stayed on after getting a second opinion and having the cancer confirmed. He told me he had learned much there about traditional Ayurvedic and Chinese medicine. He laughed as he pointed to an overnight case that barely fit under the seat in front of him.

"Would you believe it is completely full of herbs and Ayurvedic medicine?" he asked.

I eyed him skeptically.

"No, really. I have enough there to last through Japan, India, and my trip south to Sai Baba's ashram."

"And what if His Holiness's private physician gives you more? What will you do then?" I inquired.

George rolled his eyes. "Give it the place of honor on top, of course." he said with a laugh.

I got back to my seat just as the complimentary beverages were being passed around, and settled down with juice and a book to make the time pass more quickly. Several chapters later, Barbara stopped by to talk about her plans to stay with Sai Baba. She had been having some very realistic dreams about him and felt drawn to be in his presence. Our trip to India was the perfect opportunity. Barbara didn't seem to be the ashram type. She taught music at a school in New Jersey. Though slightly built, she made up in determination what she lacked in physical strength. I admired her courage and stamina. Southern India in the summer would be excruciatingly hot.

We were interrupted in our discussion by a stewardess announcing dinner. The usual scramble occurred while people tucked their things away and lowered tray tables in eager anticipation. We could choose between a meat dish or green noodles. I decided on noodles to prepare myself for the food in Japan. The meal came complete with soba sauce for dipping, and chopsticks as well as silverware. Chopsticks were familiar, but I had never eaten noodles with them before and quickly discovered you cannot twirl noodles around chopsticks the way you can around a fork. So I made a grab at them instead. My confidence was slipping away as rapidly as the noodles when I happened to glance across the aisle and saw a young Japanese woman struggling with knife and fork to master her Western meal. She looked up just then, and our eyes met. The woman smiled, held up her empty fork, and shrugged. I held up my empty chopsticks, shrugged, and smiled. Then I picked up my fork and started to eat. We still had a movie and several more empty hours to fill.

At last the sound of the engines dropped from a whine to a whisper as the plane pulled up to the loading gate in Narita right on time. Clearing passport control was only a matter of patience, and English subtitles on the Japanese signs made it easy to find the escalator down to our luggage. It had been neatly stacked and was being guarded by two women in uniform and spotless white gloves. They provided baggage carts and pointed us in the direction of customs. We trailed through like a line of ducks, and I could hear Justin and Mary-Margaret greeting people as they left the building.

Justin was always easy to find. He was tall and solidly built, his hair blond, his eyes blue behind his ever-present glasses. He was friendly and enjoyed being with people, although he usually appeared serious and sometimes even shy. He had an amazingly quick wit that could pierce the most serious moment. He was laughing and joking now as he and Mary-Margaret helped everyone stow their luggage and board the bus.

Even though the sun was setting, it was hot and sticky. The air-conditioned bus was blissfully cool and quickly transported us to our hotel. The rooms were small but comfortable. Three yukatas and three pairs of slippers lay neatly folded on the bed, and a teapot and cups were tastefully arranged for the morning. By the time I arrived after completing room assignments, my roommates, Judith and Emmy, were already in bed. Judith reported that Yoko had called to remind us that Yuko would meet us at Tokyo station and she would see us in Kyoto. Everything was okay. Physically exhausted, I gratefully slid between the cool sheets. The last thing I heard was the hum of the air conditioners as I slipped into sleep.

Hours later I awoke with a start. It was dark and the air conditioner still hummed. It was impossible to find a comfortable position, so I gave sleep up as a thing of the past. Since sunrise seemed imminent, I decided to take a quick shower and get a jump on the day.

As I was drying off, I heard a soft tapping sound, and a voice tentatively inquired, "Joy?"

I opened the door and found a sleepy Emmy wanting to enter.

"Didn't mean to wake you," I whispered. "Just thought I'd get an early start."

She cocked her head slightly, opened her eyes a little wider, and looked at me quizzically.

"It's only two o'clock," she whispered back. There was a short, startled pause as I absorbed this information.

"Oh," I responded meekly, "guess I'll go back to bed."

Under the cool sheets once again, I lay still and willed myself to relax. It didn't work. I finally got up and dressed in the dark. Making sure I had the room key, I tiptoed out and put on my shoes. The deep silence of slumber surrounded me. Suddenly I felt elated. I was free. I quietly made my way downstairs. The lobby was deserted, the front door unlocked. I stepped outside.

It was still, the night air warm and heavy with fragrance, the sky filled with soft, milky clouds. I took off my shoes and walked barefoot across the prickly wet grass. I felt effervescent and completely alive. The smell of warm asphalt mingled with the sigh of the wind and the song of insects. Face to the sky, I spread my arms, turning in slow circles. I'm here, in Japan! I felt time curve back on itself and brush me with remembrances just out of reach. Hastily, I pulled a scrap of paper from my pocket and quickly wrote:

Insects like Tibetan bells, softly chiming
My ears ring in harmony.

No thoughts, I told myself, *just be.*

Chapter 5

Travel, Trains, and Taxis

We had successfully navigated our way from Narita to Tokyo by subway, and stood huddled together, a small island in the midst of a torrent of swiftly rushing commuters. Before anyone could be swept away, a young woman approached us. She carried a large purse and wore slacks, a sleeveless blouse, and low-heeled shoes. With a smile, she introduced herself as Yuko Takaki and explained that she had found us easily because she recognized Mary-Margaret from her picture in the *"Brother"* book.

After a short conference, we decided to go directly to platform 6 and await the arrival of the 11:10 bullet train. Once there, we lined up facing the tracks, luggage in hand, packs on back, like horses at the starting gate. The train pulled in, the doors swished open, and we charged. The maneuver was successful, although unnecessary, as we found ourselves standing in an almost empty car. Obviously, we had managed to avoid the famous rush-hour crush.

The doors closed, and the train clacked its way out of Tokyo station, picking up speed as it entered the suburbs. Our luggage was safely resting on the floor, in small overhead racks, and on several empty seats. Bart bags 1 through 4 would travel by truck from the hotel in Narita to our hotel in Kyoto and would not be arriving for several days. There was nothing to do but relax and enjoy the $2^3/_4$-hour ride to Kyoto.

I was seated almost knee to knee facing an older Japanese couple. They were intent on keeping their packages from touching me or my luggage as the train banked around the curves. If a bag shifted, the husband would make a grab for it while glancing up at me. His wife sat quietly, hands folded around a purse in her lap, until a box followed gravity's law and slid a few inches, coming to rest against my foot. She nudged her husband, who leaned down to rescue it. They talked a little between themselves. I tried to smile reassuringly from time to time, but found myself unable to relax, uncomfortable with their discomfort.

We were all relieved when they gathered their parcels together and, with the slightest suggestion of a bow, scurried from the train. I sighed, made myself comfortable, and gave my full attention to the images flashing by. We were traveling above the rooftops, which marched in an orderly progression of heights and patterns to join low hills in the distance. Here and there a patch of green or splash of color hinted at hidden backyards and gardens. Bamboo and weathered fences were interrupted at intervals by small wooden gates. Periodically, the houses would give way to cultivated fields, where occasionally a figure in baggy pants and wide-brimmed hat could be seen bending over, pulling and planting. The sky remained a flat, hazy, white backdrop in front of which the scenery unfolded. From time to time, another train would whoosh past from the opposite direction, seeming to suck us toward a dangerous embrace as we flew by.

The sound of luggage being pulled off the racks and a hubbub of excited voices signaled our imminent arrival at Kyoto Station. Once we unloaded, Yuko suggested we take taxis to the hotel. She found out the cost, and we began squeezing people and bags into the small vehicles. Yuko gave the drivers the hotel's address and off we went. She and I shared a taxi, and I took the opportunity to tell her how grateful we were for her very timely help. The fact that she spoke English made it even easier. It turned out she had studied the language at a school in Berkeley, California, and taught English in Tokyo. She had already been to India and said her experiences there helped to open her mind and heart. We talked about publishing. She told me that she had started her own company, Mahoroba Art, and published her first metaphysical book several years ago. I was very pleased that she would be spending this time with us.

It was only ten minutes to the Travelers Inn. By the time we arrived, there was a flurry of activity as room keys were handed out and directions given. Above the noise I heard Mary-Margaret announce that we would have a short session with Bartholomew in her room before dinner. We had just enough time to get settled and freshen up before the meeting.

Chapter 6

Kyoto: Day One–an Opening Statement That Takes Us by Surprise

At four P.M., 20 people squeezed themselves into every available empty space in Mary-Margaret and Justin's small room. Mary-Margaret sat quietly on the bed, legs crossed and eyes closed, as silence descended on the group. After a few moments her eyes opened, and Bartholomew looked around. Rubbing his hands together, he smiled and said, "Well, my friends, good afternoon. We keep meeting in strange and exotic places, do we not? But not often in Mary-Margaret and Justin's bedroom." He laughed.

Then, eyes flashing, he began speaking in earnest. "You have two unique opportunities, here and also in India, to awaken to that state of consciousness which you have been looking for, for so long. The intention here is to awaken you to the continuous flow of awareness that is always present, so when you are in the Himalayas, you will have relaxed into the present moment sufficiently to be able to let go into the fullness of enlightenment."

Bartholomew paused, observing the sudden astonishment that appeared on several faces, then leaned forward, asking, "And why not? *You* are the ones who don't think you can do it, and I am here to say you can and let us do it *now*. How many more meetings like this do we need? How many more countries must we visit? How many more tours can we organize?

"It is time to do it and get on with it, and I would like to tell you precisely what we mean by 'do it.' You have been *looking* for God, forgetting that what you are *is* the God experience. You have decided that the life you are now living can't be 'It,' so you name the experience something else, and then spend endless time and energy searching for the 'something.' In truth, *this is it! Your experience as you are experiencing it now is It.* You miss it by denying the reality of this statement. You like to believe the God experience can't be present in the midst of your irritation or your boredom or your judgmental response to the heat or your worries or your relationships.

"By the end of the next three weeks, you could know that these things are also a part of God-ness, if you will remember, on an ongoing basis, to drop into the moment and allow yourself *to feel the moment exactly as it is without thinking about it.* You can spend your time hearing without judgment, seeing without judgment, and being without judgment. Allow yourself to experience the simplicity of what I call your natural being, *your* naturalness, in the naturalness of the moment. You are trying to find something that is already fully, totally present. Remember, the greatest obstacle to your enlightenment is the *belief* that you are not already enlightened."

Bartholomew straightened, and his gaze softened. "I know you have often said you don't want enlightenment if what you are experiencing now *is* enlightenment. But this is because you are missing it. You are missing the Light in your own experiences. I want you to discover what that means, my friends. You are never going to feel the Light by looking for it someplace 'other' because it is already present in the state of what is happening right now. Do you understand?" He stopped and looked at us, sensing the tension in people who wanted this understanding so desperately.

Leaning back, he continued. "All right, let's use an example. Say you are aware of feeling hot. As a human being aware of feeling hot, you may have fluctuating moments of irritation, replaced by feelings of guilt over being 'unspiritual' because you are irritated, replaced with the desire for a drink of water, replaced with whatever comes up next in your consciousness.

"Tomorrow, for your first assignment, I would like you to experience this ongoing fluctuation of thought. I would like you to observe thoughts and responses as they rise and fall. Be aware that thoughts and feelings occur *in your body,* and if you can, become aware that your body and mind are also 'occurring' in something else. Everything is going on in something, and it is that mysterious something you are all seeking.

"For this first day, I want you to practice. This is an exercise in Enlightenment. Practice awareness, and as your feelings rise and fall, share with each other whether or not this is working, how it is working, and what your experience of it is. Ask yourselves, 'Who is angry? Who is hungry?'— ask yourself but don't answer. Just stay intensely alert with the question 'Who?' Don't think you know it all." Bartholomew leaned forward and gazed upon us intently.

"I would also like to suggest a second exercise," he said. "You have been taught to view everything as separate, to see the universe as consisting of separated forms. Let us test that theory. Stop and look around, and tell me if you can find anything really separate from anything else."

He waited while we all looked in vain to find something truly separate. The chair was connected to the floor, the floor to the wall, the bodies to the floor, then to each other.

"All right," he continued. "As you go about your day, I want you to notice that all of the seemingly separate things are connected by something." He held up a hand. "Do not get intellectual and call it space or emptiness. Try not to name it; just become aware of it. Everything you look at is contained in something. Of course, when you look at a temple, you will notice that the building is connected to the ground, the trees, the sky, and the people, but please become aware of the vast 'something' that 'all of it' is nestled in. Pay attention, and you will experience a deep sense of the immensity in which all things are contained. Stretch yourselves to meet it. It is good practice.

"Follow these two simple directives as consistently as you can. Remember the rule: What you put your awareness on reveals itself. Use your awareness to help you awaken."

Bartholomew looked at us closely. "Does everyone understand?" In silence we each digested the information and instructions just given.

"My friends, you cannot *think* yourself to God, and the more time you spend in your thinking, judgmental mind, the further you distance yourself from what is happening right now! The mind is the one most constant deflector of awareness. It is true that the mind is a magnificent vehicle capable of amazing things. But just as taking a bath feels wonderful and relaxing, sitting in the tub 24 hours a day, 7 days a week is no longer an exciting event. It's the same with your thoughts.

"Pay attention to how much time you spend in your thinking mind, and you will want to break free from what I would call the tyranny of your mental process. It is a process that takes you out of the moment. On the one hand, it returns you to the past, which is filled with guilt. On the other, it catapults you into a future filled with fantasy and possible terrors. You are caught in the middle, trapped between these two polarities, trying desperately to be happy. It is this feeling of being caught in the middle that you are running from. The way out is to *pay attention.* How many times have you rerun the conversation you had with the person next to you on the bus? How often are you back with the problems you left at home? For all you know, the United States might have blown up and all your problems with it."

Bartholomew smiled. "I am in jest, but do you get the point? They are non problems because they are not here. Don't fuss over them, and don't talk about them. Do not slip into the future either. The future is unknown, and you can only spin fantasies about it. What *do* you know? One thing, really. You are sitting in this room, listening to this windbag, and that's all you know. So we start and end with this moment. There isn't any other. Snuggle down into the moment, and you can stop your relentless thinking. Pay attention. Keep track of how often you slip out of the moment. Listen to your conversations. How often do you talk about past and future? What would you talk about if you were just talking about the present? Try it!

"Awareness is aware of everything, and as the days go on, it will become easier to feel this awareness. If you practice this consistently, I promise, at the end of three weeks not one of you will ask what awareness is. You will know. Whether you choose to use that knowledge is up to you, but *you will know!* We have some exciting days ahead, so stay with it." Bartholomew looked around again, a smile lighting up Mary-Margaret's eyes.

"Practice as much as you can before we next meet. I would appreciate hearing about your resentments and frustrations over this exercise. I prefer you to come in swinging than not to do it at all. That at least will let me know we are engaged in this process. So I will see you again tomorrow."

Mary-Margaret stretched and removed the microphone from her scarf. "Okay, everyone," she said. "Let's meet in front of the Inn tomorrow morning at 7:15, and our friend here will lead us to a cool, quiet, shady spot to have our meeting."

She patted my shoulder, ignoring my raised eyebrows. *What's this?* I thought.

Smiling mischievously, she turned to me directly. "It occurred to me you might like to take a walk in the cool of the evening."

Cool of the evening, my mind echoed. It's 85 degrees.

"And find us a nice, quiet, shady spot to hold the meeting in tomorrow," she continued.

Quiet, shady? I thought to myself. *In the middle of the city?*

"And pretty close by," she added, tapping me on the arm as she turned to go.

"Sure," I said brightly to her retreating back. "No problem."

I grabbed my roommate Emmy, who was innocently passing by at the moment, and dragged her out the door and across the street. I explained our mission as we started walking along the canal that ran parallel to the Inn.

Soon we crossed a stone bridge and followed a path that took us to a large pond surrounded on three sides by small pine trees and rhododendron bushes. We discovered a lattice-covered arbor supported by concrete pillars close by, under which were several benches. This was relatively shady, quiet, and nearby. For coolness we would have to see. We looked at each other and nodded in agreement.

I glanced at my watch. "Fifteen minutes from start to finish," I said with satisfaction. "Let's go back." We turned and headed for our air-conditioned room.

Chapter 7

Kyoto: Day Two—
the Trying Practice of
Being in the Present

T he following morning we were joined by Yuko, her friend Chien, and
Chien's smiling baby, as we gathered at our chosen meeting place and
were greeted by a large flock of gray and white pigeons. A small, wrinkled man dressed in white undershirt and gray trousers was busy serving them
breakfast. His feet were bare, and he hummed softly to the birds as he fed
them. Soon we and the cooing pigeons had all settled in together.

We sat awhile, listening to the sounds of early morning. A rumble of nearby traffic and the slap of sandals meeting sidewalk mingled with the patter of
falling grain and rustling feathers, all blending in quiet harmony. As we
relaxed against the concrete and stone, Mary-Margaret straightened up and
opened her eyes.

"Good morning," Bartholomew began with a smile and a question.
"Would anyone like to volunteer their experiences from yesterday and their
responses to them?"

Patricia spoke up in her dry, Northeastern accent. "I was recalling all the
trouble I had getting here and felt anger rising. I thought I had forgiven everyone connected with that, but I guess there's a level of forgiveness I haven't
reached yet."

Bartholomew held up two fingers. "When you die, you will be asked two
things: How much have you loved, and how much have you learned?" he
responded. "Learning does not mean how many Shakespearean sonnets you
can quote; it means, how much do you know about reality and about
energy itself? It also means, how much have you faced the dark side of your
own psyche?"

He leaned back and continued. "My friends, if you are angry at someone and you have a feeling of 'How *dare* they?' this 'How dare they' is a sign you are not finished facing a difficult part of your own nature. A perfect example of this is the violence you see projected on the television. People watch others acting in destructive ways while they sit safely in their living rooms, surrounded by a comfortable life. It is easy to watch world events and become outraged at 'other people's' violence. But ask yourself this—if you were the one who had everything you cherished taken from you, or had been completely humiliated, what might your response be?"

The answers came immediately. "Indifference, righteousness, judgmentalness, irrationality, pain, fear, anger."

Bartholomew continued. "Remember one of the basic laws of human consciousness. That which angers you has something to do with you and is therefore connected to you! Stop trying to always be holy, spiritual, and wise, and you will begin to see this. You all have moments when you treat others in ways they resent or are hurt by. Is there anyone here who feels they are impeccable in their thoughts and actions toward others? Sometimes you act with love, understanding, and forgiveness; and sometimes you act outraged, judgmental, and violent. It all coexists in the human psyche.

"Please understand, as these next days unfold, you are going to be mirrors for each other; you will see yourself reflected in each other. You do not come on tours like this only to see temples or even the Dalai Lama. *You come to see yourself.* You come to face yourself: the good, the bad, and the ugly, and to learn how you deal with all of it. Let's have a little bit of humor. Try to let go a bit. See yourselves and others as human, too. What a surprise!" He laughed.

"Can you entertain the idea that under certain trying circumstances you could do, and probably have done, some of the same awful things you are so outraged at 'others' for doing? There is a certain irony in all of this. The world provides endless faces for you to deal with. Do you understand? You and the world are one. Claim all the faces the world provides as your own, with as much humor and letting go as you can. Is it a difficult lesson? Absolutely. Is it an essential lesson? *Absolutely.* This is the essence of understanding the human condition. If you really feel 'you' are better than 'others'; if you think you could never do what 'they' have done, you are fooling 'yourself.' Under certain intense circumstances, you are all capable of both amazingly beautiful and exciting actions and those that are less than exalted. It's the spectrum of humanity. When you admit all the similarities, your outrage toward people and circumstances will begin to taper off."

He crossed his arms. "Is there anything else from yesterday?"

"It was the internal, unceasing mind chatter that drove me crazy," I blurted out. "I was concerned about the things that were difficult yesterday and the day before, as well as what was going to happen today, tomorrow, and the rest of the trip! I could feel the tension. I was struggling to drop all of it and be in the moment. The more I tried, the worse it got."

Bartholomew laughed. "Did you hear that?" He seemed pleased. "She said, 'I tried to be in the moment.' With that statement comes a new set of rules, the major rule now being, 'I have to be in the moment.' You might as well say, 'I have to climb Mount Everest.' There are no rules! No 'have to's! If we create another 'have to,' we are back where we started. Being in the moment is not something you *have* to do. It is something *you are always doing and cannot cease to do.* You are not aware that it is a constant, ongoing occurrence, and therein lies the difficulty.

"The so-called doing is already done because this moment is where you are, and this moment is all there is. It is what is. It *is* what's happening. To help you remember this, watch the rise and fall of your breath, and observe the ongoing passage of 'thinking thoughts.' Become aware of the *act* of simply hearing, not judging what you hear. These things will put you right in the moment.

"As an example, let's use this 'act' of hearing. Do you will yourself to hear? Do you consciously make that decision, or is hearing something that happens, which you then become aware of? How about thinking? Do you decide to think? You may decide what to think, but do you decide to *think?* Do you decide to breathe or see, or are breathing and seeing sensations you become aware of in the present spontaneous moment? There is something going on in this moment that you are responding to all the time. There is something alive that you need to learn to become aware of and begin to relax into.

"I want as many of these kinds of relaxed moments as you can experience today. Again and again and again, I want you to be aware that hearing, seeing, breathing, and thinking are spontaneously rising and falling. Be aware of all of it. Don't struggle with *how* to be aware. Do not think you have to start being aware of awareness. You can't be aware of awareness; you can only *be* awareness.

"These are simply words until you have the experience of being in the moment. How do you experience anything? By using what you have. You know you can hear. You know you can see. You know you can breathe. And you certainly know you can think. Stay with what you know. Don't tell yourself stories; don't 'make things up.' Don't get fancy; stay with what is intimately surrounding you for the rest of the day, and we'll take it up again tomorrow."

A hand was raised, and Bartholomew turned toward Linda. "Let me tell you what I did last night," she exclaimed. "I didn't think about anything! I just tried to figure out what it was all in. I was absolutely amazed to find that behind it all was this . . . I don't know how to describe it, but it was like ecstasy."

Bartholomew smiled. "The true nature of the human 'Being' is complete bliss and ecstasy. It is a total, full state of well-being. In the midst of any difficulty, any pain, rejection, loss, misunderstanding, confusion, or doubt, there is an absolute, ongoing constancy that those who experience it call ecstasy. I have been talking about this ecstasy for years, and I am very grateful to you for expressing it. Behind all the ever-changing ego drama is the bliss, the well-being of Being."

He spread his arms wide and beamed. "And that's the reason I am one of the best friends you will ever have. What do I want for you, my friends? I want you to experience ecstasy, bliss, and well-Being. I am not taking you down this path to suffer, suffer, suffer. We are here in this beautiful city because it is filled with the knowing of the natural. The natural self is beautifully filled with natural well-Being. Sit in the moment, as best you can with the rat-a-tat-tat barrage of past and future hammering at you, and breathe, see, and hear in the moment, as it 'naturally' is."

The Body's Language

George, who was sitting on a stone bench surrounded by his cameras, lenses, light meters, and extra boxes of film, spoke up. "What about the people you have difficulty with, people you can't say 'no' to? How do you deal with them?" he asked.

"Most of you still believe if you can get your external world to smile and tell you you're a good and worthwhile person, you will be happy," Bartholomew replied. "My friends, if you are paying attention, you must realize that the world smiles at you some of the time, frowns at you some of the time, and sometimes doesn't even know you are there. Every time you attempt to relate to another person, all the games of human separation come up. You consciously or subconsciously begin to ask, 'Do they like me or not? Am I accepted or not?' It is a constant mental chatter that begins instantly. Instead of this kind of 'mental' interaction, I suggest you drop out of your 'thinking mind' and learn to become aware of the vast space you and this 'other person' are occupying."

Bartholomew leaned forward, pointing to several people for emphasis. "If you look at these bodies from a *spatial* point of view, you will see how small they are compared to the space they are resting in. Most of the time when people are engaged with each other, they are watching the eyes, the mouth, or the body of 'the other person,' waiting for some response from them. There is no relaxation, no happiness, no bliss possible in that intimate moment, just a watchful waiting, like a cat at a mouse hole. It might get you dinner, but it's not going to get you much else," he said with a laugh.

"Once you become aware of the incredible space surrounding every 'thing,' whether it's an idea, belief, opinion, object, or body, you will relax and allow yourself to see that the interaction between you and 'it' is more interesting and spacious than you imagined. There is so much more present, you will not mind so much if the person frowns instead of smiles. Everything both shrinks and expands to its proper perspective, two small little bodies in the midst of an immense, vast, marvelous space. It's the importance you attach to the response of this 'other person' that causes pain. When the person becomes part of a vaster reality, they are no longer the only focus. The tension arising over, 'Did I do it right? Can I do it right? Am I safe?' will begin to ease. Then you can decide what you need to do."

Bartholomew turned to the rest of us. "All of these questions are very minor. In the end, what you like and dislike are just ever-changing parts of the human condition. Your beliefs and attitudes rise and fall all the time. When you see they are less interesting than the experience of the vastness in which they rise and fall, *which is the space,* you can begin to develop a sense of humor around your ever-changing desires. Then someone can tell you they don't like what you're doing, and, instead of jumping up and throttling them, you can smile and say, "That's an interesting point of view' and mean it, instead of, 'How could you possibly say that?'"

Bartholomew leaned back and relaxed. "Can you feel the tension of trying to force the external world to meet your ever-changing picture of how it should look? In the end it's relatively unimportant. I know the ego rebels at such statements, but your likes and dislikes are really unimportant in the light of your true nature. You change your point of view more often than you change your clothes, *but you are not aware of it.* Today you would fight to the death to keep a point of view that you may give up tomorrow at the drop of a hat. So let's relax around all of this and recognize that each one of you is a disappointment to someone. Can we start with the knowledge that you are *all* part of the human race, and allow yourself the wonderful let-go of being part of that wholeness?"

Laurel, who had been taking notes, looked up and said, "I try to be aware of myself, but I realize how afraid I am most of the time. How can I really be aware of myself in the midst of that fear?"

Bartholomew was quick to reply. "I think you are afraid because you have defined yourself as something very small. People who need to be aware of themselves are identifying with a limited kind of personality, something dark, unworthy, or 'less than' others."

He looked around. "Do you understand what she is saying?" Turning to Laurel, he continued. "If I'm wrong, please correct me. What she is stating is this: Oftentimes when people have been trained by difficulties in early child-hood, they have to be on their guard about their environment, more than other people. They have to be very watchful because they feel their environment can turn against them at any time. They become very good at reading signals from the people around them so they are not taken by surprise. As they get older, they would like to drop the defensiveness because it is a stance that causes separation from others, and that causes stress in the physical body."

He leaned forward and looked at her lovingly. "There is no one in your environment out to get you like that anymore, my lovely one, and there is certainly no one in this group who is out to get you at all.

"You have an opportunity to practice with this group for three weeks. You can relax without having to be on guard against anyone. During that time, I want you to be willing to look at everything with a nonjudgmental response. Tell your body to relax. It is very tense, so give it that message again and again. Practice with people you already feel a bit relaxed around. Don't go to the hardest person on the tour and start with them. Start where it's the easiest or most gentle for you."

Addressing the rest of us, he went on. "Let's get back to basics for a moment. There are at least three trillion cells in the body. These three trillion cells are constantly listening for messages from your mind. While *you* may not be paying conscious attention, the cells are always listening. And they hear all the repetitive trivia that goes through your mind. They respond to what they hear by expanding or contracting. When they hear something that makes them feel safe, they expand. When they hear something fearful, they contract. Give your cells the conscious command to relax and expand, relax and expand. Let this be a sweet, gentle mantra through all your tense moments, and the cells *will* begin to relax and expand in the midst of anything. The ongoing message of safety given to the cells can be the greatest help you receive.

"When your cells relax, you have more options, you see more 'might be's,' and you want more options. You want to be able to choose different responses. You want to be relaxed, no longer 'uptight.' You want to be open and alive to the moment. Humanity is finally beginning to realize that bodies and minds are interconnected. The mind gives the body messages, and the body responds. It's the body/mind combination that can bring you a feeling of well-being, love, and light; or a feeling of tension, fear, and separation. It's up to you what message it receives."

Jim raised his hand. "We talk a lot about being nonjudgmental. What is the difference between indifference and being nonjudgmental?" he asked.

Bartholomew paused a moment. "People are constantly 'reading' one another," he responded. "It's like mental braille, your mind interpreting what your eyes take in. In response, you can give yourself any number of directives. One is to be indifferent about what you have observed. This produces a feeling of deadness or flatness. You have already made a judgment but buried it behind this indifference. Another directive you might give yourself is to simply decide to see what's 'really there.' That is being nonjudgmental. That is the willingness to see what's in front of you just as it is, without comparing it to anything."

He rested a hand on the concrete pillar beside him. "Most of you see/think. All I am asking for is seeing, without the need to think about your seeing. It's like looking at this wonderful pillar. Your mind can be filled with questions. What kind of pebbles are in it, where did these pebbles come from, how strong is the pillar, what kind of concrete did they use, how long did it take to make it, who made it, and where does that person live? You see, the *pillar* is no longer here. It no longer is as it is; it is as you 'think' it. But if you are willing to simply look with the full awareness of 'seeing,' all of a sudden you will see it and the space around it differently. It doesn't have to tell you anything. You don't have to go out and join it. You're already joined. There is only One. Simply rest your awareness on it, and it will come to life for you, in its own 'is-ness.'

"There is a big difference between being nonjudgmental and being indifferent. You feel this difference in your body all the time. Love, or being nonjudgmental, is a relaxed accepting of the moment, exactly as it is, without the need to change anything. Indifference is a barrier between you and what is happening in the moment. You have a need to distance yourself from something, so you are not totally present. You have vacated the premises, which are your bodies. For whatever reason, you don't want to be in the moment, so you are just not there."

Bartholomew patted the pillar affectionately and turned toward us again. "As you go through the day, I'd like you to watch the rise and fall of your acceptance and rejection of whatever is happening. Watch yourself approve or disapprove of what is going on. Don't scold yourself; just take note of it."

Leaning back, he studied the folded hands in his lap and spoke slowly. "I want to talk for a few minutes about the physical body. There is a way to be totally immersed in heat and perspiration and be absolutely blissful at the same time." He stabbed a finger at us. "Your happiness is not determined by the state of the weather or any other external condition!" he exclaimed. "If today you immerse yourself in feelings of being uncomfortable, you will miss out on some of the most incredible beauty you will ever see or experience. So instead of worrying about how hot you are, just breathe and allow yourself to fully feel the heat and whatever else is going on at the same time."

He gazed at us thoughtfully, then smiled. "I want you to experience the bliss of being hot, the total excitement of being saturated with sweat, the satisfaction of dunking your head in the water whenever you need to. Physical misery is one of many miseries, and if you can get into close rapport with physical misery, the other, less observable miseries become easier to bear. Are you going to be hot? Yes. Does it matter? No. Don't run away from the feeling of being uncomfortable. If you let yourselves be trapped by your physical comforts or discomforts, you will miss some life-changing experiences."

His blue eyes sparkled. "I would like a bliss report on misery tomorrow." There was uncertain laughter from the group. "I am in jest," he continued, "but please, my friends, don't separate yourselves from it. To try and stop being miserable about being hot is the best way to be totally miserable. Stay with it, and we will meet again tomorrow."

Accentuating the Positive

Mary-Margaret unclipped the microphone. "Today is the day we have a bus to take us to some of the outlying temples," she announced. "Everyone please get your things together, and meet in the lobby at 8:45. The bus will be ready to leave by 9:00. Don't forget your water bottles and bandannas!" she added as everyone headed back to the Inn.

The front door of the Inn opened directly into a small reception area made even smaller by several counters filled with colorful brochures and postcards. The lobby was a state of mind rather than an actual location, and left little room to fit 20 people and their day packs. We overflowed into the restaurant, which, luckily, was empty. Everyone checked sunglasses, hats, umbrellas, water bottles, and each other, preparing like an expectant army about to take to the field. Here and there, sun-blocked noses were thrust deep into city maps, and pockets bulged with essential supplies such as tissues and chocolate chip cookies.

At last we were all accounted for. Yuko led us out to the biggest, shiniest bus I had ever seen. We were met by a smiling, uniformed hostess and were ushered aboard. After everyone was settled into the waiting arms of the soft, reclining seats, the driver, who was strapped into the captain's chair, straightened his perfectly straight tie, gave a final tug to his immaculate white gloves, and thumbed the starter. The engine throbbed into life. He flipped a switch, and a small TV monitor lit up, showing him a view of what was behind the bus. Checking the screen and each rearview mirror, the driver backed neatly into the street, swung the nose around, and we were on our way.

Like a cruising ocean liner, we sailed down broad avenues, navigated narrow passageways hemmed in by tall buildings, and finally emerged into the clear green depths of the open road. The houses, shimmering in waves of heat, receded into the distance, while schools of people on the hot pavement swam from pool-like shadow to pool-like shadow. That would be us tomorrow, but today we cruised in air-conditioned comfort.

The day unrolled in a kaleidoscope of new sights, sounds, and experiences. Our explorations began north of the city at Kusama. Massive and grounded in its own serenity, the 1,222-year-old temple welcomed us. We strolled its paths, drank its water, and sat in the shade of its shrines, not one of us unmoved by its presence.

South and west of Kusama, the silence of monks meditating had long since saturated the small sub-temples at Daitokuji. Daisen-in reflected a stillness in which a sudden footstep became the beat of a heart, and the sound of shoeless feet gliding over wooden floors, a reminder of its past. The dry sand garden, an ancient chronicle of nature and man, was as soothing to our sight as the silence was to our spirits. Time stopped. We sat, breathed it in, gave it back, breathed it in, gave it back. We left the temple and ate ice cream cones while standing in the heat. We flowed with the day, and the day inevitably took us home.

At dusk, Justin, Mary-Margaret, and I went in search of dinner. We stopped at a small noodle house around the corner. Its open sliding door was an invitation to enter. It smelled delicious. Neither man behind the counter spoke English, but our Japanese was impeccable.

"Soba noodles with tempura, please, " I rattled off.

"Biiru," or more precisely, "Asahi," Justin added.

"Arigato," chimed in Mary-Margaret with a slight bow.

Along with many gestures, these words magically produced large bowls of thick, steaming soup filled with buckwheat noodles and plump, breaded shrimp. This was accompanied by several very large bottles of icy-cold beer. We lingered over our meal, enjoying the food, the people, and the surroundings. Our dinner finished, and satisfied in every way by a deeply beautiful day, we strolled back to the Inn.

Chapter 8

Kyoto: Day Three— See No Judgment, Hear No Judgment, Speak No Judgment

The room was pitch black as I fumbled among my clothes, searching for the mini-flashlight tucked somewhere in my shoe. The air conditioner hummed, and it was pleasantly warm under the quilted covers. Emmy was still asleep a few feet away. Between us we almost filled the Japanese-style room we had moved into late yesterday. I sat up, flipped the switch on the flashlight, and checked my watch: 3:52 A.M.—again! I lay back down in disgust, worrying about the lack of sleep, and wondering where we were going to put the furniture.

Mary-Margaret, Justin, and I agreed that the park had been a lovely setting for the meeting, *and* it was too uncomfortable. We needed someplace quieter and cooler. Especially cooler. Darcy and Sharon had volunteered the use of their room, which they said was a tiny bit larger. The plan was to move as much of their furniture as possible into Mary-Margaret and Justin's room before the meeting began. And here I was, busy at 3:52 A.M. trying to picture where to put it all.

Having driven sleep completely away, I carefully worked my way out from beneath the covers. The room was chilly, and I hastily grabbed my clothes and stepped over the high threshold into the small bathroom. I dressed, brushed my teeth, and checked my watch again: 4:10. Tiptoeing the few steps to the door, I impulsively snatched my Walkman on the way out.

Downstairs all was quiet. Through the front door, trees were just beginning to appear in the pearly light of morning. I left the Inn, slipping on the headphones and attaching the player to my belt. After I punched the play button, the opening sounds of Kitaro's "Ten Years"[6] slid into the space between my ears. Everything slowed. I looked around. Bells shimmered in my head. I walked. Leaves danced before my eyes. The air was opalescent. My feet fell between the notes. Everything I saw bowed, swayed, bent, flickered, shook, flowed, ran, and burst open in time to the music. These were precious moments of perfect harmony, strung together by the emptiness of early morning. Alone with Kitaro and Kyoto, filled with gratitude, overflowing with appreciation, humble with happiness, I returned to the Inn.

A few early-morning risers were gathered in the restaurant sipping tea and quietly talking. I found Mary-Margaret, and together we knocked on Darcy's door. She and Sharon looked bright, cheerful, and well scrubbed as we began to move their furniture, backpacks, duffel bags, and collection of assorted fruit next door. Their room emptied quickly, and Mary-Margaret's began to look like the inside of a thrift store. We carried in the last bed frame, pausing in the doorway, wondering where to put it.

"Hey, are you going to put this thing down, or do we hold it all morning?" Darcy grumbled good-naturedly from her end of the bed. We squeezed into the room and stacked it on the other frames, piling the mattresses on top. Mary-Margaret arrived with the last table lamp and gingerly placed it on the pinnacle of the precarious-looking heap.

"Good Lord," she said, "I certainly hope I haven't left anything I need by the window."

"The hotel staff is going to think we're crazy," came Darcy's disembodied voice. At this moment, Sharon stuck her head in the door. "Anyone want a banana?" she asked, a lopsided grin on her face.

"I really think it's time to begin," Mary-Margaret suggested helpfully as we filed out the door. Everyone had found a seat in the almost-empty room when Bartholomew greeted us.

"Good morning, my friends," he said, rubbing his hands together. "I am sure you have all practiced feeling the space we talked about yesterday. I would like to hear your experiences of how you worked with the simplicity of seeing, hearing, and thinking without judgment. I would be grateful for any response."

He looked around and nodded to Lee, who carefully put her pen down, clasped her hands together, and looked at him thoughtfully. "There was a temple with a monk praying," she said. "It was an ongoing monotone sound, and a baby was crying right next to me, and people were talking all around me." She paused a moment, then continued. "And my expectations when I came here were, as always, that I will be totally centered in all these foreign countries, and this particular building would be all mine, quiet and still. It never happens, and I don't know why I keep expecting it to be that way. So I stepped back and really allowed myself to hear all these sounds going on, and soon it became interesting. I used to get upset about being disappointed at not having conditions the way I wanted them. This was a good exercise for me," she ended. "I needed to do it."

"That's beautiful," Bartholomew responded. Turning to the rest of us, he inquired, "Did you all have the same kind of experience?" He waited to see how many hands went up. "You see," he went on, "this is an external lesson that reflects an internal truth. You cannot organize your lives to always look the way you want them to. You cannot get the outside world to be silent. The baby will always cry. The people will always talk. The dog will always bark. Things happen. Please understand; the job is *not* to choose between the chanting monk and the crying baby. The job is to learn to allow it all.

"Being able to really do this is tremendously helpful," he continued. "Actions rise and fall. Events rise and fall. Sounds rise and fall. Emotions rise and fall. Sometimes we smile, and sometimes we frown. Everything rises and falls in the midst of a vast 'Something.' Pay attention. Don't get stuck on whether you like or dislike what happens to be rising and falling in a particular moment, because in the next moment it will be different."

Bartholomew held a finger to his lips. "It was as if someone said, 'Shh, Lee needs to be quiet.'" He smiled. "When you say 'Shh, I need it to be quiet,' it doesn't happen, but when you invite it all in—the children, the noise, the discomforts, even the people applauding you and the people booing you—something happens." He clapped his hands together and spread them wide. "All of a sudden, that wonderful open space in which things rise and fall is experienced, and you no longer have the tension produced by wanting everything to look a certain way.

"You see, one of the difficulties of trying to control the external world is that the body pays a tremendous price." Bartholomew shook his head and repeated softly, "A tremendous price. And when you finally allow all things to simply happen, the body begins to relax. It can then breathe its own breath, with its own rhythm, expansively and deeply. The experience in the temple is the experience of your life. When you take journeys like this, you do tend to have greater expectations that certain external events will take place. When those expectations are not met, you have the opportunity to observe your response.

"Expectation is one of the things that gets in the way of love. You expect other people to be wise or loving enough to know what you want or need. But can they, really? This is a trap you fall into over and over again. Then add to it your own expectations for yourself. If *you* were only loving enough, you would not have resentment or get upset over such little things."

Hands on knees, Bartholomew leaned forward. "The fact is, ladies and gentlemen, sometimes you are loving and sometimes you are not. To pretend that you can, with your limited egos, sustain an ongoing state of love is the height of arrogance, and I ask you to stop it. It is the ego that says, 'I have to be the perfect lover.' Oh, really? By whose definition? Yours! And what if the other person doesn't agree with your definition of 'a perfect lover'? What if they had something totally different in mind? Please realize, an expectation is based on what the ego likes or believes, and *that's all it is."*

He leaned back again. "I would like to talk about another assignment for this afternoon. Will you play with the concept of getting excited about hearing points of view totally different, even abrasive, to your own? I would like you to focus on the *excitement* of listening to and *appreciating* other people's beliefs, ideas, actions, and desires.

"You want to stretch spiritually? That is a good stretch. If someone is saying, 'blah, blah, blah,' and you don't believe in their blah, blah, blah, try finding a place in your consciousness where you drop out of your judgmental mind and join with them. A place where you can relax and allow other opinions, beliefs, and other points of view to exist alongside your own. A neutral place that actually finds these differences interesting. If you are willing to relax and be open to 'others,' and to the moment just as it is, you will begin to have a sense of safety. This can lead to the place where you are joined as one."

"I would like to feel that joining," Ellen responded quietly. "What is so painful is when I feel I am being harmful."

"There is only one question I would ask you, lovely one. In these events when you experience yourself as harmful, do you set out to do harm? Is your intention to 'harm' another? Or is *harmfulness* a word that arises when *certain specific conditions are present?* This is a very important point. There is only one question at such moments: 'What is my motive?' If it is, 'This morning I am going to find so-and-so and shake them until their teeth fall out,' that could be experienced as a harmful act. It is the *decision* to do harm that is harmful. Most of what you call *harmful* are responses that feel uncomfortable when certain events are happening.

"Please realize that each of you is going to do things other people feel are harmful. It is part of living with other limited egos. What you usually mean by 'being harmful' is that the other person doesn't like what you are doing. But is that a real definition of *harmful?* Many people say that someone yelling at them is harmful. Yet, at times, to yell at someone may save their life or awaken them to their own inner truth. So, let us agree it may be possible there is no one definition of what is harmful.

"I suggest you begin relaxing into 'what is' by realizing that there are moments when you *are* considered harmful. That is the way of egos! By no longer being fixated on the view of yourself as harmless, we can move to a deeper, more creative level. Dealing with the feeling of "I am being harmful' is really a question of dealing with the inevitable clash of what your ego believes and what others believe. It is possible to move past the ego's limited interpretations of both definitions and rest in the natural state of true harmlessness."

Mary-Margaret stretched, and we took a short break. As we settled back into our places, Patricia and Mary-Margaret were talking about love and serving others. Mary-Margaret clipped the microphone to her scarf, settled into an upright position, and Bartholomew began again.

"I hope one of the markers I leave behind will be one that says that growth doesn't have to come through suffering. It can come through compassion and through sweet, gentle, immediate love. Let's talk a minute about this. Someone in New Zealand asked a question about 'service.' He said he believed service was what bound lives together, what made life worth living. Service, as defined by this particular gentleman, was his loving action in the world brought about because he wanted to be a good person. He further felt he could 'gain points' by doing such service. But is that true? What is real service?"

He leaned back and settled himself more comfortably. "Real service is an action that arises spontaneously when love is present and feels an action would be appropriate. It doesn't call itself service. It is the action of doing whatever 'needs to be done,' with no concern for the results. There is a world of difference between this and 'service to produce a certain end.' If you see yourself as a server, please be careful. It may be your ego doing the serving. If so, your ego is what will get the benefits, and the benefits are a fatter ego! Until you understand this, laugh a little at yourself, and realize you are doing things that look like service because they make you feel better and you like that view of yourself.

"If someone says, 'I must serve. I must love. I must be kind,' it is the limited ego 'I' talking. Let me give you an example. A woman came up to Krishnamurti at the end of one of his lectures. 'Oh, we have the same job,' she said, because she gave lectures all around the world as well. 'There is a difference,' he replied. 'You do it because you need to. I do it because I have to,' meaning, she had a need that was being served by lecturing, while he lectured because the action of love would not allow him not to. Krishnamurti didn't say, 'How wonderful, another year of lecturing' or 'How awful, another year of lecturing.' It was his life at the moment, and that spontaneity could change at any moment."

Patricia spoke up, "Do we need clashes of egos in order to grow?"

Bartholomew smiled. "At the ego stage we are talking about, it is the most obvious way. It is relatively easy for people to observe a connection between what is happening outside and what is happening inside. The external mirrors the internal. This is usually thought of as a painful process. But the other, the beautiful side of mirroring is rarely thought about. For example, if you are standing in front of a great work of art and find yourself responding to its beauty and power, that is *also* you. But rarely do you see this as yourself. You angle the mirror so you perceive all the negative aspects as a reflection of who you are, and all the wonderful, wise, positive aspects of who you are not. So the dog droppings on the sidewalk may be a mirror for you, but the beautiful gate through which you walk will almost certainly not be! This is *selective choice*. What you need is to embrace it all. Allow your whole being to open and relax into 'Aaaah,' in gratitude and awareness that whatever is happening, is you. Stretch into the 'ah' of all life a little more."

The Relief of Relaxing into the Moment

Bartholomew slapped Mary-Margaret's abdomen several times. "You know what they say in Zen. There is a blind Buddha in the hara, so make it see. That's what we are talking about. You have to see in a new way, a way that sees life fully. You have to allow yourself to see from a place other than the limited ego, which is always postulating polarities: right and wrong, smiles and frowns, male and female, pleasure and pain.

"When you were meditating in the Zen garden yesterday, you may have noticed something interesting. If you gazed softly and long enough, the two mounds of raked gravel disappeared. There was just one long expanse of unified gravel. What had been separated was now joined. Then a few moments later, the two mounds reappeared. Whoever created this garden knew that separation is illusory and also had the awareness to create a visual field so others could experience this transformation. The skill of the Zen masters who created those visions is continuing to help others allow the blind Buddha to see. Separation, then Oneness, then separation. This is the way the world really is. Both ways of seeing are possible. All of a sudden, as you look at something, a seeming miracle takes place—you awaken to a new way of seeing. It takes willingness and practice to do this. The ego will resist, but that's all right, too."

Judith, who was sitting directly in front of Bartholomew, leaned forward and said, "I felt the desire yesterday to see and feel in a certain way, and I wanted to be detached from that desire."

Bartholomew looked at her fondly. "When stated that way, desire and detachment are two sides of the same coin. What you are really looking for is the state in which desire and detachment can both be present. Usually, desire means you are moving toward something, and detachment means you are moving away from it. We need a word that embraces both and yet has neither of those connotations. It is more like a total acceptance of everything. What most people mean by detachment is a withdrawal of life force, interest, and involvement from the situation. In reality, the one who is truly detached is so totally present that all of their interest and attention is readily available.

"Detachment is the gift of the great gurus, the great teachers. They are unconcerned with the next moment because it holds no fear for them. They can be totally present with you and the situation just as it is, with no separation. Instead of saying they are detached, you could say they are totally engaged. What they are detached from are the results of that engagement. What you do as a result of their teaching is really of little interest to them. Your response is entirely up to you. You could throw their advice back and say, 'It's useless,' and they will say, 'Fine,' or you could tell them, 'It's wonderful,' and they will still say, 'Fine,' So instead of the usual sense of detachment, meaning withdrawal, we would like to encourage you to be more present. Stay in the moment. Listen and see without judgment. Breathe, with the awareness of breath. Let it all come in."

Looking around, Bartholomew nodded to Eleanor. "I'd like to know your experience," he said.

Without hesitation, she replied, "I found a lot more bliss in the heat than I thought I would."

"I'm very glad," he responded. "Talk about that for a moment."

"Well," she said, "I anticipated that it would be really difficult, and it turned out not to be a big deal. I just kept reminding myself to be open to what was happening. I did really well during the day, and then we went to dinner." Eleanor shook her head. "And I never gave it another thought," she finished ruefully. We all laughed. "It was really wonderful in the temples and gardens to find those moments. But in the end, back in the human interchanges, it was no longer so easy to remember."

"Well done!" Bartholomew exclaimed. "Let's go back to the blind Buddha within each of you. The goal is to make the Buddha see. When someone becomes enlightened, they have the ability to see things as they really are. They do not need to change them, weigh them, or analyze them. Love dwells in the midst of that kind of clear, present acceptance. The awakened Buddha says, 'I will be joyfully present this moment, with whatever persona you are manifesting now, whether you love me or hate me. Being with your Being is enough.'

"But please understand, it often takes time and practice to see like that. I am asking you to keep on practicing. You *can* see without judgment. And again, let me suggest that one of the most helpful ways to do that is to allow yourself to become aware of the space that surrounds the person in front of you. Allow your awareness to expand into the spaciousness they are standing in over and over again. Allow it to expand out amongst the trees, past the buildings, the clouds, and the sky. Cultivate that sense of easy expansion. It will help tremendously, because whatever the limiting situation is, you will be able to see it as quite small when compared to the vastness you have become aware of."

Bartholomew shifted his position. "Let us say you are having difficulty with someone at home. You have some kind of unfinished business with them. If you are responding the way most humans do, you try to *think* your way through the situation. You analyze, weigh, and judge. Who is right? Who is wiser? You keep thinking about what you can do, should do, must do, are going to do. Then you become aware of what they might do, could do, should do, are going to do. That kind of thinking is relatively useless, so I would like to suggest something that might be more helpful. Begin by remembering that each of you has so much more help and guidance available than just your thinking process. Additional information comes from your intuitive knowing of the entire situation, as well as the 'felt sense' in your body in the moment.

"When you are in difficulty with someone, instead of thinking about the problem, please use these 'other parts of your Being.' Feel how they feel. Sense their fears. Be aware of the vastness of space around them, as far out as you can. Allow your body to 'feel into the moment,' picking up so much more than thoughts. I know this sounds trite, but you might also consider sending a loving thought to them, saying something as direct as 'I want all to be well between us.' Then drop it and move on to what is next in the moment. Even if nothing changes between you, *you* will benefit greatly from this effort. Your body and mind will relax, release, become vaster, more spacious, and less constricted.

"Unless you intervene in a conscious way, you will keep replaying the old 'negative' interactions over and over again, and there will be no clarity or space for real healing. Send them the message you *really* want them to receive, which might be, 'I wish you happiness. I care about you and yearn for us to work through this situation.' See the space, see the happiness, see the relaxation of their body, and *mean it when you wish them well.* You cannot do this if deep inside you don't really have these wishes for another. It is only possible if you *truly* wish for peace between you."

"What happens if it's not a person but events you are worried about?" interjected Emmy.

"It is a little more difficult when you are facing abstract worries about the future. Remember, we talked about the tyranny of the past through guilt and the terror of the future through anticipation of disaster. Difficult events take place in everyone's life. So it is best to begin by acknowledging that life has such potentiality. Do not hide from such an obvious truth. Haven't such events already happened? Perhaps they have not been world-shaking, but they have shaken your world. They have certainly been enough to land you flat on your back, frightened and helpless and scared. Is this true?" Many of us nodded in agreement as Bartholomew continued. "Be aware that part of your consciousness is fearful because of past memories. When fear comes up, I recommend a very basic response. *Simply be aware that fear has now been activated in you.* Name it. 'Total, complete, and utter terror is present.' Even the saying of it seems to lessen it.

"Along with the fear, and often hidden by it, there is also an *excitement* present. The human consciousness knows it is through change that life expands and unfolds in new ways. As fearful as any changes in your life might seem, please be aware that there is also the potential for exciting movement. Even when you speak in terms of big Earth changes, do you not also feel an anticipatory kind of excitement at the possibility of the old collapsing, allowing something new and more interesting to arise?

"To admit this excitement is very difficult, because you know that these changes will also bring tremendous pain and suffering. But try to be courageous enough to face the possibility that world changes will bring great opportunities. Think for a moment what it might be like to live in a 'future' world where equality was the goal rather than the amassing of power."

Bartholomew smiled and raised an inviting hand to George. "You had some interesting experiences yesterday, did you not?" he asked.

George looked down at his hands for a moment. "I was taking pictures in that first large temple at Mount Kurama. Then I sat down and leaned against the inside wall of the temple, and the tears began to flow," he answered. His voice reflected his amazement. "That whole day, each temple we went to, I would start to cry again." He touched his swollen right cheek. "Each time I cried, what made up the swelling seemed to dissipate." George fell silent.

"Yes, my friend," agreed Bartholomew, "because you are an intelligent man, I know you have already stumbled onto one of the keys to your healing." He pointed to the right side of his face and continued. "One way to talk about the blockage in this area of the face is to say it is where you hold your tears. Unfortunately, your society says it is unmanly to cry. So all of the unshed sorrows are held back. I think it is vital to good health to allow everyone to do what they need to do to cleanse the pain out of their physical bodies. Crying is one of those ways. I would suggest to you, my lovely friend, that you cry your eyes out for as long as you need to. In so doing, you will begin to wash out the locked-in pain, and when that pain goes, there is a chance the dis-ease can also go. Keep crying, and the rest of you people, please, when he cries, leave him alone. Just give him your loving, steady, yet distant, support. That, and an occasional tissue."

Bartholomew leaned back and was silent a moment. "I would like to conduct a little experiment today that might bring up some resistance. I want you to pay close attention right now to how you feel about your body." Everyone closed their eyes in order to follow this directive.

"When you are in touch with the feeling of how you actually feel about your body," he went on, "I want you to say to yourself, *I totally love and accept my magnificent body.* This statement may be the furthest from your own, but do it anyway. Then wait a moment and allow yourself to feel that acceptance. Don't make it a mental exercise. Try it and see what happens." We were silent as we all tried to get in touch with *having* a magnificent body and then loving and accepting it totally. The silence was broken by a giggle.

"What's the first thing that happens?" Bartholomew asked.

"Relaxation." "Radiance." "Warmth." "Joy . . . bubbles of joy," were some of the answers.

"Thank you. Now, I want you to give yourselves this message over and over again for the rest of the day. Say it with focused awareness, and then wait a few moments to have the body receive it. Do it hundreds of times today. Ladies and gentlemen, I mean *hundreds,*" he repeated emphatically. *"I totally love and accept my magnificent body.* It is a message your body may not have heard in its entire lifetime. If you had treated any friend of yours with the same amount of judgmental scolding with which you treated your body, they would have left long ago. You have subjected it to long and continual internalized verbal abuse year after year. Do you hear me?" he asked sternly.

"If any of you have any kind of physical or mental difficulty you are trying to heal or understand, this is the exercise for you. In the end, the presence of dis-ease is partly a resistance to the bliss and beauty of God-Consciousness. Your mind will say, 'I don't think my body is magnificent.' Do not worry about what your *mind* thinks. I want you to let your *cells* hear this message. They are waiting like parched desert sands for the water of your approval and gratitude. Without the cooperation of your cells, healing is very difficult. So let's give your cells a new message, and watch what happens as you go through the morning, the afternoon, and on into the evening. Notice the differences. *Pay attention.*

"You do not need to run from any feelings this brings up. In fact, it would help to notice them as they come and go. You might experience boredom, discomfort, disbelief, resistance, embarrassment, shame, whatever. Feel it, don't think it. Don't run, don't change, don't avoid anything; just be present. All you ever have to do is stay focused totally in the present, paying quiet attention, and the *natural* truth will make itself known. So stay with it, and I will see you in the morning."

Win Some, Lose Some

People left quickly, and we returned our meeting room to some semblance of its original order. Half an hour later, we met in the lobby with full water bottles, wide-brimmed hats, and umbrellas as protection against the sun. We shouldered our packs, left the cool oasis of the Travelers Inn, and walked half a block to catch the local number 5 bus to Kyoto station. This morning we were taking the train to Nara[7] to visit some of the best known temples in Nara-Koen Park. Our group boarded the bus with confidence. After all, we already knew what the train station looked like, even if we couldn't read the street signs or communicate with the driver. All we had to do was enter the bus from the rear, make our way up front in time to get off, drop 150 yen into the collection box, and exit. Simple.

The only hitch came when the bus stopped in front of a subway we mistook for the entrance to Kyoto station. The bus door slammed shut behind us as we realized our error. Luckily, it took only a few minutes of disoriented panic to agree that the solution to our dilemma was to catch the next number 5 bus headed in the same direction. We finally arrived to find Yuko had located the correct platform and was waiting for us to appear. We flashed our rail passes at the turnstile guard and ran for the train.

As we left the Nara station, a blast of fiery-hot, humid air greeted us. Maps in hand, we set out on foot for our destination. After a few blocks, my heat-sensitive body was on the brink of rebellion. I was seriously practicing the mantra Bartholomew had given us that morning: "I totally love and accept my magnificent body." The resistance was overwhelming. *This is very ironic,* I thought. *Not only can't I stand high temperatures, but I am now adding greatly to my physical discomfort by being in conflict about this mantra.* Plain stubbornness carried me along for several more blocks. Other people were also having difficulty, so we decided to stop in the shade of an open-air restaurant and have something cool to drink. Larry, who has had much outdoor survival training, looked at my bright red face, and, taking me by the arm, steered me toward a table in the back, ordering ice water as we went.

Twenty minutes later, everyone felt better. We resumed our march to the park, and I tried another mantra, as my body once again threatened to succumb to the heat. "Relax and release." Relax and release the heat, relax and release the pain. And yes, relax and release the irritation at my body for responding in such an unsatisfactory way. It was a moment-by-moment struggle to stay big enough—not only to allow what was happening in my body, but also to be aware of what was going on around me—and accept it all without resistance.

I only marginally observed the three- and five-storied pagodas as a blur of red and gold through aching eyes, when a nearby rectangle of cool darkness beckoned. Our close proximity to the East Hall of Kofukuji Temple promised relief. Yuko purchased tickets for the group as Mary-Margaret tied a wet kerchief around my neck and led me toward the building. Giant wooden doors stood open, revealing a dim interior. We stepped inside and seated ourselves in a row along the high inner threshold. The building contained a space within itself that was filled with cool silence, a faint smell of lingering incense, and the powerful presence of the Four Deva Kings and Twelve Heavenly Generals who surrounded the main altarpiece. I sat leaning against a doorpost, wet scarf around my neck and a wet hat on my head, simply breathing, waiting for my heart to calm and my blood to cool.

We left the temple and approached the entrance to the park. The broad, leafy walkway was surrounded on both sides by small stands where post-cards, carved statues, cool drinks, ice cream, booklets, posters, and fans were sold. Several children left one stand clutching cellophane packages of over-sized wafers. We soon discovered the wafers were not for the children, who were clustered in a group, laughing and shrieking as the beautiful red deer nuzzled and butted its way toward the treat. Soon deer were everywhere. Large white spots on their bodies made them look like overgrown fawns. Many were friendly to the brink of obnoxiousness.

I knelt in the shade of a tree to change the film in my camera. Totally absorbed in this task, it took me a moment to realize that my map to the park was being lifted from my back pocket. I turned, coming face to face with a large antlered deer, who was now dining on my map. I grabbed it and pulled. The deer pulled back. "You can't eat that!" was my rational exclamation. Large, brown, liquid eyes gazed calmly back at me as the deer continued to munch on the map, several inches closer to the hand that was feeding it. I pulled harder. The deer pulled back. I pulled again, and the deer jerked its head. The map tore, and I went sprawling. The deer, still chewing, looked thoughtfully down at me. I scrambled to my feet, eyeing the remains of my map. Time to leave this deer to its fate. I picked up my hat and camera and left in search of my fellow travelers.

I caught up with them at Todaiji Temple. The Main Hall or Daibutsu-den is home to the Great Statue of the Buddha. At a height of 53 feet, it is the largest bronze statue in the world. The building itself was reconstructed in 1707 at *two-thirds* its original size, yet it remains the largest wooden structure in the world. It is approached by way of a gravel path bisecting an immense lawn of clipped grass. No trees distract the viewer, so it stands totally exposed. From a distance, the two-tiered white building with its age-darkened wooden beams is impressive yet austere. Once we set foot on the path, I became more aware of its true size with every step. It is an odd feeling—do you shrink, or does the building grow to meet you? Pausing at the entrance steps, I looked almost straight up, 155 feet, to catch a closer glimpse of the two gilt *kutsugata* (shoe-shapes thought to ward off fire in ancient times) that adorn the twin peaks of the roof ridge.

It was even more stunning to climb over the threshold and come upon the Great Buddha. The statue has its own presence, energized by the adoration of hundreds of thousands of worshipers over the long span of centuries. Heat and exhaustion melted away in the healing coolness of the dim interior. The very air was saturated with a penetrating stillness. We circled and circled the Buddha, drawn like planets to the orbit of some quiet, far-distant yet ever-present moon. Wrapped in deep stillness, we left an hour later, taking taxis back to Nara station. We caught the train to Kyoto, where several of us elected to ride the number 5 bus for the ride home. No mistakes this time. Everyone easily recognized the red Torii Gate of the Heian Shrine as our stop.

Many of us ate dinner at the Inn that night. Everyone was tired. I grabbed a cold Asahi beer from the hall vending machine as I made my way to our cool room. Emmy went in search of a rumored hot tub in the basement, as I curled up under the quilts with my beer, book, and aspirin. The last thing I heard as I drifted into peaceful sleep was the sound of my own thinking . . . *I totally love and accept my magnificent body.*

Chapter 9

Kyoto: Day Four–Body, Mind, and Healing

The barest trace of gray was visible through the opaque window of our room when I awoke the next morning. Today's meeting with Bartholomew would last three hours, and we had decided to move the location once again. We did not feel that it was fair to the staff to continue moving furniture back and forth between rooms for the next several days, so Emmy and I had volunteered the use of ours. It was smaller than the others, but we thought we could create the necessary space by cramming almost everything into the hall closet.

I threw on my yukata and disappeared into the bathroom, where I hastily wrung out and hung the two blouses I had left soaking the night before. Brushing my teeth and splashing my face with water brought me to the state of early-morning semi-alertness perfect for a walk. I dressed and quietly made my way downstairs. It was only 4:30 as I let myself out the front door, but the sky was already turning a hazy white. I had come to love these solitary mornings before the city roused itself to meet another humid day.

Turning left, then right, I headed toward the huge Torii gate that signaled the approach to the Heian Shrine. An automobile came up behind me and unobtrusively passed. It stopped at the end of the street, and a man climbed out. Walking quickly, he paused to stand on the sidewalk facing the shrine. He stood in stillness for a few moments, then clapped his hands sharply together three times and bowed deeply. Straightening up, he jumped back in the car and made a quick U-turn, disappearing back the way he came.

I felt a strong burst of joy and laughed out loud as I danced a quick two-step to the corner. Slowing down, I breathed in the returning silence, worshiping a leaf, the curve of a bamboo gate, a cool patch of shady moss, the flash of bright orange glimpsed through the trees.

Suddenly the sound of wild screeching filled the air. I crossed the street to discover some white birds roosting in a broad-leafed tree, prevented from escaping by a thin wire mesh. The pungent smell of animals told me I was passing a small zoo. I turned and crossed the river where a large white egret walked, head down in search of a meal. The egret spread its wings. Taking flight, it passed directly over the captured birds, a moving speck of freedom against the milky sky.

A thin thread of anxiety unraveled inside me, tugging at the surfacing fear that I would forget these meaningful encounters. Stuffing them into my psyche, I felt like a miser hoarding each golden moment, accumulating a fat bank account to draw on in times of pain. This fear of a future internal poverty dissolved my joyous present like acid eating its way through polished metal. As I returned to the Inn, I pondered this simple lesson.

Still bemused, I climbed the three flights of steps back to the room. Water was running as I opened the door, and Emmy stuck her head out. "Good morning," she said with a cheerful smile. "I'm almost through with my wash, and I'll hang it in the tub, where it will be out of the way. Do you want to get the room ready before or after breakfast?" she asked.

"Let's do it now," I answered. "That way we'll be sure it's done in time."

Emmy gave a last stroke to her reddish-brown hair and emerged from the bathroom. "Where can Mary-Margaret sit?" she asked.

"How about the TV stand we stored in the closet? We can put it in the corner, next to the window, " I replied. "Do you think it's strong enough?"

Emmy disappeared headfirst into the closet. I could hear grunts and mumbles as pillows, clothes, and suitcases began to ooze out into the room. "Here it is," she said triumphantly, passing me the TV stand as she backed out of the closet. The TV stand was made of wood and stood about three feet tall. I set it on the floor and sat down.

"It's sturdy enough but not very comfortable," I said, making a face.

"Try this," Emmy said, tossing me a pillow.

"Perfect." I looked around. "We can open the futons and spread them out on the floor."

"How about against the walls so people can lean back?" Emmy asked.

"Good idea. I'll get the rest of the floor pillows and fill in the spaces,"

I responded. "I like the tatami mats much better than the carpets anyway."

We hurriedly shoved our things back into the closet. Emmy removed the clothes hanging in bunches on the air conditioner knobs and distributed them between the shower and the bathroom door. Surveying the room, we looked at each other.

"It's fine, and I'll bet it will hold everyone comfortably . . . if one or two people don't mind sitting in the entryway," she enthused.

"The closet door is definitely bulging," I observed thoughtfully.

"Don't touch it. Let's go to breakfast," suggested Emmy.

The rattle of dishes from the kitchen, the mingling smells of toast and soba broth, and the hum of mixed languages greeted us as we entered the lobby. Laurel and Lee were filling empty bottles with ice water from the tap behind the front desk as Jim refilled his teacup at the counter. Yoko was waiting for us. She had arrived late last night, and this was our first opportunity to meet each other. We all squeezed into a group at one of the tables. Emmy ordered a Japanese breakfast, and I ordered Western. When hers came, she broke her raw egg into her bowl of rice and added some pickled vegetables, stirring half her small bowl of soba broth into the mixture. Using chopsticks, she began to eat daintily.

"It's very good this morning," she said, sipping her tea. "I wonder what the little purple things are."

Just then Yuko passed by. Emmy stopped her and asked.

"Small pieces of salted pickled cabbage," Yuko answered, with a smile. Emmy put several pieces in her bowl and went on eating.

My breakfast arrived, and I smeared jam on the two-inch-thick slices of buttered toast, shelled my hard-boiled egg, and added milk and sugar to my coffee. Judith nudged me with her elbow as I took a large bite of toast. "Don't you like rice and pickles?" she inquired.

"Actually, I do. I'm just taking a break from yesterday, when I poured my tea instead of my soba sauce onto my rice and raw egg," I replied, regretfully.

Judith laughed as we pushed back our chairs and headed upstairs.

A lineup of shoes was already by the door when we returned to our room. Inside, the window was open, and people were gazing out over the tiled rooftops. Mary-Margaret sat down gingerly on our makeshift stool and wiggled around, testing its sturdiness. Roberta and Larry lay sprawled across the futons, and much good-natured jostling flew back and forth as others looked for a comfortable place to sit.

Mary-Margaret finally clipped the microphone to her blouse, took a sip of water, and arranged her brightly colored skirt about her legs. She leaned against the wall and closed her eyes as we finally settled down.

"Well, then, my friends, good morning, and I am pleased to see you," Bartholomew began. "I think for our three-hour session today we will go for an hour and a half, take a break, and then reconvene after ten or fifteen minutes. This announcement of future events is just to let your bodily functions know that help is available in the not-too-distant future," he smiled, catching us off guard. Then, eyes sparkling, Bartholomew continued.

"If you can understand how the cells within the body function, you will see how the combination of body and mind work together on the Earth plane. To help with this, I would like to ask Mr. Moore to present a short synopsis of a very important story about healing."

Justin is an excellent storyteller and thoroughly enjoys that role. We all settled back in anticipation as he adjusted the microphone, laced his fingers together around his knees, and began.

A True Story about Cellular Transformation

"About six weeks ago, Mary-Margaret received a copy of an article that appeared in *New Age* magazine last year. It's a true story about a lady named Niro Markoff Asistent.[8] Her story begins in 1984 when she was working very closely with a meditation center on the East Coast that was associated with Osho, also known as Bhagwan Shree Rajneesh. She met a man named Nado at one of the meditations who came up to her and explained that he'd had a series of dreams about her and from them had recognized her during meditation.

"It wasn't long before Niro and Nado were living together, but after a while he began to lose interest in the relationship and became more distant. She thought initially it was because he was a dancer, a poet, and an artist, and needed his own space. In time she suspected something else was probably going on as well. Over the next year or so, she began to develop strange physical symptoms. She would perspire profusely at night and run a temperature of 104 degrees. She also experienced very intense aches and pains and a thing called thrush, as well as diarrhea. The doctor couldn't help, and her physical condition was deteriorating. At first she preferred to ignore this and continued her duties at the ashram, acting as if everything were normal.

"When instructions came from Oregon headquarters to close the center, Niro went to Spain, where she did some very intensive breath therapy. It released many things: her perceived denial over what she really wanted to do with her life, her anguish over her relationship with Nado (which hadn't developed the way she'd expected it to), and the final recognition that she was really sick.

"She returned to the United States and continued to live with Nado; they were caretakers at a large beach estate in New York. While there, they received word from the center in Oregon that Nado was HIV positive. Niro realized immediately that the symptoms she had been experiencing might be from the HIV virus, so they went together to be tested at one of the state clinics. During the six weeks it took to get the results, she went through self-denial, incredible rage at Nado for infecting her, and hope that it really wasn't AIDS.

"On receiving the news that she did indeed have AIDS, she again experienced anger and denial and the feeling of being a victim. She went to her own private physician, and he told her the facts—no cure existed. By hearing this from her doctor in a matter-of-fact way, she was finally able to accept the truth of her situation. At this point, Niro realized she couldn't tolerate the stress of living with Nado and asked him to leave. She needed to establish the appropriate environment for herself in which to live out her remaining days.

"One day, looking at the calendar, she saw that according to her doctor's estimate, she had only 451 days left to live. At that moment, she had the revelation that every moment is precious because the clock is always running. This was not an intellectual understanding for her, but a cellular recognition.

"She started doing what she deeply felt she wanted to do. She wanted to meditate more because it felt right. In her meditations, she started receiving impressions about a daily routine that would be appropriate for her. One aspect was to accomplish three things each day when she was awake and moving around, and to set realistic goals. So it might be that she would balance her checkbook, do some sewing, and manicure her nails, but every day three things would be on her schedule.

"One day, as she was doing a Rajneesh kundalini meditation involving lots of loud music and movement, the power went out, suddenly ending the music. At that moment she saw inside her body. All her internal organs were covered with a yellow-green slime. She was so repulsed by this that she started visualizing—not just a gentle little golden flow to wash the organs with—but a veritable Niagara Falls, and flooded her body until the organs became a nice pink color.

"Then she decided she wanted to change her diet. She went on a high-protein liquid diet because it felt right, and she figured she might as well die in a beautiful, thin body. She did this for several months, and then went back to solid foods. As part of her daily awareness routine, she would ask herself from moment to moment, 'What is happening now? I am standing in the kitchen. I feel the cool tiles under my feet. I am measuring flour.' She began to stay totally in the moment, doing 'What is happening now?'

"She also decided to take two walks a day, one in the morning and one in the evening. One day in March, she was walking on the beach and realized that the ocean was her teacher. The ocean was teaching her several very, very important lessons. Each wave would come in, and each wave was different. Then it would go back to the infinite ocean, and another wave would come in and take its place. This was the cycle of life. It was like a heartbeat with an expansion and a contraction. She would have these expanded moments, and then go into the future and realize, 'Oh my God, I'm going to die. I have no reason to feel this good,' and then clamp down on the expansion.

"Realizing this, she began to relax and allow the inner moments of expansion and contraction. One day she was walking on the beach, intensely aware of each step she took. It was as though each step was the last step, the only step. She stopped and turned to the ocean and raised up her arms, and Osho appeared in front of her. She noticed he was no longer greater than she was. They were at the same level, equals. They embraced, and she had a satori, an opening, and realized that however she died, whether by AIDS or an automobile accident, she would die consciously. Beyond that, there wasn't anything to get excited about. This, too, was simply one more expansion. It was all perfectly normal, perfectly ordinary.

"At this point, Niro decided to go back to the clinic and be retested because she no longer had any of her former symptoms. She did this, and the counselor called to ask if she would agree to be retested yet again. She went again and was found to be HIV negative. This is medically impossible. *She no longer had HIV antibodies; she was HIV negative.* She knew then that a miracle had occurred out of the process she had been engaged in.

"Nado got back in touch with her when he was in a hospital dying. She spent his remaining days with him, loving him, massaging him, and talking to him. In the end, they had both received healings, but chose to take two different paths. She chose to live, and he chose to die."

We were silent as Justin finished, each person lost in his or her own thoughts of what healing is. Bartholomew looked at us and spoke softly.

"What I hope this story brings up in all of you is the realization that mysterious things *can and do* happen that your mind is not able to understand. Every moment is filled with so much more mystery than the limited faculty of your thinking can grasp."

He leaned forward, excitement edging his voice. "There are obvious things that brought about—not a healing in the usual sense—but a total *transformation* of this woman's cells. What were these tools of transformation? First, there was the ongoing, constant visualization of the powerful, cleansing flood of what she called 'Niagara' awareness. Remember, you have at least three trillion cells in your body, and these trillions of cells are always listening for the creative power of the mind and heart to give them guidance. Cells are not the thinking part of this body/mind union. They are the receptors, and their function is to await the directive of the mind and heart. *"What you give as a directive is what the cells will pay attention to,"* said Bartholomew, emphasizing each word.

Your Body Is the Best Friend You'll Ever Have

"Remember yesterday, when I asked you to get in touch with the ongoing mental abuse you give the cells of your body? This self-abuse has been going on for years, and yet your cells are still alive and functioning. They haven't abandoned *you*; they haven't given up! You can greatly help yourself change this abusive behavior. Every moment of your life you have the opportunity to flood your own cellular structure with gratitude, love, and appreciation, even when there is something in the body you do not see as perfect. The cells alone do not create health or illness. It is a combination of many things, many beyond your mind's limited understanding.

"Most people in Western society have been trained to believe that the mind is here," Bartholomew said, pointing toward his head, "and the body is here," he continued, thumping his chest and legs. "This presents you with a diagram of the thinking mind separated from the rest of the physical body. This idea of separation gives rise to the belief that mind and body have nothing to do with each other. To further complicate the separated situation, you often see your mind, your body, and any illness in it as isolated from one another.

"With these beliefs, you have created three separate entities, and there always arises the possibility of making a potential enemy of whatever is seen as separate. Whenever you choose to create a boundary of any kind, you have a potential war zone. So illness is seen as a separate entity, an enemy, which necessitates bringing in something from the outside to heal or kill it. What would be most helpful is to awaken to the truth. There is no real separation among mind, body, and illness, and you can use your mind to help heal the body. You do not have to wait to be ill to bestow this gift on yourself.

"It is interesting to note that the woman in our story did not set out to heal herself. In this way, her situation differs a bit from the usual healing story. She was not able to visualize herself as getting well, since getting well was not a possibility in her belief system. The belief was that AIDS has no cure. But she did cure herself!

"How did she do it? Let us remember a story you may have already heard. A valley in China was filled with death and dying because of a severe drought. The plants were dead, and the animals and people were dying as well. The people prayed for help. One day a monk walks into their village and moves into an old hut on the outskirts of town. There he spends his time sitting in meditation. The villagers know, without knowing how, that the appearance of this monk is terribly important. After a few days, it begins to rain, and with great rejoicing they go to him and say, 'Thank you for the rain! What did you do?' He says, 'What do you mean?' They say, 'You brought the rain. How did you do it? Did you pray for it?' His answer is, 'No, I didn't pray for the rain, I harmonized with the drought.'" Bartholomew paused. "I'll say it again: *'I did not pray for the rain; I harmonized with the drought.'* Do you understand the difference? Harmonizing means a total acceptance of whatever is before you. For him it was the drought. In the acceptance of things as they are, they can change. Remember the current quote, 'What you resist persists.'

"In the case of illness, many of you say you can never get well if you are not willing to fight your illness. This is resistance. Using the image of fighting an illness is to invite defeat. Just as in warfare, if there is an enemy and a battle, one of you wins, and one of you loses. Images like this produce tremendous fear. And when fear is foremost, harmony is distant. You need to look at things differently. You can begin by remembering that illness is a stuck energy lodged in the cells of your body. This stuck energy is made up of emotions, beliefs, and past experiences. To move it, you need another kind of energy. What helps most is to keep filling the cells with the visualization of love and gratitude, light and clear power. In so doing, you are not resisting the stuck energy manifesting as illness; rather, you have accepted its presence and are giving it your attention. You simply focus on another energy to enter and do as it will. No scolding the 'bad' and praising the 'good.' Just an easy acceptance of one, and a gentle movement toward another kind of energy.

"The constant, delightful input of nourishment, gratitude, and apprecia-tion brings relaxation to the cells, and you know what happens then. Relaxed cells open and expand. Remember in the story how Niro experienced two things: expansion and contraction. She was willing to expand but did not want to contract. What she finally learned was the wonderful rhythm of life that includes both. Try breathing in without breathing out, and see what happens.

"There is a rhythm of inbreath and outbreath, of expansion and contrac-tion, of one energy following another, of a duality that is reflected everywhere you look. It's the dance of life. The delight is to be aware of it all, leaving nothing out. When you begin to relax in this manner, not only are miracles possible, but miracles become the order of the day."

Giving Yourselves the Gift of Nourishment

Bartholomew stopped and pondered a moment before continuing. "Some of you want a nourishing physical and emotional relationship with another person, and you become upset when it doesn't happen." He leaned forward, gazing at us intently. "I would like to make a suggestion. While you are wait-ing for that relationship, flood your body with the gift of loving nourishment clear down to the cellular level. A gift from you to you. Do this, and you will begin to feel the incredible presence of a loving vibration deep on the cellu-lar level. This is an experience you have been waiting for. And it won't be a gift dependent on someone else, something that can be withdrawn if you don't do what the other person wants. With this gift *that you give yourself,* you become self-reliant, meaning reliant on your Deep Self. A self-reliant person is not someone who knows how to get around a large city, but one who knows how to meet their own needs, fill their own life, and nourish their own body."

We laughed over the reference to 'getting around a large city,' as that was exactly what we were trying to do. A smiling Bartholomew turned toward Yuko. "Which brings us to our gratitude to you, my friend," he said, bowing slightly. "I think we would have lost the entire tour," he laughed, "in varying stages, in various trains all over your beautiful city, if not for your help," he concluded. Turning back, he addressed us again.

"When you realize the depth and simplicity of being reliant on the Deep Self, it gradually ceases to matter who comes or does not come into your life. However, when you energize your cells with this magnetic hum, you *do* tend to draw people into your life who like feeling that hum. Then don't be surprised if you happen to get all the love affairs or friends you can handle. Electromagnetically align yourself with the power of love, and you begin to *embody* love. It zings in you. Other people feel the warmth and are drawn to it. They enjoy being in your presence because the throbbing, pulsating, amazing love energy is always in and around you. And the cells are the focus of this amazing activity.

"Please do not confuse this love energy with the human phenomenon known as 'falling in love.' You give yourselves very confusing messages around love and sex and the physical. On the one hand, you believe sex will take you to heaven, and on the other, that sex will send you to hell. Between these two extremes, you have every possible variation—you shouldn't do it but you want to. You yearn to do it but you don't know how. And on it goes. There are very few areas in the human psyche as confused as the sexual. But in the end, it is really very simple, and the cells of your body know this. When you have a sexual orgasm, it is not in your mind, is it? It is in the body! Your cells burst open in a rambunctious letting go, and you experience it as an amazing physical pinnacle." Bartholomew smiled at us.

"You can also have *spiritual* pinnacles if you are willing to give the dry, gray cells of your body the nourishment they need," he said. "Spontaneous awakenings can take place, not only in the body, but also in the mind. You can have awakenings where the mind literally opens, and the confusion of the brain disappears. Clarity is experienced. The new replaces the old. Remember that 95 percent of the thoughts you think today you will think tomorrow. If that doesn't depress you, it should. It is like taking a bath in the same water every day. You put a small amount of fresh water in the tub and think it will make a difference. Well, does it? When you pay attention, you will see how lukewarm, repetitious, and boring your mental process is. If you would stop thinking *all* the time and think only as needed, you would experience spontaneous awakenings in the mind." He dropped his hands to Mary-Margaret's knees. "Does anyone have questions about any of this?" he asked.

Darcy's hand shot up. "I sense enlightenment is possible in this lifetime," she said, "and I sense what it's like. I also sometimes see the gnarly beliefs attached to fear, and I hold back. But one of the things I don't know much about is, what happens after you reach a permanent state of enlightenment? What would happen to my life?" she asked earnestly.

Bartholomew paused, gazing at something we could not see. "The state many of you are capable of reaching now, and which will deepen day by day, is to break through some very strong illusory beliefs and to really know who you are. This is awareness itself. With that knowing, the mind will be filled with light and the heart with love. You will move through your life with grace, humor, lighthearted integrity, and fullness of being. You will be fearless. All kinds of events will rise and fall, and you will be at ease with all of them. You will be in a state of well-being that is not dependent on others, or on the pleasant events in your life, or on certain relationships continuing. At the same time, you will fully love those who are in your life, and you will also love everyone else fully." He looked around. "You know what I'm going to say. You continue to chop wood and carry water. Your life goes on. The difference is, you do everything from such a vast space within you that all aspects of the external world fit into that space. You don't try to get rid of anything or add anyone. Everything in your world is poignantly marvelous!" He smiled into our silence. "I recommend it," he said. "That is as brief a description as I can give you. I suggest you find out for yourself."

Lee cleared her throat and spoke. "On the subject of the mind, I am wondering if you ever get to the point where the mind stops chattering and there are long spaces in the thinking process."

Bartholomew leaned forward. "Good question," he said. "You stay in your small mind because you believe it is your mind that controls your happiness and peace. You stay in your mind because you fear that, unless you do, you will be out of control, mindless, and your life will fall apart! But you can fall out of your mind again and again, moment after moment, without losing your life or your sanity. You can fall into the space all around you. Fall into simple hearing and simple seeing. Fall out of the old mental patterns and still be here. Get *out* of your mind; don't *lose* your mind.

"Your brains get overheated because you use them constantly. It's like running a car continuously. The engine overheats. But when you repeatedly drop out of your mind, for as long as you can, it becomes cooler, more detached, and like your car engine, it works more efficiently. The strength of the focused mind is laser-like and extremely quiet, so the spaces between thoughts are much longer. No one ever ceases to think. The great enlightened ones still think, but there are long spaces of what I would call 'mysteries' in between their thoughts. When thinking needs to happen, it does; if not needed, it doesn't. There's an open awareness to what is present, and then, if thought is appropriate, a thought arises."

He looked back at Lee. "There will be a time when the two fields—thought and open, spacious awareness—will reverse themselves. The space will be the predominant vibrating awareness, and the forms will be secondary. Now it's the opposite. Now you are focused on the forms, and the space is secondary. You have to allow space to open itself up to your awareness. If you keep practicing, it will work. You become aware of vast space and that forms move *within* that space. This is a very different way of seeing, and it results in your enjoying each moment just as it is."

Bartholomew leaned toward Greta, who always sat quietly, straight up, and sometimes with her eyes closed. Right now they were open, looking directly at him. "Yes, my friend?" he inquired.

"You mentioned the phrase 'the heat of the mind.' I have an image that, as it drops away, that heat will relocate, say lower, in the abdomen. I guess I'm looking for some clues about how to facilitate this," she concluded.

"In the East Indian tradition, the kundalini rises from the base of the spine and travels up through the head, and enlightenment is the result. But in other systems of awakening, there is no mention of the kundalini, although full enlightenment is a result. So how can we understand this? The kundalini is a very useful and valid image, but not the only one. In systems that do not hold the belief in the kundalini, we find that the followers experience the energy moving in other patterns. It can enter from the top of the head, like a fountain, and spill over the entire body. It can be experienced as a flame in an open, radiant heart, or in the abdominal area called the hara. There are no rules with energy, so whatever your belief is, your experience with energy will likely follow that belief. Energy follows your thoughts, but you can always change your thoughts." Bartholomew grinned as Greta smiled and shook her head from side to side in bemusement.

He leaned back. "I would like to ask today for a repetition of yesterday," he said to all of us. "I would like you to become space beings in the deepest, most wonderful sense of those words. I want you to become aware of open hearing and open seeing, without any kind of desire, selection, or judgment. As best you can, be conscious of the ever-changing rise and fall of seeing, hearing, and breathing, and the awareness that it all happens in the wonder of space."

We relaxed as Bartholomew turned to Justin and said, "All right, then, let's take a short break, and we'll come back and discuss yesterday's adventures." Mary-Margaret stretched and removed the microphone. People began to move around. Some headed for the bathroom or a drink, while others stretched out on the floor or wrote in their notebooks. Soon we were gathered together once again, shoulder to shoulder on the floor.

A Point of View Is Only a Viewing Point

"Now then," Bartholomew began, "I would like to hear about your responses from yesterday. I am particularly interested in that part of the assignment where I asked you to expand enough to hold your point of view plus the view of another. Did anyone work on that and with what results?"

Emmy raised her hand. "Of course I noticed the pressure," she began thoughtfully, "whenever somebody didn't agree with what I was saying or thinking." Her laughter joined ours as she went on. "I watched and was amazed at how many times 'mine versus theirs' came up. I got into trouble when I forgot it was simply a point of view (mine) and started reacting like it was 'The Truth.' Just noticing this gave me more space than I had before."

Bartholomew nodded and smiled. "Everyone has a different point of view, and most of the time you see the world from yours. The words 'point of view' are perfect because it is the point from which you view the world. Just like this." He held his hands up to the sides of Mary-Margaret's face like blinders on a horse. Peering around at us, he said, "Everyone else, of course, is doing this as well." He leaned over to Justin, almost cheek to cheek. "The idea is to get as close together as possible in the hope you can share the same view. But even then, there will always be a sense of separateness, because no matter how close you get, your view will always be slightly different."

Bartholomew straightened up, dropping his hands. "You approach a person or event with your own bundle of varied experiences and responses. And you bang up against another person who has their own bundle of responses. You versus them. Theirs versus yours. Who is right? How do you dissolve these differences? In the end, the only thing that dissolves the boundaries between you and them is what you call Love. Are you willing to love the person in spite of what you believe they have done to you, in spite of the mistakes you think they have made, or the different points of view they have? Under some very difficult conditions, are you willing to see what in them is love itself?

"And I am not talking about that lofty, superior point of view when you decide to forgive the person for all the seeming 'wrongs' done to you. This kind of forgiveness usually means that you, in your great piety and righteousness, look down on the other person's failings and, from that position, decide to forgive them. Do you understand? That is condescension and has nothing to do with love or forgiveness. And it *feels* like condescension to you and to the other person. But love feels like this," Bartholomew spread his arms high and wide. "Love says, 'Yes, I'll love you. Yes, we have differences, and I still love you.' When you make the choice to love, without even understanding what that means or how to do it, conflicts can dissipate, and space begins to open up between you. This creates the possibility of developing a point of view that joins the two of you into a unit of 'oneness,' and this feeling of 'oneness' brings peace.

"Now, most people would say their point of view is the 'right' one, and that it has to override the other 'wrong' one and obliterate it. And so they war. This produces fear, and a sense of desperation. When one person finally gives in, there remains a large amount of resistance to and resentment against the 'winning' point of view. The result is not harmony, but angry submission. What is necessary is to have the two spheres of opinion come together, so between them a third dynamic is created in the middle space, one they can share. This can be a third way of seeing, a third solution, or a third kind of understanding that doesn't say A is right or B is right. With willingness, what arises is what you would call a loving solution that neither validates nor invalidates either side. It is a blending, an 'us' rather than a 'me' or a 'you.'

"But how to do this? It must begin with a mutual willingness—a deep commitment to *cooperate*. You must both be *willing* to begin this process. Then one person presents their way of seeing the difficulty, and the other person listens openly with as little mental judgment as possible, after which the second person presents his or her point of view while the first person practices open listening without judgment. Then you sit with what you have heard for just a little while. What oftentimes arises, if not a perfect solution, is a deeper understanding of what created the other person's point of view. This new intimacy leads to a gratitude toward the 'other' for being willing to make the attempt to really hear your deepest voice.

"My friends, you don't always have to reconcile conflicts through deciding on a unified action. You can reconcile deep things through a unified understanding of another person's point of view. Each one may end up doing what they need to do, feeling their point of view is the one they intend to uphold, but they are now able to go forward through a middle ground where they have joined in a vision of understanding.

"As you begin to develop this gentle art of joining, you will come to realize your speech is all-important. Use heart words, not mind words. When you enter that space, willing to speak from your heart, and the other person does the same, you might find yourself saying something like, 'I felt abandoned, felt nobody heard me, that my view was unimportant and was being overridden.' These words indicate that in the end, the events are not what really matter. It is your feelings about the events that count. So the other person may respond, 'I was so frightened by having to tell you what I had to say that it came out forceful, overbearing. I was in such a fearful place I had to say it in a hurry.' Do you understand? The event was not the problem.

"When you present only *your* interpretation of the events or 'just the facts,' and the other person presents only theirs, you cannot blend them because you are never going to agree on what you saw. You are both looking at the same event from different points of view, and the view will *always* be somewhat different. So, do not focus on the events. Be willing to listen to the feelings behind them. That is where the pain lies. You will fall into compassion as you recognize the fear of the other, because you have fear within yourself as well. If you have an issue with someone, sit quietly together. Don't go over the history of the event in question, but simply present your deepest feelings, and then see what happens." Bartholomew looked at us thoughtfully. "I wonder if any of you are willing to risk it," he said softly, "because in order to do this, you must be willing to let go of the 'I'm right' separation. That is very difficult for the ego. It is *you* who must choose—the ego, left to itself, never will.

"All right," Bartholomew said, taking a sip of water, "is there anything else about yesterday? Any other people's experiences?"

Darcy raised her hand. "What happened for me was similar to the story you tell about the wise man who gives you an elixir and tells you that if you drink it, it will bring enlightenment—but the only condition is you must not think of monkeys while drinking it! As soon as you mentioned conflict, my day was full of conflict." We laughed as Bartholomew responded.

"Well, today I have said *love*—so love, love, love. If you followed that pattern yesterday, be consistent, and today you will see only loving."

With a grin, Darcy continued. "I couldn't quite get to that space of understanding, so I just did 'damage control' on the conflicts. At least they didn't get worse. I did the best I could. The solution wasn't so expansive, but at least I didn't add to the problem."

Bartholomew clapped his hands together. "Excellent. Now, all of you please remember, you are not going to find ultimate solutions. Remember, I've said life is not a problem to be solved; it is a mystery to be experienced." He stood up and looked around. "I would like to talk about a concept that is the basis of many Buddhist teachings. This concept will arise again and again in our next days together. Some of you might have difficulty with this, but please see if you can be open enough to hear it."

Who's There When You Ask, "Who's There?"

"Zen states that upon close observation of the continuous person you call yourself, you will eventually discover there is no continuous person present. When examined closely, that which seems to be a continuous person having continuous experiences is found to be just a series of unconnected images, responses, and thoughts that rise and fall in an ever-present, present moment. These images, responses, and thoughts are like silver fish leaping out of a vast lake, flashing in the sun, and returning again to the lake. They are not connected each to the other; nor is there an overall meaning of the different movements of each fish. They just rise, flash, and fall. So it is with a seemingly connected 'you.' What makes you believe you are a continuous person is *memory*."

He paused and paced a few steps. "I want to talk about memory, because it is an interesting subject and very misunderstood. I know we are going deep, but it's important that you understand this. You say you are sure there is such a thing as a past, your past. And if I ask you how you know, you will tell me it is because you can remember it, that you have a memory of it. When pressed further, you could go on to describe the temple you visited yesterday, and you could get others to agree on that joint experience. So, when you put them together, you can say you are sure the past is real.

"But stop a moment. Go into your memory and pull out an event from yesterday, anything at all. All right, are you really experiencing yesterday's event, or is it possible that what you have just done is recreate something that itself is new this moment, right now?" The group only tentatively agreed.

"You say, 'I remember,' and here comes the memory. But in reality, you have just created a brand new event in your mind, right here and now, which differs in many respects from the reality you had when you had the original experience.

"If you could compare that remembrance to the original, you would find that they are not the same. You have *not* recreated the same event, exactly as it occurred, and the farther away you get in time from that event, the more vague the memory becomes. So when people say they remember what happened to them when they were two, I would like to suggest what you remember has been endlessly covered over by all of the events that have happened since. Where are the true events of the past? You recreate the two-year-old again and again as you 'remember the past,' and each time you do, you have created something brand new." Bartholomew paused, aware of our confusion. "It's a puzzle, not easy to grasp, but I ask you to dwell on it."

Greta spoke up. "When you asked for that memory, it was a feeling I went back to and brought to you in this moment."

"Yes. Thank you."

Sharon tilted her head and looked up at Bartholomew. "From the way you just said that, I wonder why we feel the need to remember our past."

"Well, I never said you did," Bartholomew responded with a smile.

Sharon continued slowly. "If you stay in the present, maybe there is no need for the past. There is a memory of what happened that we're creating but if we're not really living it, there's no need to even . . ." She shrugged. "I mean, why not just be in the moment and not be so concerned with what we've gone through?"

"Exactly!" Bartholomew exclaimed, sitting down again. "When you deal with the past, you are dealing with fantasies and dreams. And people who think in terms of karma have compounded the problem tremendously. Not only do they talk about the immediate past, but they are also now going into what they call past lives to bring forward trace fragments of very vague remembrances and much fantasy. These 'memories' of past lives are often creations in the moment used to explain the unexplainable. How many times have you heard things like, 'I don't get along with my mother because in a past life she abused me'? Well, maybe she did, and maybe she didn't, but does saying this help resolve the issue, or does it just give you a comfortable 'answer'? Do you deal in the moment with whatever is going on, as it is being experienced in the moment, or do you keep creating what I call 'story lines'? Karmic story lines may be fascinating, but they are not very useful. Paying attention to these vague trace patterns is like watching a movie. You can believe the characters and events existed, or you can just view them as a creative expression of the imagination.

"Now let us apply this idea to that part of you that you see as 'me' when you say 'me'—your so-called continuous self. Because you are not paying attention, you miss the obvious spaces between one 'you' and the next 'you.' You are not aware of the open, empty 'between' moments when no continuous identity is present. Is it possible that what you do is bring forward into each moment a fragmented image of what was created in a 'past' moment?

"It is important to remember that the past contains guilt, and the future instills fear, and you are inexplicably wedged between these two poles. The way out is not to move to either pole or resist the habituated flow of thought that takes you into either past or future. In short, the solution is once again to stay in the moment. Then, what is *really* happening now reveals itself. You do not have to know how to *do* this, just be *willing*. I mean something very specific by this. Be aware of breathing, hearing, and seeing. And please be aware that you don't have to think all the time. For a few moments you can fall into a state of nonthinking, a state that is full, alive, and peace-filled.

"Then, what is present in the moment, which is not the past or the future, which is not the small self but which is no-thing, where the wondrous abundance of what *is* there reveals itself and is yours. You do not have to 'get there' or 'go anywhere.' You do not have to *do* anything. You simply have to be awake in what is always happening every moment.

"When you find you are making your false self a drama king or queen of your universe by dragging the past or future into the moment, please relax, and have a little lightness about it. This 'past or future king or queen" can be tyrannical. It longs to be right, and it yearns for power. Don't resist it; just relax around it all, and stay in the moment. Breathe. Watch the thoughts as they rise and fall, hear the sounds as they come and go, see the ever-changing vistas pass before your eyes. Be fully present. Then you will begin to get a sense that it is just one moment following another. You will know that your reason for living is to enjoy each moment with its pure, natural, exciting, amazing, pulsating life. The Christian model instructs you to become like little children. Why?"

"Because they stay in the moment," came an answer from the back of the room.

"Absolutely. If you try and draw a child out of the moment, they may indulge you by doing so for a while, but they will return to the moment as soon as is safely possible. For the little one, there is nothing else in the whole universe except what they are seeing, smelling, feeling, tasting, and hearing. They do not *think* about their environment; they want to *experience* it fully and completely. This is a beautiful, peace-filled state. All that is really necessary for you to be able to experience the same state is the willingness to interface in the moment with whatever is before you, just as a child does.

"How many of you really know what things smell like? You are so busy trying to decide if it is pleasant or unpleasant, the smell is gone before you have really fully experienced it. How many of you really know how it feels to chew, to taste? Try it. Be simple. If you are eating an orange, be aware of the smell, the color, the texture, the taste, the juice, all of it. When you are feeling heat, feel heat. Give those things you don't like the same close attention as those you enjoy, and you will be surprised at what might happen. In the midst of everything—things you like, things you don't like, and things that distract you, stay with the willingness. Do not abandon the field of your awareness. Be conscious of what you are 'being,' and be it with the delight of experiencing it fully."

Laurel, who was leaning against the wall, spoke out. "I can understand not being able to recreate the past fully because that is of the mind, but don't the body or the cells remember?"

Bartholomew paused. "This process of body/mind works so quickly that it puts your modern-day computers to shame," he said. "It is the mind that instantly gets a picture and tells the cells how to respond in the moment. The mind triggers the body, but it happens so quickly that one feels like the body reacts first.

"A camera can show you a scene that takes in a whole valley, a town, and the mountains beyond. That vast part of you, your awareness, does the same for the other parts of your Being that you are not always aware of. That is why something can be happening behind you, and you will still sense it. Your awareness senses what's happening; the mind translates the message and passes it on to the body. You often short-circuit this process by not accepting those 'nonmental' images you are constantly receiving. You use only your brain to try and understand events, emotions, and relationships. If you will practice periods of dropping out of the mind and give your overheated, hot brains a rest, you will be able to begin picking up direct promptings, knowings, and inspirations. You will become alive and present in your world in a fuller, more vast, more awakened way.

"This brings us, I think, to another of the tools that Niro Asistent used for the total transformation of her cells. Remember, she did this so well the HIV virus was not to be found. It was not lying dormant; it was gone. A medical *impossibility—it was gone!* You know what happened, but let's speak of it once again. When Niro awoke to the tyranny of the past and the terror of the future and realized they both held nothing but fear, she also discovered that the only place she felt safe was in the moment. So she did everything she could to stay in the moment, which means when she walked, she was simply walking. When she made muffins, she was totally present mixing the batter. Did it take awareness? You bet. We are talking about many months of total concentration. As she became aware that the moment was the only place she could have peace, she sought that place again and again, not as a practice, but as a place of refuge.

"Your dilemma, my friends, if I can be blunt, is that you are not miserable enough. But you need not sit around waiting to get more miserable in order to awaken. I have told you; you can awaken through love, with joy and delight. You do not have to haul yourselves there through illness, loss, grief, resentment, self-pity, or any of the other painful experiences you are so good at creating. I am asking you to awaken out of joy because it is so delightful! Do it—not for any great cosmic reason, but because it's going to feel so wonder-filled. Bliss, the realization of your connection to the Divine, *is inevitable; it is your destiny*—and aren't you glad!

"You are all miserable but don't want to acknowledge it, so you do your best to find things to distract you. The deepest misery all humankind shares is the feeling of 'separation' from God. Great awakenings happen when people can no longer distract themselves from this knowledge. You may be lying in a hospital bed and realize you are about to die without finding out what the Earth journey was all about. That's misery. Remember what the Buddha says? He says (now I am paraphrasing), 'All right, you can awaken in seven lifetimes, seven years, seven months, seven days, seven hours, seven minutes, or you can do it now.' It is always up to you. Do it now, or do it later, but you *will* do it.

"In fact, Buddha is a perfect example of this process. He literally sat in the moment under a tree and did not move. The pressure of his consciousness placed him in that position, and in the stillness, the awakening happened. It is the pressure of your consciousness that places you in those pressure-filled moments of life. When you feel the pressures around you, be still and allow it to happen.

"If you were to perform an autopsy on the body of an enlightened one, you would not find some kind of guru switch inside. There is no divine little button to push that is labeled The Enlightenment Button. A guru looks just like you, nothing special. So to attain their understanding, you need to do what they did: stay in the moment, allowing yourself to hear without any kind of judgment, see without choice or translation, breathe without anything other than breath happening. This is the most exciting way to spend your time before you open to full realization. If you stay present, you will not have to wait long to feel the ecstasy of being in the moment. When life is experienced clearly, fully, and directly, it is blissful *no matter what is happening*. It is the experience of that particular moment of life that brings bliss—not the content of that moment.

"Scientists have been finding that people in extreme pain, when guided in precise ways into that pain, have still felt the incredible bliss and excitement in that moment of living. Yes, pain is still present, but when awareness is there, the whole experience changes. In the past, the medical profession has tried to suppress the physical pain, when in truth what brings the release and relaxation around pain is to add awareness to it. Bring your awareness to the physical pain or the throbbing emotional pain of guilt and sorrow, and you will discover that pain is not the only thing present. I know this seems to be a paradox. Pain and bliss appear to be opposites, but are they? We suggest that it is pain and pleasure that are the opposites in your belief structure. Bliss stands *outside* them and has absolutely nothing to do with your physical, mental, or emotional bodies. *Bliss is the experience of your true nature.* It is love; it is knowing you are not separate. It is what blends and unifies opposites such as pain and pleasure.

"For those of you who are dedicated finders, I ask you to give yourselves a year of dropping into the moment as we have described, and find your answers for yourself. Where is bliss? What is bliss? Bliss is what *is*. It's always present. You can't earn it; you simply allow yourself to be aware of it. You are like a fish swimming in an ocean looking for water, or like a bird flying through the sky searching for air. Know that and be free!" Bartholomew relaxed.

"Then, as a side effect, you may heal yourself of your mental, physical, and emotional traumas—as a side effect. But the first order of business is to enlighten your life, your mind, and your heart.

"So let us go back to Niro's transformation through AIDS. Who was the guru here? AIDS. Who was the savior? AIDS. You can see whatever affects you either as your enemy or your friend. It is up to you. You cannot run away, but you can choose your response. You have crafted your lives very carefully to bring you to enlightenment, so be willing to embrace all of your creation and be thankful, even if you have forgotten that you created it."

He paused and leaned back. "Are there any questions?"

Gratitude and the Bean Jar

"When we flood our bodies with gratitude, is it to get rid of the dis-ease?" asked George.

"The dis-ease is not necessarily something you have to 'get rid' of," Bartholomew answered. "When you flood the body with an awareness of gratitude, you are not excluding giving gratitude to the dis-eased part of the whole. On the contrary, when you flood all parts of your being, you will come to realize what you are most thanking is the dis-ease. It is the dis-ease that can bring about your awakening. I have told you since the beginning of our work together that when you reach enlightenment, you will be on your knees in gratitude to the people and events that gave you the worst trouble. Yes, you'll be grateful for those who loved you and for the wonderful events of your life, but it's the ones that knocked you to your knees that will receive the most heartfelt thanks. You have the words for it, do you not? 'No pain, no gain.' The history of enlightenment and awakening is filled with that belief.

"I wish to remind you yet again that it need not be so. There is an exception to this idea I would like to give you as inspiration. Let us go back to the Buddha. When he was born, his parents were told that he would become either a very great ruler or a very great spiritual teacher. Since they were rulers of a very small principality in India, they yearned for him to carry on their princely line. To ensure this, they kept all of the dark things out of his life. He never saw death, decay, or illness. He had beautiful women surrounding him. He was able to enjoy whatever he wanted, pleasures of the senses without limit. His life was filled with ease and pleasure—on a limited level.

"Then one day he left the palace grounds without his parents' approval and saw the pain, illness, death, and grief waiting outside his little island of pleasure. In an instant, he realized how unreal his life had been and began his search. So he came from the opposite point of view. His path begins with pleasure, moves through pain, and eventually embraces it all.

"We hope that one day you will experience gratitude for your physical body, for the pleasure and the pain of it, for all the ways you have moved in the world and all the choices, 'good' or 'bad,' that you have made. If you leave the diseased part of your body and your life out, you totally miss the wholeness of your path and keep the cells of the body from the one thing that will balance them. They are in stress because they have not felt the nourishment of your unlimited consciousness and gratitude.

"If there is a painful area in your body, give it focused attention, because that's what it is looking for. It's looking for the nourishment of your awareness. I know this is opposite from the medical model, which tries to distance your attention from the area that is painful. It encourages you to become numb and to ignore the entire situation. Sometimes it distances you by not allowing you to even know of your illness, while what the dis-ease really needs is your total intimacy with it.

"So, we suggest you become as fully aware of the situation as you possibly can. Then, if you have the willingness to act to create something different, you can take advantage of the incredible power that awareness holds within it. You have to realize that without awareness you know nothing. You don't know why you bring these things on yourself. You experience yourself as, perhaps, stupid, foolish, dead, and unaware, perhaps feeling yourself as a robot that God is punishing for past sins. But you can move to experiencing yourself as a conscious, dynamic, alive, creative being. If the latter is true, you and God together are creating something wondrous that has as its basic thrust the full knowledge of the God-Self. You can choose whichever vision of yourself you want. You can acknowledge that whatever dis-ease is present has a perfect reason for being present in that moment. And you can give the cells what they yearn for, the light of your awareness.

"The cells of the body are like the three little jars of mung beans some students at Vista Grande School[9] were experimenting with. The beans were all from the same source, and the jars were all the same size. Each jar got the same amount of water and the same sunlight. But there was one main difference. The children were instructed to give the beans in the first jar statements of 'We love you. You are going to grow tall and strong.' They were told to ignore the beans in the second jar, giving them physical nourishment but no words. Then for the third group of beans, the children were directed to scold and discipline the beans, telling them they were ugly, useless, and of no value. Obviously, the number-one jar of beans grew the best. But it is very interesting that the second jar of beans, which was ignored except to be given water and light, grew the least, and the ones that suffered verbal abuse did far better. What does this have to do with the cells of your body?

"The principle is the same: If you choose to ignore your cells, they will fail to relax, to expand, to come alive with energy. You ignore your cells at the risk of having them wither and dry up. I really recommend that you treat your cells like the children treated the first jar of beans. You are like a walking bean jar, and you can sprout and grow, or you can wither and die.

"You know, they have found that people stay healthier when their lives are focused on love, even when all other so-called necessary things are missing. Why? Because when you are surrounded with loving people, one person is flooding the other's awareness with acceptance and appreciation right down to the cellular level. The cells receive this silent message and are nourished. This is one unconscious reason why many people keep creating new love affairs. On some level they realize that, for those few brief months, they are in an expanded state where their physical, cellular, mental, and emotional bodies are receiving total approval. The result is a deep sense of well-being.

"You can continue to move from one love affair to another, or you can give this same nourishment to yourself. In Justin's story, Niro shows that through constant nourishment and caring for her cells, she plus Life bring about a total transformation of them. She took care of her own energy field by removing herself from an environment that kept pulsating with negativity, knowing the negativity could not help her. In the midst of a relationship that keeps bringing up your negative attributes, it is very difficult to come to God-Realization. So please, if you care about someone, show them your gratitude and love as often as you can. Be willing to appreciate the other person for who they are, to feel that wonderful Oneness, in spite of your differences. In that appreciation things can sweeten, relax, and unify."

"How do you release the negative feelings when it's someone you really, deeply have trouble with?" asked Patricia.

Bartholomew turned to her. "First, you need to decide if you really *want* to release them," he explained. "If you do, and if you can stay with it long enough, and it is important enough, you will find out exactly what it is that triggers your negative responses. It is *never* what is before you. It is a mirror of the past. The trigger may be as simple as the look on a face, or the way a person is walking, or words someone says. The instant memory traces connected to such subtle responses can repulse or please you, but they have nothing to do with what is before you. Watch them. Acknowledge to yourself that repulsion is present. Tell yourself it's *interesting* instead of moving your responses into 'good' or 'bad,' 'negative' or 'positive' categories. These categories are only ways to justify your judgments.

"In the end, you will see that all things change. You move away from a negative response to a happy, pleasing one and think, 'How lovely.' Trying to get an accumulation of 'how lovelies' and stay away from the 'repulsives' is what is keeping you on the karmic wheel of life. You can live without being on this wheel, you know. The rise and fall of dualities is only a very small part of the amazingly vast wonder of who you are. As you awaken, you will come to realize dualities are just temporary; here this moment, gone the next. In the end, it's greater fun to be enlightened than to continue to travel the wheel. I recommend it over all other experiences.

You want to experience bliss? Be aware of enlightenment. How? Stay in the moment. Stay in the ever-present, empty, immense center of the moment and from there, observe it all."

Bartholomew stopped and looked around. "You've been wondrously patient," he said. "Let's take a break, and then we'll come back and jump into the mind."

Big Mind, Little Mind

When we returned, Mary-Margaret held a piece of paper in her hand. "I would like to read you something I found in a friend's bathroom in New Zealand. It's by Goethe,[10] and I thought we could all relate to it," she said, settling herself on the padded TV stand.

> Until one is committed there is hesitancy, the chance to draw back, always ineffectiveness. Concerning all acts of initiative and creation there is one elementary truth, the ignorance of which kills countless ideas and splendid plans. The moment one definitely commits oneself, then Providence moves too. All sorts of things occur to help one that would never otherwise have occurred. A whole stream of events issues from the decision, raising in one's favor all manner of unforeseen incidences, meetings and material assistance which no man could have dreamed would have come his way. Whatever you can do or dream, you can do. Begin it. Boldness has genius, power and magic in it. Begin it now.

Mary-Margaret paused. "I think we can all benefit from hearing this," she said quietly as she picked up the microphone. Clipping it to her blouse, she closed her eyes and relaxed. "All right, then," began Bartholomew, "I would like you to spend the next few moments in the quiet observation of 'thinking.' Simply relax and experience what it is. You think all the time, but few of you are conscious of what that process is really about. So allow yourself to be aware of thought, and then we will discuss the interconnection of mind and body." Bartholomew stopped as we attempted to observe this familiar, yet relatively unknown, process.

"Thought," he continued, "is a wave of electromagnetic pulsations of a specific range of frequency that moves through the body and is focused in the brain. The resulting action is what you call *thinking*. Thought waves that are not 'yours' also move through you, as do the ones that seem to originate in 'your' mind. Usually, you pay attention to those arising from your ego—'your thoughts.' It helps to relax into the possibility that thoughts, vast and small, move through you, rather than 'these are my personal thoughts.'"

Bartholomew leaned forward as he spoke. "I want you to understand what a creative process your life is. The marvelous vehicle you call the *mind* is filled with many wondrous things. One is the possibility for *inspiration*. When you let the mind sit quietly, simply being aware of 'what is present,' you create a space for inspiration to arise. This is where meditation is very helpful. In meditation you are not required to think. It is possible to simply sit silently and be present. When you keep thinking the same old thoughts, the mind is activated in the same old way. Stop the constant thinking, and the powers of deeper awareness within the mind have a chance to play *on* you and *with* you. You might experience them as openings of the chakras or flashes of deep knowing.

"These openings are all valid, and you can be inspired through them. The third eye, for example, is a point of vast inspiration." He pointed to the middle of Mary-Margaret's forehead. "The mind has flashes of creativity which the third eye can 'see.' However, if you are caught behind it in thinking mind, the opening of the third eye will rarely happen. All the chakras can inspire you with their own particular wisdom."

He slapped Mary-Margaret's abdomen below the navel. "Here in the hara you will find tremendous creativity," he said. "It holds grounded, powerful inspiration and willpower that ignite the quiet mind and show it how to bring its ideas into form. The hara gives you the strength to do things, to make dreams happen. Don't be afraid to take creative chances, to try new ideas, or to create new realities for yourself. The energy of the hara will help you." Bartholomew leaned back and smiled.

"I am often asked to define God. One way to do that is to say God is *undifferentiated potentiality*—a potentiality filled with limitless possibilities, including limitless, undifferentiated thought. It moves through all the various chakras in the human body. This is why we can say you are connected to all levels of awareness because the body itself, in the chakra system, is connected and open to each of these levels."

Electromagnetic Grids—Choosing Your Blueprint

Bartholomew continued. "In our work, we refer to these chakra openings as electromagnetic grids, or joined lines of power. Before you come into birth, you set up the electromagnetic currents to connect strongly with certain specific energy fields you wish to experience. You select various patterns you wish to live through in your Earth life, and together the patterns form what I have called your *blueprint*. Blueprints are electromagnetic choices, chosen in an expanded state before birth. For example, you decide beforehand the probability of having children, being a millionaire, or any one of the hundreds of possibilities that will go to make up the events of your life. As the undifferentiated energy of potentiality moves into form, it personalizes into 'your life,' 'your interests,' 'your desires.' Do you understand?"

Bartholomew paused, looking around at the faces. Some were puzzled, some bright with understanding, and some very confused. "All right, let's go at it another way. Let us go back to the duality of attraction and repulsion," he said. "What do you think attracts you to certain people who are ready to jump into your life, for good or bad, for fun or pain, or any combination thereof? It's the electromagnetic pulsating of the grid, which sends out a signal that is recognized by that corresponding frequency. What you call *soulmates* is just a fancy word for the coming together of two electromagnetic grids. It's not as glamorous to say it this way, but there it is," he said with a smile.

Emmy spoke up. "How much leeway is there for change?" she asked. "Are we stuck with what we have arranged for ourselves before coming in, or do we have choices? What if I've programmed something I no longer want, or want to experience a little breakdown in a past grid decision."

Bartholomew broke into laughter. "I love it, a breakdown in a grid decision! That's marvelous. You will never, until you reach full enlightenment, ever fulfill the total potentiality of your grid. There is *always* room for movement, deepening, and creative change. The grid of potentiality is so immense and pulsates with such power that there is room for all types of change. This is why scientists can say you are living at 10 percent of your potential capacity. They are talking about the incredible, vast possibilities of the grid compared to the small amount of it you have actualized. Much more is possible. So, please, don't ever worry. Just keep stretching. The grid is immense. You will not reach the edge and hit a wall. Keep moving.

"When you create these grids, you create them from the deepest part of Awareness with as much help from other energies as you need. Please understand, unlimited help is available prior to coming into life, just as it is in this life. When you choose to go to some place far away, you spend a lot of time getting the advice of experts. You find out what kind of supplies are necessary. You go to the person who is the most knowledgeable and say, 'Please help me. I have six different water bottles; which one is going to work the best?' When you begin this life journey, do you think you just hold your nose and jump in, hoping that everything you need might be there? When it comes to choosing the potential equipment available for your life journey, you literally have unlimited wisdom to draw on.

"This is why, for example, if it is not in your destiny to birth a child, you can do whatever you want, and you will not give birth to one. Conversely, if it is your destiny to have one, you are not going to be able to get out of it. At the same time, when you have learned the necessary wisdom contained in a certain pattern, it is possible to then create something new and different. Don't try to guess your future—just live each moment fully, and let Life take care of the rest. Remember, Life is living you!"

Emmy looked at Bartholomew expectantly. "The example you just used has been an issue for me. When I was pregnant, I was certain I was going to have a girl. I knew her name, and I could feel her around me. I even talked to a psychic who agreed. I had a boy. Did I make the whole thing up?" she asked.

"No, you didn't make the whole thing up, and it raises a good point. You must realize that these things are not so cut and dried. There is tremendous flexibility and abundant creativity and delight in the choosing of all these things. You had to have a child. And when you look at your son, you see someone who has a beautiful blend of masculine and feminine—a very lovely Being. You could easily have 'felt' the feminine parts of his balanced psyche.

"All of you place certain 'have to's' in the grid, things you have to do. Some of you 'have to' gain experience through relationship. Some 'have to' experience through children. Sometimes you even 'have to' experience losing a child," he added softly. "Children run your life for a long time. They are not just a little incidental extra, here today, gone tomorrow. In the midst of these firm areas is a lot of play, a lot of give and take, and beautiful mergings, awakenings, and understandings—far more than the limited, finite mind can imagine. Remember, Life is a creative process, and as you awaken, there are greater and deeper knowings awaiting you."

Darcy leaned toward Bartholomew and spoke out. "I'm getting confused here. Are you saying some children are 'have to's' and some aren't?"

"Yes, and the particular one you've got is a 'have to.' Then there are children who are not 'have to's because of some deep change in you, some shift of focus or intent. When the child does come, it could be said there is an agreement between you. It's the same as if you've agreed to meet at the corner of Hollywood and Vine on the 20th of October. You do that on the Earth plane all the time. One person comes from Tokyo and another from Cairo. You meet in Los Angeles to plan events together, and don't even think it's unusual.

"Oftentimes, when you have been tempted by relationships and dropped out of them before they really got going, you are experiencing one of those 'Well, let's think it over' times. If you decide it's a 'no go,' it doesn't happen. The idea that your karma is a choiceless path you walk down without looking to either side is a boring, limited, uncreative, nondynamic point of view. When you move to greater potentials, allowing yourself to risk, to relax, to become more loving and aware, that movement takes you to another crossing point in the grid where the next potential lies. If, at that place, someone comes along whose frequency no longer fits due to your expanded state, or theirs, the joining does not take place. The point here is to realize you are living a dynamic, creative life each moment, filled with the potential to be ever-expanding and full of ever-new joy."

"Could the grid be affected by the bombardment of thought waves that I often feel passing through it?" asked Emmy.

"Only if you connect with them through mutual agreement. If they don't find some similar energy in the grid, they will not remain to be assimilated," Bartholomew replied. "But don't forget, the potential of the grid is vast, and it *always* holds the potential for full enlightenment, when you become interested. The 'ever-present possibility' of realizing the God within could be called 'God's Grace,' and it is always present as a potential for *all* humankind. Remember, God has no favorites."

Patricia waved her hand for attention and asked, "Who determines these 'have to's in our life?"

"In the deepest sense, the creative potentiality of consciousness determines the grid. Or, if you'd rather, it all comes out of God. But within that creative power your own 'personal' grid is also to be found. It comes into being through your own potential and your own necessity. It is both impersonal (God) and personal ('your' past or 'your' karma or 'your' desires). You are aware consciousness manifesting as whoever you perceive yourself to be. 'You' take a body to experience the total potentiality of what it is to be a fully awakened human. So 'you' will put those things in the grid you have not yet experienced and need in order to do that. Those things 'you' have already experienced and understood, 'you' will leave alone.

"For example, let's say you have had a past life as a monk. Let us also say some 'monkish' things were uncompleted in that life. Since there needs to be completion for the whole understanding of 'monkness,' that unfinished understanding comes back in another life to finish it out. You have all been or will be all the faces of humankind. In the end, those who are totally finished are those who have experienced all of life, who have gained enlightenment through life's experiences, and who no longer have anything that either attracts or repulses them. They rest in what is beyond both.

"If there are still things that so repulse you that you could never dream of doing them, they may be what you will have to experience at some future time. If you wish to avoid this, relax around those things you find difficult by allowing yourself to entertain the possibility that you also contain traces of that 'repulsive tendency.' Once you allow yourself to feel the possibility that you are not separate from the repulsion, you will understand what is contained in the tendency. Then you can see yourself as fully human, full of all human potential. When you really experience that which repulses you, the repulsion simply becomes a potential possibility, not a fearful future."

Bartholomew relaxed. "My friends, if you could truly get to know the person or feeling you so strongly dislike, the antipathy would be gone. You are repulsed by things that frighten you, situations you have not allowed yourself to imagine as possible for you. Being freed from having to live out a fearful situation by experiencing it comes from the willingness to fully feel and understand it. It comes from dissolving the unreal boundary that separates you from the situation, or from someone who is currently playing out that part of the whole. Be grateful *they* are doing it. It gives you the opportunity to see yourself mirrored in them, and releases you from the need to create that experience directly.

"Whenever you empathize with or have compassion for anyone in any way, you are no longer separated from them." Bartholomew smiled at us as he leaned back. "I have told many of you that the one person you should sit next to on the bus as often as possible is the one you most dislike on the tour. Do it enough, with a nonjudgmental mind, fully willing and open to see who is really present, and you will breathe a sigh of relief when you realize that another part of you is no longer separate."

Patricia looked up from the notes she was taking. "What I do when I experience repulsion is to stay with the person long enough to find out what it is the person is mirroring to me," she commented.

"Wonderful," Bartholomew responded, "as long as the person is in your presence. You see, many people feel repulsions that have nothing to do with what or who is right in front of them. They are repulsed by different lifestyles or ways of being. For example, in the so-called modern Western world, many people feel a repulsion to what they see as the uncontrolled violence of some Third World countries. Thinking they could never be that violent, they bemoan the actions they see taking place elsewhere. Were anyone to place themselves in some of those very desperate situations, instead of sitting comfortably in their living room watching them on television, they might understand how people, including themselves, can be driven to violence. You might directly experience that for yourselves if it meant the difference between your child eating or not eating, or living or dying. Under those conditions you could conceivably perform the same actions. With this understanding comes compassion, and the judgments dissolve. Words, ideas, and beliefs are the most separating. When you are willing to imagine yourself in another person's situation, you experience the reality of the moment in a very different, intimate way.

"Whatever you are afraid of, find it and experience it fully—now, in yourself, in this very moment. I've said it before, no matter who or what or how distasteful it is, if you can see it, think it, or imagine it, it's *yours*. Otherwise you wouldn't see it, think it, or imagine it. Judgment is released when you realize if something repulses you, it's in your grid and you need to fully stay with and experience it."

Uncovering the Shadow

Justin turned to Bartholomew to ask a question. "Why would millions of people agree to come together in a place like Somalia to starve to death?"

Bartholomew put his fingertips together and closed his eyes for a moment. "Painful events, but a good question," he said. "One of the basic dualities on this planet, my friends, is the difference between those who have and those who don't. It goes way beyond automobiles and air conditioning. I am talking about basic necessities such as food, shelter, medical attention, clean water, and safety. Millions of souls have chosen to uncover what we consider to be *the* governing shadow of this planet, which is the determination of some people to have all they want and to enjoy life, while allowing others to suffer and do without even the basic necessities.

"With relatively few exceptions, the people on this planet are unwilling to share what they have, even though the desperation and cries for help are thundering throughout human consciousness. So now we have situations like those in Somalia and much of Africa. These difficulties created by poverty and violence have been present for centuries, but now they are presented in such a vast, spectacular display that people will finally be forced to acknowledge the disparity. The immediacy of this display is due to the wonder of television and all such worldwide communication. It thrusts you into the middle of Earth-plane reality. As you sit comfortably in your living room with your feet up and a cool drink at your side, watching these intense dramas unfold, you must eventually feel a wrenching in your heart that you will no longer be able to explain, ignore, or put aside. You will begin to wonder if maybe there is something one needs to do in order to bring about a better balance.

"It often takes tremendous courage to choose to live the life of poverty that then brings up the shadow of human greed to all of humankind. If you could look into the eyes of many of those small children in Somalia, you would find some of the wisest, most conscious people on this planet. These and similar difficulties will bring more and more of the shadow of imbalance into your consciousness. It is part of some of these children's grid, this dedication to revealing the inequality among peoples. Children die of starvation in Somalia, are put to death at birth in India, or are the recipients of brutal child abuse in the United States. These events have been taking place on this planet for a long time. Now, the playing out of these events is being chosen by those who have the inner centeredness, strength, and courage to face these conditions. Some of the darkest events are being played out by some of the greatest human lights.

"Things like a so-called individual's karma can no longer be used to explain away these tragedies. The idea that the abused must have been an abuser in a past life is not necessarily true and does not solve anything. It is possible that something very different is going on. Try asking yourself what that might be. Do not be so quick to judge others. Look closely and deeply at yourself when you do. People who are able to take such difficult events and work on their responses until they feel compassion for the offender are greatly helping to remove shadows that have long hidden under rocks of ignorance. Everyone who has reached any kind of understanding or state of forgiveness for the one who has done the abusing is expanding the light on this planet. Such a person is not a victim, but a victor."

Bartholomew leaned back and paused. "You have been very tolerant and patient with our cramped space here," he said, "so let us close for now. But before you go, I would like you to extend yesterday's assignment into today as well. As best you can, for as much time as you can, stay in the moment. Explore what it means for you, in your own way. See if you can involve your bodies in it even more than yesterday. As you go from temple to temple, walk with awareness. That does not mean you can't talk, but it does mean you pay attention while you talk, and while you walk. The aim is to learn how to walk and talk and be aware at the same time.

"Here is something to think about as you go through these temples today. There is no other culture in the world where the awareness of space and form exist together so beautifully. The magic of sacred Japanese architecture comes from the recognition that space is the most important part of any structure. Subordinate to it are the forms that enter and occupy the space. The space itself is the sacred essence, the sacred substance, and the objects are carefully sculpted to fill it in a particular way. Form and space work together, so what you call empty space is the womb in which forms rise and fall.

"Notice these marvelous spaces today as often as you can, and allow yourself to flow into that emptiness. Then you will be able to actually experience a basic spiritual Truth: The things that fill the space come and go, are born and die. But always, the space remains."

Mary-Margaret removed the microphone. She stood up and stretched. "Let's meet in the lobby in an hour for the trip to Sagano," she said. The session was over.

Spaced Out and Out of Space

Later that day, I walked toward the dark black rectangle that delineated the entrance to Tenruy-ji Temple. My sense of space was already tweaked as I approached a doorway set in a wall slightly left of center, climbing steps set even farther to the left of that! Inner space beckoned. Space as the "final frontier" hovered above us. *If the night sky was just a dark veil filled with holes, would we be looking at the light beyond it?* I wondered. *If space could be compressed so totally there was no space at all, would we pop through into another universe? What happens in the body when we have emotionally run out of space? Is it all in the mind?* The wind, messenger of space, nudged me gently toward the darkness. I entered, expanding in an inbreath that held the scent of old wood and spices. I exhaled into the space of the inner gardens.

Yoko smiled and lightly tapped my arm. She had given her camera to Darcy and wanted a picture taken. She, Mary-Margaret, Yuko, and I arranged ourselves on the edge of the wooden veranda. Yuko leaned back and laughed. Mary-Margaret and Yoko sat shoulder to shoulder, smiling at the camera. I knelt behind them, leaning against a post as the shutter snapped, wondering if our bodies would leave a soft imprint in space the way our feet left footprints in sand. We followed the gravel path around a building where playful ceramic frogs frolicked in a coin-tinted pool of splashing water.

Geometrical symmetry, asymmetrical harmony, and formal yet playful exhalations of space greeted me. No accidents here. Every angle, every vista, every curving roof, rock, bamboo railing, tree-clipped hedge, stone lantern, and reflection was carefully orchestrated in a formal, natural, expansive setting. *Do they never get tired of contemplating raked gravel and rocks, or is it really the space surrounding them that is so enticing?* I wondered.

I turned a corner, and the gravel path split in two, leaving me standing at one end of a narrow, covered walkway. It had no walls, but carefully placed posts and long lines of wooden slats set in the ground led my eye to an opening far away. Step by step, each space between the posts revealed a changing scene. Bushes bursting with flowers were set behind a lawn of soft, dark-green moss that spilled and tumbled over rocks and lapped at the shore of a bubbling stream. Waterfalls echoed the splash of colorful orchids that lined the path. Gray patinaed tile outlined rooftops compressed by space with breathtaking intensity.

I seemed to shrink to the size of my thumbnail, and I walked through this landscape as through a still-life painting. I was ecstatic, intoxicated by space and form. Space bubbles burst in my blood until I no longer knew if I was breathing space or space was breathing me. *I wanted more!*

This fatal slip from 'beingness' into desire imploded the space around me. I was stunned, shocked, and battered by the rushing weight of this implosion. Space settled heavily into place between a single breath. A momentary feeling of desolation passed through me like a scorching blast of wind. In my desire to hold on to the space, I had lost it. My grasping mind had done it again!

I rejoined my friends and followed the gravel path through a gate into a forest of green bamboo. The space shifted to a vertical axis and took off like a rocket, leaving pale green contrails behind. A bamboo fence lined the path—cut precisely to a similar height but awesome with individual beauty. The golden stalks shimmered in the sunlight, dappled in rich, tawny colors by shadows streaked with mellow, earthen browns. Tiny bamboo shoots with yellow leaves were busily rustling together. Behind them, thick green trunks rose in delicate, precise curves toward a crown of dancing leaves. The milk-white sky lay just beyond their reach. The soft sighing of leaves being rubbed together by the wind hummed in harmony with the sharp clacking of collid-ing bamboo trunks. Color, perfectly muted, absolutely analogous, bursting with ripeness when pierced by sudden shafts of light, lay dormantly waiting. Sunlight arced across the space and ran like green lightning down the trunks.

Some of us were startled into extravagant praise and others into silence. We passed through the thinning groves of bamboo into the quiet back streets of Sagano and home again. I wondered if I had been seduced by the beauty of the forms within the space or by the space itself. Had I moved out of a fanta-sy and into the moment?

❧ ✳ ☙

Chapter 10

Kyoto: Day Five—Farewell and a Late-Night Performance

The group arranged itself on the floor of our room for the last time. Mary-Margaret made herself comfortable on the TV stand and clipped the microphone to her blouse. She took a sip of water and closed her eyes.

"Good morning, my friends," Bartholomew began. "We will not meet again until our second day in India. Therefore, I would like to talk about what is going to happen so you can begin to get ready to receive the blessing of the Kalachakra. The energy generated in this initiation—not only by His Holiness the Dalai Lama, but also by all of his very intense associates and devoted monks—will set up an amazing hum. This hum, plus the natural energy of the Himalayas, combined with being seated beneath Mount Kinnaur Kailash, Shiva's[11] 16,000-foot winter home, will provide you with a golden opportunity for transformation." Bartholomew laughed mischievously.

"Whatever happens," he continued, "you will not return home the same as when you left. We have spoken many times of allowing yourselves to remember that the cells of your body can relax and open to whatever energy is present. They will do so when you give them that sweet and gentle directive. This is what I am asking for in India. You will be responding to new sights, sounds, smells, and tastes. Some of them you will find painful or difficult to accept. I want you to watch carefully how you allow your senses to affect your responses to what is present. The choice between welcoming these new experiences with delight, or censoring them through judgment, is entirely up to you. You are moving into a culture that is so different from what you are used to that all of your alarm buttons may be activated. The potential for separation will be present. At the same time, there will be a wonderful opportunity to be open to every moment with awareness, interest, and full participation.

"If you allow yourself to be put off by your judgments because things do not agree with your idea of 'the way things should be,' you will miss the wonderful dance of life bursting forth in this country. Remember, it takes only a moment of awareness to realize that you can be at home in unfamiliar surroundings. You can easily move to a more spacious inner place where you are totally present and can allow this amazingly diverse and spiritual culture to play upon your psyche.

"I ask you not to waste two weeks of your lives only to go home and realize what you have missed. Just relax into it all, and be aware of your judgments. Do not try to push them away or pretend they are not there. Ease into being a part of the human condition as it is manifesting itself in front of you. It's all you anyway! Laugh at yourselves because there will be many times when that kind of laughter is the only appropriate thing to do." Relaxing, Bartholomew paused and took a sip of water. "Are there any questions about this?"

Darcy raised her hand. "I have heard and read about the poverty and hardships in India," she said. "I don't want to turn my back on that, but it seems overwhelming. How do we deal with those things?"

"India is a perfect place to learn about seeing without judgment. If you can allow yourself to experience it all, in the midst of what you see as pain and poverty, you will find delight and acceptance. Look for the children laughing and scrapping in the streets, the women chattering in the markets, the men gathered together as friends. Watch for the things that reflect the rambunctious consciousness of life, as well as what you have defined as hardship.

"Are poverty and pain out there? Yes, but don't forget that it's in your lives as well. Their pain is your pain. You have your part of it, and they have theirs. And the excited, joyful consciousness you have, they have as well. Look for all of it 'out there,' and you will be able to feel all of it 'in you.' This is a delightful and complicated country, full of different ways of overcoming various difficulties. The people could not have survived otherwise, and I want you to come to appreciate their creative cunning. This may result in a difference of opinion during your financial transactions. Don't worry, leaving a few extra rupees behind will not hurt you," he said, laughing.

"These people enjoy much in the way of spiritual benefits that you do not. The entire subcontinent is one of the strongest spiritual areas on the planet.

The gods and goddesses are alive and equal. They dance, play, and do all those 'naughty' things together that most Christians wouldn't dream of their God doing—and they enjoy it tremendously. A child born into this culture believes in some form of deity, or in the reality that God exists. They needn't spend the first 40 years of their lives wondering if there is a God, and, if so, where to find it. Their problem may be which one of the gods they should pick to love, honor, and merge with. Merging is always a real potentiality, full of the possibility of bliss and joy.

"In the next two weeks, every moment will contain the opportunity for expansion of your physical, mental, and emotional well-being, and suggestions will be given as we go along. I would like to begin by asking you to continue to be aware of the responsibility your mind has for the well-being of the cells of your body. Your cells and your bodies are tight from the mental directives you give them to keep you safe. Let the mind give the body the directive to relax and open, to feel that all's well. Then allow yourselves to enjoy the cellular relaxation and inspiration that come with this directive.

"I wish to emphasize the need to be aware of these relaxed moments. I know it is hard for you to realize how long your cells have been operating under maximum tension. When the directive is given to relax, it *will* be done instantly. It may not last longer than a moment, but it will be there. Do it again and again. Material that you have not been willing to face before will be released. Do not make the mistake of projecting it outward onto others. Stay with the feelings and mental pictures that arise without judging them good or bad. Simply be aware of them and relax.

"You may react to events so quickly that it feels like an automatic response, just like your leg jerking in response to your knee being struck by a rubber hammer is automatic. You may respond verbally without thinking, or find your body recoiling without consciously knowing why. This 'knee-jerk' response seems to bypass the brain and happen 'on its own.' Watch for these responses and remember, whenever you are relaxed and open, that there is a possibility of letting go of old, hidden material. Be gentle, and have as much love and compassion for yourselves as you can. Don't forget to laugh. It will go a long way toward dispelling your anxiety and doubt.

"As you move to the higher reaches of the Himalayas, you may also experience the effects of oxygen deprivation. This can be very helpful for releasing material. And if you have ever wanted visions, this is the place for you to have them. The visionary light is in the very air and mountains themselves. Allow the process to work on you. Be willing to allow change to happen. You have already done everything necessary to place yourselves in this position of potential transformation. Many of you have seemingly sacrificed tremendous amounts of emotional, mental, and financial energy, so let's get the maximum experience from the situation. Don't sleep through it.

"The chances are good that you will start to feel totally vulnerable, exposed, and unsure of yourself. For the human psyche, hearing the words 'totally vulnerable' can produce fear. You usually equate vulnerable with being in an undefended position where someone can act on you in a way you will find difficult or destructive. That is not the kind of 'vulnerable' we are talking about. I want you to be vulnerable in the deepest sense of allowing yourselves to be open to the unknown—to the power and mystery of something exquisitely different and nonmental. In the next few weeks, let this appreciation pour out of you. Let it rest on every flower, every physical deformity, every mound of excrement, every mountain and river that you come in contact with. Make no distinctions. Appreciate it all. Be open to it all. You can do this because, seen with the eyes of deep appreciation, everything is beautiful."

Bartholomew paused a moment. "I'm sure you have all come to know you have just touched the surface of this magnificent country you are leaving tomorrow," he said. He leaned toward Yuko and Yoko. "My deep gratitude to you both for all your generous help and support." Turning to Yuko, he continued, "And my gratitude to you as well for your willingness to publish a book you cannot be sure your world will accept.[12] Some people will benefit greatly; others will find the material somewhat bizarre. But in the end, the job is to simply get it out into the world. I am very grateful to you for taking this risk. Thank you."

Bartholomew turned to us and continued briskly, "All right, my friends, I would appreciate your using the next two days to the maximum. You have gone through a lot of trouble to get here. Don't miss it. I can say with certainty we will never have this opportunity again. And remember, you don't have to *do* anything. Be present, be open, and be willing to allow the energies to change you. Leave the rest to God. You are in good hands," he said with a final smile.

One Last Temple

Everyone quickly scattered after the meeting. This was our final full day in Japan, and no one wanted to waste it. Emmy and I had just enough time to return the room to its original condition before she left, and I went to join Justin and Mary-Margaret. After lunch, we took a taxi to Ginkakuji Temple, the Silver Pavilion—*my* Silver Pavilion, a temple I had fallen in love with in an art history class many years ago.

In this city of extraordinary sights, my expectations had been more than met. I was grateful for my sense of vision above all others, as my eyes drank in and devoured what my mind had longed to see. My body, my friend, always on the verge of shorting out, has continued to support me and somehow maintain its circuitry intact. Because of these miracles, joy has invaded my body. Passion has run rampant through my veins and along my nerves, leaping synapses in a single bound, thrilling my neurons with the reckless abandon of its passing. It has hit my mind in bursts of appreciation that have brought my thoughts to their knees. Zinging through arteries down to the smallest capillary, it has leapt into the void between the darkest cells, exploding them into mad applause with its wild daring. And now, the Silver Pavilion!

Our taxi dropped us off in the midst of a parking lot crammed with orderly rows or large, closely packed buses, patiently awaiting the return of their passengers. Upon entering, we were immediately swept away by a torrent of laughing, chattering, camera-clicking Japanese tourists. Mary-Margaret retreated to a quiet, shady spot overlooking the gardens while Justin and I turned against the tide of good-natured humanity. We rested in an eddy of people caught against the barrier of a bamboo railing. We turned to find ourselves facing stillness—in the contrast of splashing waterfalls, glistening rocks, moss, and flowers.

Within minutes the tide had turned, and we were left alone. Crowded walkways were now empty. Space appeared to open up and reveal the classically intimate, yet expansive beauty of this one-time personal villa-turned-temple. The softness of weathered wood, the sensitive proportions of structure to space, the linear beauty of gravel paths, the intimate embrace of living garden and raked sand stilled the mind and opened the heart. No wonder the shogun and his company had spent nights here under the full moon, looking out at the waves of carefully raked white sand sparkling silver in the moonlight. They must have sat quietly listening to the higher octaves of running water and splashing carp, transported inward, deeply into the moment, down and away from the daily intrigue and war of feudal times.

We found Mary-Margaret still sitting in the shade, contentedly fanning herself, looking as serene as her surroundings. She joined us and we left the pavilion, walking the ancient Path of Philosophers back toward the Inn. Washed thin by the heat and filled with the experiences at Ginkakuji, I gratefully sought the refuge of my air-conditioned room once again.

For our last night in Kyoto, the group would meet at Gion Corner to experience the aesthetic delights of traditional Japanese arts. We felt this would be the perfect way to end our stay in Japan.

A Late-Night Performance

One can only admire, if one is aware of such things, the marvelous ingenuity of an evolutionary system that can produce such a miracle of survival as the backward bending joint of a bird's leg. What a delicate, perfectly formed, carefully constructed hinge the heel of such a slender leg has become. What dexterous feats of balance the bird can perform with the assistance of this small joint. Sideways hops, pigeon-toed struts, splits, backbends, two-point landings, upside-down swings, flutters, and crawls are only part of a bird's large repertoire. This miracle of body management magnificently serves the bird's major interest, which is the accumulation and ingestion of food.

That evening a bird of unknown species took to the air above the city. Having spent a day exercising that extraordinary ability birds are so prone to take for granted, this one had been successful in unearthing worms, snatching rotten vegetables from the outdoor market, and, in general, scrapping with others of its kind over similar tasty treats. The bird flew over Hanamikoji-dori and circled a brightly lit, colorful building. Perhaps it was distracted by the lights, or perhaps the day's feast was weighing heavily on the bird's small stomach, but it made what could only be described as a very sloppy landing on the curved roof of the pagoda-style structure. It was saved from further embarrassment by one claw, which had hooked itself underneath a tile.

Meanwhile, in the building below, our group had taken their seats in front of a dimly lit stage. An expectant hush fell as a kimono-clad woman came from behind the curtain and sat down. Her precise movements introduced the austere simplicity of the Zen tea ceremony, a ritual only highlighted in the program we had come to see at Gion Corner.

This ceremony was followed by the solemn music of a 13-stringed instrument known as the Koto, which in turn was replaced by a man standing alone on the stage next to a small table holding a two-foot-tall vase. He performed magic as he constructed a beautifully energetic yet serene arrangement from a profusion of flowers and leaves he had placed on the floor.

As the curtain rose, the Koto reappeared, joined by a drum and several flutelike instruments. The sound of Gagaku[13] filled the room. A man appeared, wearing an embroidered costume of brilliant orange and gold. His head was covered by the brightly lacquered mask of a mythological beast, and the strong, stylized steps of the dance were mesmerizing in their movement.

The last sounds of music faded away as a backdrop was lowered and a feudal lord stomped to the center of the stage, speaking the first lines of a Kyogen, or ancient comic play. As the play unfolded, the exaggerated mannerisms and broad humor of the actors surmounted the language barrier with comic action, and the foreign audience was left laughing as the curtain descended.

Then, from the wings, two beautiful and beautifully dressed *maiko* (Geisha in training) slowly emerged in time to the sound of a single Koto. They bowed, bent, and turned with the grace of young aspens in a summer breeze, performing the Kyoto-style dance known as Kyomai.

Once again the curtain rose, this time on a bell tower set center stage. A man entered carrying what appeared to be a three-foot doll. He was joined by two others, whose faces were covered and who were dressed completely in black. This was the classic Bunraku puppet theater performing the final scene from an 18th-century love story. The complex movements of the kimono-clad heroine were so realistic that the puppet's skillful manipulators soon faded from view. The final curtain fell on a happy ending amid loud applause, whistles, and stamping feet.

Exiting into the parking lot, the group scattered, everyone seeking their own transportation back to the Inn. Several people, Judith among them, decided it was a good night to walk home. In search of something cold for dessert, they headed down the street in the direction of their own peculiar destiny. A late-night snack stand was open, and the travelers stopped to purchase ready-made chocolate-covered ice cream cones. Laughing and chatting together, they turned down a nearby dark, winding side street.

Up on the roof, the bird, which had been quietly drowsing, lurched into the air in an effort to reorient itself. Still filled with food, its flight was clumsy, but it circled slowly and climbed to 50 or 60 feet, where it leveled off. Fate vectored the bird onto an interception course with the group walking below. Judith was busily talking and eating her ice cream, when she heard a soft plop. Looking down, she realized she had just dropped chocolate on her brand new white skirt.

The bird, greatly relieved, flew away in search of a friendly tree in which to spend the night. Without thinking, Judith lifted her skirt and licked the chocolate off. It had a very strange taste and it took only seconds for her to realize the "chocolate" had been left by the bird!

☙ ❈ ❧

Chapter 11

Moving On

O f course, I didn't hear this story until the next morning at breakfast, when I did my best to be a sympathetic rather than a hysterical listener. I asked Judith what she had done and how she felt about the whole incident.

"I couldn't say a word; I was so appalled," she said. "I started gagging and spitting into the gutter. The others thought I had suddenly gone crazy." She laughed. "I think it was the first time I realized I was not going to be in control of what happened to me on this trip."

I chopped up my egg and spread it carefully on my toast. "Well, I suppose there is a lesson to be learned from this experience," I said innocently.

She looked at me, blue eyes open wide. "Yes, yes there is," she said softly. "Give up chocolate ice cream."

To keep myself from laughing, I turned to Mary-Margaret. "Where do we go from here?" I asked.

"To the airport, I hope," she replied. "Justin, Barbara, and I are off to Nagoya, while the rest of you go to Osaka. Hopefully I'll see you in Singapore," she added.

Justin and Mary-Margaret had learned the day before that, although they were our tour leaders, they had been accidentally placed on standby and would be leaving from Nagoya airport rather than from Osaka with us. Yuko was going with them to make sure they caught the right train. It was time to say good-bye. The group broke up and shared hugs all around. Yuko negotiated the fare with our bus driver, and the others climbed into a taxi. No telling when we would see our Japanese friends again.

We waited two hours at Osaka before taking off, but a pleasant reunion did indeed await us in Singapore. As we disembarked, Mary-Margaret and Justin came to meet us. My roommate, Carolyn Lake, was also there. She had arrived from the States several hours before and was waiting for us. Her favorite camera was on her hip, and our duffel bag lay at her feet. We caught up on the latest news from home as we waited for our flight to be called. One cocktail and two coffees later, we were securely fastened into our seats as the airplane took off on the final leg of our journey to India.

PART III

India

August 1992

Chapter 12

The Journey Begins—Again

We landed in Delhi at 9:30 P.M. local time. It was dark and hot—sticky, smelly, diesel hot. We dug through a jumbled mountain of luggage in the dim light to recover our bags, then joined the ragged lines waiting to clear customs.

A small group of people stood on the other side of a low wooden barrier about 30 feet away. Some of them were waving and shouting hello. The Australians had come to meet us. As I passed through the gate, a woman with long, dark, curly hair came up to me. "Hi," she said with a shy smile. "I'm Lin Bell." Lin had introduced the Bartholomew books to Australia, and I was delighted to meet her after many years of long-distance correspondence. As we hugged, a man approached, fairly crackling with energy. It was Sol Singer, eyes sparkling and white teeth flashing in a huge welcoming grin. Over his shoulder I recognized Chai. I had last seen her in Taos, and here she was, tall and slim, looking relaxed and very much at ease in "her" India. She introduced her partner Russell, a tall, handsome young man with black hair and beard.

"Are you all here, then?" Chai asked with a smile, as she grabbed a nearby suitcase. Without waiting for an answer, she took Mary-Margaret by the arm and started off. The rest of us followed, staggering toward the exit. Twelve hours of air travel and a hefty dose of jet lag had left us docile and disoriented. Somewhat revived by the wind whipping through the open windows of our two "air-conditioned" buses, we were even further energized by small squirts of adrenalin as the driver serenely zig-zagged his way through heavy city traffic.

Arriving at our destination, the group spilled noisily into the quiet lobby of the Marina Hotel. We sprawled across all available chairs and sofas as Chai and Russell checked us in, passed out room keys, and made sure everyone knew how early we were leaving for Shimla the next morning. The group quickly dispersed, tiredly lurching up the white marble staircase in search of their assigned rooms.

Carolyn and I entered ours, dropped our bags, and looked around. The British influence was apparent in the high ceiling, wooden wainscotting, and long narrow windows of the large room. But the heavy drapes were torn, the carpet thin, and the dark wooden furniture scuffed and scarred. Switches that had once sent current rising to the overhead lights no longer worked. The elegant black marble in the bathroom was chipped and cracked. The toilet rocked on its base, and the faucets seemed unsure of their original function.

It smelled musty from overworked air conditioning, and the walls were stained with dampness. But it was cool. The covers were neatly turned down, and the single bedside lamp cast a soft glow on sparkling glasses and bottled water. I passed up the promise of a lukewarm shower, quickly brushed my teeth, and fell gratefully into bed.

☙ ❋ ❧

Chapter 13

Delhi to Shimla—
What We Learned about
Ourselves During Our
First Day in India

At eight the next morning, our two small buses, topped by a mound of tied-down luggage and camping gear, and crammed with food, supplies, Australians, Americans, and our Tibetan cooks, pulled away from the hotel in a black cloud of diesel smoke. As we eased into traffic, I was fascinated by the loud herd of assorted trucks, buses, cars, motorcycles, minivans, bicycles, and mopeds that instantly surrounded us. Small, partially enclosed three-wheeled vehicles were in use as taxis. Painted bright yellow and black, they darted in and out of traffic like fat, scurrying beetles.

On the sidewalks, women in brightly dyed saris and men dressed in a mixture of dark business suits, multicolored turbans, loose silk shirts, and gleaming white trousers passed by in a continuous stream of ever-shifting colors. A face or figure occasionally stood out in sharp relief. A beggar with no feet sat leaning against a building as he peered through a moving forest of legs. The dark, aristocratic image of a male profile was etched in stark contrast to his clean white Mercedes. In the street, a sweating businessman clutched his briefcase, caught in the act of climbing into a bright yellow taxi.

The city passed by in a hot swirl of motion that finally overwhelmed the senses. Sol sat calmly unpacking his newly acquired harmonium, riding backwards on a mound of supplies stacked neatly between the driver's compartment and the front seats. He pumped the bellows and fingered the keyboard, humming and chanting along with the music. The other Australians joined in. I gradually relaxed and took a long drink from my water bottle.

Eventually the streets turned into highway, and the buildings were left behind, until even the suburbs melted into open road. Bullock carts, donkeys, and plodding pedestrians joined the stream of traffic headed north. Several hours later we naively asked Chai for a bathroom stop. "No problem," she replied, as she banged on the separating glass partition to get the driver's attention. His companion turned around as Chai shouted her request. With a grin he spoke to the driver, who immediately honked his horn and pulled off the road.

We stopped at the edge of a cultivated field bordered by a line of sparsely growing trees and bushes. Carolyn and I glanced at each other and shrugged as we climbed down and stretched. The Australians piled noisily after us, quickly separating before the arrival of the second bus.

The Americans followed more slowly, looking around as Chai turned and yelled at them. "Watch where you step," she said, darting behind a convenient tree. It took several seconds for everyone to realize this was the bathroom stop. Roberta laughed and gleefully waded into the knee-high grass. The rest of us scattered, trying to get away from passing traffic, the vigilant bus drivers, and each other. Our inhibitions had been left behind, and it was a laughing group of people who gathered back at the buses.

The road to Shimla took us gratefully higher into cool pine-scented mountains. We alternated seats and stood in the aisle, drank water, sucked the juice out of small cardboard containers, munched on nuts, and stuck our heads in and out of the windows. I passed the time talking with Chai. I was curious about what she and Russell had gone through trying to organize a tour when often nothing could be accomplished without knowing the third cousin of a friend of an influential friend.

"How did this trip get started, anyway? What did you have in mind, and has it worked out as planned?" I asked her.

She leaned back against the seat, propping her feet on a sack of onions. "Let's see," she mused. "I remember when it started. Mary-Margaret and Justin were sitting on my veranda in Australia, and we were talking about India and the Himalayas. I showed them some photographs of the time Russell and I walked through Zanskar. They were amazed. Justin inquired about my other trips to India, and then Mary-Margaret asked me if I would organize a trip to the Himalayas for them. I told her I'd love to, but only if we could go to a spiritually powerful place, not just on some kind of sightseeing tour."

"How long ago was this?" I asked.

"About two years ago," she replied, popping a few nuts into her mouth. "I said okay, but I knew it wasn't going to be easy because I had never organized a group trip to India before. It's really difficult to organize *anything* in India, but I thought I'd give it a go. That's how it started. Russell and I came to India this January, and it took three months to get through all the paperwork and the bureaucracy." She sighed. "It's like pushing through mountains every-where. My desire was to spare people as much discomfort as possible. Since we've got such a limited amount of time, we cannot waste it on red tape. Russell and I knew that most people hadn't been to India before, so the coun-try and the climate would be a shock. It would be really, really hot, and Delhi is very polluted. We wanted to move people out of the city quickly and into the mountains."

"How did the Dalai Lama get into the picture?" I asked.

"Well, we set up the tour when we were actually in Dharamsala.[14] We wanted to have lots of interactions with different Tibetan teachers and hope-fully have some kind of interview or teaching with His Holiness while he was there. Then when I went to South India, I saw His Holiness's secretary, and I asked if we could possibly have time with him as a group. He said no, because His Holiness would be in Europe and then would fly to India and go straight up to a restricted and remote area in the Himalayas to do a Kalachakra initia-tion. So I asked him if we could go, and was told that everyone was welcome, but since the location was restricted, we would probably not be able to obtain permits to get there. I asked him if we got there did he think it would be all right with His Holiness? He said it would be fine." Chai laughed, her blue eyes sparkling. "Then the next day he called me over and told me it was going to be in Kalpa. So he gave me the location on the one hand, but said we prob-ably couldn't get there on the other.

"Well, that really changed things. I wanted to go to a Kalachakra initia-tion, and I was prepared to get the necessary permits and push through all bar-riers. Mary-Margaret was excited. She said that everyone was keen on expe-riencing the teachings of His Holiness and would love to be with him in the Himalayas.

"Russell and I waited until the snow melted in early March before we head-ed off to Shimla. The road was open, but when we got there, they wouldn't let us go any farther. The area beyond was completely restricted. 'No, you can't go. No, you can't get permits, and *no*, you can't just go and check it out,' they said. The tourist bureau told us they couldn't book anything for us in that region—that we would have to go on luck. Well, you can't take a group of peo-ple up there on luck, so I met with the head monk at Namgu Monastery in Dharamsala, where His Holiness lived, and asked him for help. He said,

'Okay, one monk, Dev Raj Negi, comes from the area around Kalpa, and he is hoping to organize things there. He will be coming here first, and I will instruct him to look after your group.' And he did exactly that.

"As we were pulling out of Dharamsala, someone came rushing up to tell us Dev Raj Negi had arrived late last night. I told the driver to wait and rushed over to the monastery, woke up the monk, and told him we had to set up the organization for a group in Kalpa, and we had five minutes to do it. He said, 'I already know it and have been instructed to help you.' The head monk had told him when he arrived that he was to help organize this group. So he says, 'I promise you I will organize some accommodations for your group. You have my word. I've been instructed, and I will do everything I can.'

"Right there I knew it would happen. I couldn't get any information in or out of that area, but I knew everything was going to be okay because I had this connection with Dev. Then I got a letter from him when he was in Varanesi. He said he was leaving to go to Kalpa and to please give him details. So I sent the details both to Varanesi and Kalpa, just in case. I told him the dates when we would be arriving and how many beds we would need. He received the letter, but I didn't know it at the time."

"When did this happen?" I asked.

"Months later," she answered. "I got the letter around the first of June."

I was surprised. "We were scheduled to leave in July. Weren't you running out of time?"

"Well, yes and no," she said. "I knew Dev was going to organize it because I knew I couldn't. There was really no choice because I couldn't go in there myself to set things up. I had Jamyung, my friend in Delhi, working on the special permits, and even she was saying, 'I hope they are going to come through.' She has friends and acquaintances in high places. I knew if anyone could get them, she could. She said we had a chance because the Indian government waives all special travel restrictions for the short period of time around a Kalachakra initiation so people can come and go. As for continuing on to Lau Spiti, we would have to wait and see. In the end, we got the permits through her, but they are only good for ten days beginning with the first day of the Kalachakra. The permits will actually run out when we are in Kalpa."

"What an amazing process," I said.

"Well, it is amazing because it took a lot of faith and a lot of really strong connections. Staying in Kalpa wouldn't have worked if we didn't have someone there who was instructed by the head monk in the Namgu Monastery. I mean, that's his teacher and his guru, right? He would bust his gut to follow through on the instructions that were given to him. I knew that. And he has. He's gotten the whole doctor's residence in shape for us."

Chai fell silent. I looked out the open window at the darkness that had fallen. Our headlights illuminated the road like two giant glowworms as we slowly crawled up a series of steep switchbacks in search of Shimla. Everyone was quiet, having worn themselves out trying to hear each other over the guttural grinding of well-worn gears. The air felt cool. Our driver and his companion were searching ahead for signs of the city. The tape player was mercifully silent after tormenting us for hours with the latest Indian pop music. Those of us sitting in front had threatened to dismantle both the tape player and the driver when we ran out of patience with the sound.

In the end, the driver redeemed himself by slickly maneuvering the bus through the narrow rock confines of a vertical driveway and pulling up in front of a brightly lit mansion. Chai had booked us into a Maharajah's summer home instead of one of the hotels in town. He turned off the engine at precisely 9:10 P.M., and for a moment all we could hear was the pop and ping of hot metal in the silence. We breathed a collective sigh of relief, grateful to be there. The staff surrounded us, and soon the sound of shouted instructions and the thud of dropping baggage was heard. Chai bounced off the bus. I unwound from around the sacks of onions and beans and followed more slowly. Justin and Mary-Margaret were already inside the building speaking to the concierge as we crowded into the vestibule and looked around.

My attention was immediately drawn to some photographs hanging on the dark walls. As I approached, a toothy young Tyrone Power smiled at me from above a tall oriental vase filled with flowers.[15] Clark Gable, all ears and sexy grin, leered harmlessly from a place above the beautifully carved wooden telephone stand. Abbott and Costello cavorted impishly under the curved staircase, and Jean Harlow languidly reclined on a couch in the hallway. All of the photos bore enthusiastic inscriptions of gratitude and compliments to the Maharajah. It was eerie to be so unexpectedly reminded of a time long gone, yet living on in these chemical shadows and pale highlights of faded ink.

I was snapped out of my reverie by the sound of my name echoing down the dim passageway. It was time to find our room. Four of us gathered in a large bedroom on the second floor, foreigners to the suggested opulence of a four-poster bed, settees, and large, elaborately carved wardrobes. We dropped our luggage, cleaned up, and went in search of food.

Several large tables had been pushed together in the center of an ornate dining room and were covered with white tablecloths to hold a buffet-style meal. Silver gleamed among the snowy white napkins, reflecting back the light of the overhead crystal chandelier. Tendrils of aromatic steam leaked from the covered dishes as our servers brought out tea and chapatis (crisp, flat bread) to go with our rice and dahl (a stewed lentil dish). People circled the tables, eyes gleaming, forks raised. We carried our plates to the chairs lined up against the walls. The room was filled with the sound of clinking china, subtle chewing, and mild conversation. To the ambidextrous went the reward of a hearty dinner, as we balanced the plates, napkins, and silver on our laps. By the time supper was over, room assignments had been sorted out, and we headed upstairs.

I heard a knock on the door, and Lee presented herself, nightgown over one arm, toothbrush in hand. We would often wonder in the days to come how she managed to keep her nails polished and her long, curly hair under control. Right now, she had come to inquire if we could squeeze another person into our room. "Yes," we chorused, and promptly removed the mattress from one bed, placing it on the floor to make room enough to accommodate all five of us. Soon, the sound of quiet breathing filled the cool night air.

❧ ❋ ☙

Chapter 14

Shimla–a Brother Returns

The next morning we took turns hustling each other in and out of the bathroom. The heavy influx of guests had the Maharajah's plumbing protesting in total rebellion. Water advanced and retreated in the pipes like a blindfolded army on maneuvers, alternately spraying us wildly or leaving us covered with soap under a dripping faucet. Downstairs, Mary-Margaret had chosen a small, quiet sitting room for our first meeting with Bartholomew. Several members of the group lounged comfortably against the sofas, and some early risers were already having tea.

Justin found a soft spot on the floor, while Mary-Margaret settled into an overstuffed chair. She leaned back and relaxed as the room filled and became quiet.

"Good morning, my friends," said Bartholomew, as he smiled a greeting to the Australians. Wasting no time, he began. "It is nice to see you all. Before we left Australia, we talked about the cells of the body and the part they play in releasing your awareness.[16] Since we have also been discussing this in Japan, I think we all have the same information. Therefore, I would like you to take a moment right now to 'check in' with your physical bodies." He paused. "There is every likelihood you will be aware of a certain amount of tension building. It is very important to pay attention to the messages your cellular body will be giving you in the next few days.

"Some of you may have the idea that it is necessary for you to attend all the lectures of the Dalai Lama to receive the greatest benefit from the Kalachakra. I would like to suggest that your body may feel quite differently at times. It may want you to go for a walk, sit by a stream, or take a van to town and do some shopping. To leave your mind in charge of what you will be doing while you are here would be disastrous for your body and your spiritual awakening. So let me make this absolutely clear: The only rule in Kalpa will be to follow your own inner promptings. You are free to do exactly as you please. This is *your* journey. It has nothing to do with any projected idea of what you are supposed to achieve. For each of you it will be different. Allow it all to happen. The belief that everyone needs to do the same thing is an inappropriate approach to consciousness. In these next days, it will be important to remember the assignment I left you with the last time we met. I would like to give it again. As often as possible, gently remind your cells to 'relax and open, relax and open.' Just that.

"This new environment you are in is bombarding your senses far more than you may realize. Anytime you become aware of the slightest tension, instantly relax to the deepest level. It may help to find something beautiful in nature to do this. Focus on it, and hold the intention to 'relax and open.' Look to the mountains, the rivers, the sky, and the land around you. You will find great strength, nourishment, and silence in them. This whole journey is an opportunity to practice the cellular relaxation until it becomes as natural as breathing."

Bartholomew stopped and looked around. "Are there any questions?" he asked.

Emmy responded immediately. "I feel an area of anxiety or agitation, like something unknown is building," she said.

"Well, my friend, let's look at this realistically. You have placed yourselves as far away from home as many of you have ever been. You are in a totally new environment, and you are going into an area that is restricted and in the hands of the military. This is unfamiliar territory on many levels. In attending the Kalachakra initiation, you will be in the proximity of the Dalai Lama, one of the spiritual 'atomic reactors' of the age. In addition to the amazing presence of His Holiness, many of his devoted disciples will be there, monks who have spent their entire lives preparing their bodies and minds to receive this marvelous initiation. In your words, 'This is heavy stuff!' Please do not be surprised at tumultuous feelings of anxiety, tension, or heaviness. There is just cause for it. Be aware of it all and *relax!*

"You will get what you need, and you can destroy the beauty of this journey if you let your mind decide what goal you must achieve. When you start dictating how consciousness is to move you, you end up sabotaging yourself. I ask you to simply turn it over to the Power that has been in charge all along.

This is all you ever have to do. You have only *imagined* that you were the one in charge. Get yourselves to Kalpa, sit with the Dalai Lama, or sit with the majestic mountains and rivers, and let the process take care of itself. Look at the difficulties many of you went through to get here. All of this is part of 'the process.'

"By coming on this trip, many of you are calling your spiritual 'game plan' into play. The game plan is a set of mental tactics you employ to reach a certain goal. In this case, the tactic is to get yourselves to the Himalayas with the idea that you are going to become Enlightened. This belief is deeply embedded in the psyche." Bartholomew smiled. "Everyone goes to the Himalayas to find God, because that's where it happens isn't it? Great gurus are sitting in caves, fully realized and filled with devotion." Bartholomew's smile grew as he spread his arms wide.

"Now *you* are here in the same Himalayas, and not only that, but you will be with one of the greatest spiritual teachers the world has ever known. The Dalai Lama is not just an awakened person, he is also the embodiment of a lineage of incredible power. At the Kalachakra, he becomes the vessel and the vehicle for this ancient, yet ever-new awareness. So here you are, caught up in the fear that says, 'Oh my God, with all this help, if I don't get it here, I never will. I have *really* stacked the deck against myself. I have Bartholomew, my friends, the Dalai Lama, and the Himalayas. What if I miss it?'

"Do not underestimate the fear that arises in you over this. Many of you want to awaken more than you want most things, so the fear is real, and the fear is here. Face it. Go back to the cells, to relaxing, to silence. There is no way you can put rules on the energy your cells will be experiencing. They will do what they do in accordance with an inner, unseen pattern of electromagnetic force, and you can't do a thing about it! What you *can* do is come to each moment of your life with the *intention* to be as fully present, as fully quiet, as fully relaxed as you naturally can. That is your job. Ask to awaken, and the rest is up to God.

"And, if this is not your moment to awaken fully, I want you to know that your cells will return home filled with amazing potential from your having been here. That potential will be released in its own proper time. Nothing, and no time, is wasted. Please do not go to the Kalachakra with the idea that you will wander around with your heads illuminated like light bulbs and your hearts radiating like a central heating system! You have no idea what will happen. You may come back aware of having diarrhea and nothing else! It doesn't matter. You are not here to stick your finger into a celestial light socket; you are here to fill your cells with the *prana* they have been yearning for.[17]

"Will you understand everything the Dalai Lama says? By no means! Nor is it necessary. And if you allow yourself to get trapped into thinking you should, you will be lost. Simply approach this ceremony with excited expectation, knowing you are going to be filled to overflowing. Your cells will begin to hum and buzz and sing, and for the rest of your life, the accumulated energy will play out the way it plays out. To be willing to have this happen is all you can do. So many of you have given so much in so many ways to be here, emotionally as well as financially. Please do not add to that seeming sacrifice by thinking you must get fully enlightened or this tour is a flop. You are not in charge, so let go and allow what will happen to happen."

The Fear That Underlies All Fear

Bartholomew stopped for a moment and reached for a glass of water. Taking a sip, he looked at us with compassion. "I understand your dilemma. On the one hand, you are faced with the fear of missing the perfect opportunity," he said. "And I know, on the other, you are faced with the primordial fear that there may be no God, or that you are so separated from God that you can't find your way back Home. The manifest world of form and thought you have taken such care to create is so incredibly powerful that you are afraid this reality of separation is somehow permanent. That is a lie, which is all I can tell you. No thing your ego creates is permanent, and the idea of separation from God is a creation of the ego and therefore unreal.

"In Kalpa you may alternate between these fears and the exaltation caused by the beauty and excitement of what is going on around you. You may find yourself projecting out onto silly things, like being upset because you only got one bottle of water, while someone else got two! When you start getting disturbed over such trivia, try laughing a little at yourself. Say, 'Here comes the trivia projection,' because it *is* trivia that you are treating with such importance. Try to remember you have willingly set yourselves up to face many of your fears by hurling yourself into the unknown. Tomorrow you are going into a restricted area that hasn't received Westerners for more than 40 years, and you have several military checkpoints to pass through. Of course you feel fear. Move ahead in spite of your fears and into your fears. Have the courage to let go into being totally fearful, and watch what happens."

Looking down at his hands, he said pensively, "You know, at the bottom of all fear is the fear of dying. And the fear of dying is a reflection of the fear that there is nothing beyond death." He leveled a finger at us. "You do not fear leaving one reality and moving to another. You fear you are going to leave one reality and there *is* no other! I would like to remind you in the strongest way possible that this manifest world is *not* all there is. Please remember, you are fighting against the primordial fear of all human consciousness, the fear of extinction. Let me reassure you, there can never be an end to what is Eternal, only to what is impermanent.

"Do not try to explain any of your fears away. Do not search for what it is you are afraid of, or even where your fears come from. These are just mental gymnastics, avoidances, and explanations you use to try and escape them. The history of humanity reflects this mental creation of worlds within worlds, and then the running from what you have created. You run from the terror you are afraid is always embedded in the moment. *Is there a God, or isn't there? If there is a God, will It love me, or will It judge me like every other creation I have ever thought up?* These are the basic fears, beloved ones."

Bartholomew stopped abruptly, then continued quietly. "Please be responsible for simply and naturally being aware each moment. Have as much humor about your fears as you can. Own them as much as possible, and do not blame others for what you are experiencing. Keep your projections to a minimum. If you catch yourselves in a projection, acknowledge it as yours. Laugh about it," he said, leaning back. "Laugh a lot, my friends, because laughter is very relaxing, and then go on to the next moment. Are there any questions?"

The room filled with the sound of shifting bodies. Sharon raised her hand to get Bartholomew's attention. Looking over at her, he clapped his hands in delight. "Happy birthday, my friend. May you have a magnificent, thunderously exciting, vastly expansive, magnetic year!" he exclaimed with great enthusiasm. We laughed, applauded, and whistled as Sharon turned a bright pink and plunged ahead. "I have great anxiety about being on the bus in the mountains. Is there any more I can do in addition to talking to the cells of my body? I am so uncomfortable. I would appreciate any help."

"There is a visualization you can do that will help with any fear," responded Bartholomew. "When you're on the bus, sit quietly and allow yourself to feel this mysterious fear as much as possible. Sense its shape, size, and location in your body. Experience it fully. Sit with it long enough, and you will eventually realize that something 'other' is also present. Something your fear is happening *in*. Even if this only brings a temporary release, continue it one moment at a time, and in time your fear will fall away.

"When you have any painful feelings you long to get rid of, don't waste time trying to destroy them. Instead, meet the painful feeling with your awareness. When you feel stuck, the only possible thing left to do is to be *completely willing to experience* what you cannot run from. This willingness to be with it, just as it is, will bring about the release.

"Stop thinking about *what* you are experiencing. Become aware of the joy of moving from expansion to contraction, from smiles to frowns, from good to bad, from happy to sad. You want to feel the *flow* of life, the *motion* of life—the fascinating, ever-changing fabric of *all* life. You do not want to remain frozen in one position. Even a pleasant one can become very boring in time. *Allow* the flow, and you *will* become fully aware of what all those oppositions are rising and falling *in*."

Roberta cleared her throat, and Bartholomew looked at her. "Fear is something that has been really intense in my life," she said.

"Yes," he replied. "Unfortunately, the level of fear is increasing on a global scale, and as *you* become more expanded and open, you run right into it."

"If the fear is increasing, is love also increasing?" asked Roberta.

"No," said Bartholomew, "love is constant. This planet is totally filled with love—totally, completely, and utterly. It *couldn't* have more love in it because it is an absolute, total manifestation of light and love. That is the only reality. Are you asking if more people are beginning to feel this love? I would say yes. Since love cannot increase or decrease, it is humanity's experience of it that expands or contracts. This presents an interesting possibility. As people begin to feel the increase of fear and the discomfort it causes, many are awakening to the possibility of going within, the only place where release from their fear can be found. Eventually everyone will realize there is only one way 'out,' and that is 'in.' You cannot use your mind to get out of fear, and blaming others for your fear does not help. All you can do is drop into the sea of ever-present love. In that moment you become like the fish aware of itself swimming in the sea. The sea does not increase, but the fish's awareness of what it's swimming *in* is vastly increased."

"Is anger also increasing?" asked Lee.

Bartholomew turned to her. "Fear always produces anger, my friend. As fear increases, anger and violence increase. Here we have a lovely Roberta, who has dealt with many aspects of energy and is certainly not unconscious. She admits to having difficulties with these inner energies. If all of *you*, who are consciously working to transform these inner shadows, are having difficulty, you can imagine how someone feels who is still unaware of this. All they know is that they are filled with anger. But they are so far removed from the source of that anger, which is themselves, they don't know where it comes from, what it is, or how to work with it. They are blind and in great pain. They see it all as outside themselves and out of their control. The response is to destroy what they believe to be the source of their pain."

"So, can we think the anger is moving us toward love?" responded Lee.

"Absolutely! Wonderful thought. Everything is moving you toward love or awakening. All events come to you for a reason, although that reason is often beyond your mind's understanding. It is all absolutely useful, and is it volatile and sometimes dangerous? Yes, and at the same time, it is very exciting."

Clare set down her cup of tea. "Are pain and fear the same thing?" she asked.

"No," said Bartholomew. "Fear is a thought experienced in the body. The body responds by contracting. This contraction is what you experience as pain."

Judith, head resting on her knees, asked quietly, "Are the earthquakes that I'm afraid of inside myself?"

Bartholomew looked squarely at her. "Yes," he said. "If they happen to manifest outside, that is a secondary happening. All of you have access to the information of possible disasters. You have heard that there are likely to be earthquakes, tidal waves, and other major catastrophes. Some people decide that one of those may be a possible reality for them, and they do what they can about it. They either move or accept the possibility of disaster. But if you become fixated on the *fear*, unable to either rid yourself of it or accept its possible reality, then something else may be going on. It may well be that the fear of an external earthquake has shaken open an inner one. It has to do with each individual's response. If it's very direct and very vehement, it's your own inner earthquake, your own inner disaster.

"Do you understand the difference here?" he asked her. "The earthquake may or may not be real. Your *response* to it is what is important. If your body and mind are trembling, that says something about you. Will the external quake occur? Perhaps, and perhaps not. But if you find yourself always obsessively going back to those thoughts, look for another fear you are afraid will shake the very foundations of your life."

Bartholomew straightened up. "All right, my friends, I don't want to take up any more of your time." He laughed. "I know you have wondrous shopping to attend to, and what are cosmic guests in comparison to that perfect gift you need to buy? I would like to meet with you again tomorrow before you begin your next adventure. So let's pick an appropriate time, and I will see you then."

Relax and Enjoy

The group scattered. Shimla beckoned. This was our first opportunity for exploration in India, and no one wanted to miss it. The town was within walking distance. The road was steep, lined on both sides by tall trees and luxuriant undergrowth. They added a breath of sweetness to the cool, damp air. Monkeys chattered at us from the rusted metal roofs of concrete houses as we passed in and out of the thick shadows beneath the trees. Some people smiled at us when we met them coming up the hill. Some frowned, some ignored us, and some said, "Good morning," in soft British accents. The sun followed us down, intermittently setting the colorfully painted buildings aglow.

No cars were allowed on the streets in town. It was easy to see why. Shimla seemed to tumble down the side of a mountain. Narrow streets were lined with shops, and multilevel buildings crowded together for support. Every so often they would part to reveal a set of almost vertical stone steps leading to the next level.

We kept meeting each other coming and going. Five of us found ourselves together in the umbrella shop, testing umbrellas for the rain we had been warned would come. Farther down the street, we found a store filled with Tibetan goods. Inside, Laurel and Roberta were jockeying for position at the tiny counter, as Judith came away with a beautiful coral necklace. Larry was buried in the clothing, inspecting woolen vests, and Lin was deep in serious contemplation of the beautiful Tibetan jewelry. A lot of good-natured pushing and shoving to get in and out took place in the small shop. Everyone wanted to support the Tibetan refugees. Carolyn started talking to a young girl about the Dalai Lama, whose picture was hanging near the ceiling. It turned out that he had been in the store only yesterday on his way to Kalpa, and the Tibetans were impressed that our group was also going to the Kalachakra.

We strolled on, poking around the small shops, savoring the rich aroma of Indian cooking, until we came to the end of the buildings. The only place left to go was up, and I was panting heavily by the time I reached the next street. There we bumped into Barbara and Patricia, who were trying to decide which of the hundreds of colorful two-sided Shimla shawls they should buy.

We joined another group of friends clustered together outside the bank. They were discussing the best way to change dollars into rupees, when Mary-Margaret came shooting out of a store after escaping the clutches of a handsome, overzealous clothing salesman. George was seen everywhere. He seemed to gradually disappear under increasing layers of new and exotic clothes and jewelry. By the time we all climbed happily back up the hill, the town was much richer. And so were we.

An Unexpected Welcome Visit

I had just come down the stairs, still wrapped in the last remnants of a sweet sleep, when Chai came bursting through the front door. Her grin was wide, and her blue eyes sparkled with excitement.

"He's coming. He's coming tonight," she burst out. I couldn't help but laugh with her.

"That's great!" I responded. "Who is?"

"The Nechung, Kuten La," she said, clapping her hands together.[18]

"That's great," I repeated. *"Who?"*

She came over, her grin even wider. "The State Oracle," she exclaimed.

I was amazed. "Here, he's coming *here?"*

"Yes, yes," she answered. "He's coming to speak to us at six o'clock, and he might stay for dinner."

I glanced at my watch: 4:30. "Isn't this a bit unusual? Having the State Oracle drop by isn't something that happens often—is it?" I peered at her, wondering at the coincidence.

Chai laughed outright. "I suppose not," she said, "but I've had quite an afternoon."

I took her by the arm and led her toward the sitting room. "Why don't we make ourselves comfortable, and you can tell me all about it," I said.

She tucked her legs underneath her and relaxed in an overstuffed chair. "It *is* amazing," she said, "because my secret heart's desire has been to introduce the group to *him*—even more than the Dalai Lama."

I looked at her in surprise. "Why?"

"Because I've got a really strong connection with him," she replied. "He plays the same part as Bartholomew, right? And he's got the time and is totally present. Whereas, His Holiness has such a packed schedule that, even though he makes the time, it's limited, and there's not the space to feel really connected.

"I saw the Nechung in Dharamsala when we were there and asked him if he was going to the Kalachakra. He told me he was going early to help clean the energy for three days. Then just now I saw him standing at the side of the road." She looked at me in amazement. "To bump into him like that was unbelievable. We were standing by our bus, fighting with the porters, who had just carried all the supplies down to be loaded. Our cooks, Jumpa and Neima, were arguing with them about the payment. They were blatantly trying to rip us off, right? I was absolutely exhausted, wishing Russell were there. I just wanted to go and lie down because I felt so terrible. Then, out of the corner of my eye, about 50 feet down the road, I saw this flash of rose, and I knew it was him! I said to myself, that is Kuten La, and I felt my energy explode. I wasn't tired anymore, and I said to everybody, 'Let's go, let's go! Let's get in the bus! Let's go!'"

We both laughed at the picture of Chai hustling porters and cooks into the bus.

"I told Neima and Jumpa not to worry about the porters," she said, and I told the driver we were going now! He got in the bus and started the engine. The porters were still fighting. They turned and jumped in, and they were *still* fighting *in* the bus. The bus was so full of vegetables you could hardly move, but I leaned against a window and looked out. The Nechung was standing there, and he saw me, and we waved to each other. I said, 'Stop the bus. Stop the bus!'

"I opened the door and dragged him in over the sacks of onions and the fighting porters. I found a seat and sat him down, and he's laughing away. A buzz—a buzz of who he was—went around. The porters shut up immediately. Everybody shut up! There wasn't a sound from anyone, just the Nechung and the two other monks from his monastery. Kuten La told me he wasn't going to the Kalachakra. He had done his work and was going back to Dharamsala. He had some time to spare and yes, he'd love to come and meet everybody. So that's what happened," Chai said, eyes shining, "and that, to me, is the biggest miracle of all. Well," she said, jumping up, "I have lots to do before he comes." As we parted, Chai called back to me, "Don't forget."

Ha, I thought to myself, *not very likely,* and went off to tell the others.

That evening a small group gathered in the sitting room. At exactly six P.M., the State Oracle and two younger monks entered with Chai and Russell. His smile was radiant, and he bowed to us over clasped hands as he sat down. We couldn't help smiling back as we bowed in return. He had a youthful exuberance, but also a quality of quiet power. Kuten La had joined the Nechung

Monastery when he was 14 years old and was divinely selected as the 14th medium of the Nechung State Oracle at the age of 30. He had already been advising the Dalai Lama for five years. An aura of well-being surrounded him as he spoke to us through his interpreters, explaining the procedures one would follow on the Buddhist path to Enlightenment. His movements were graceful and his voice pleasant as he answered questions about meditation and other practices. I soon lost track of what was being said and happily succumbed to the power of his presence.

Suddenly, I became aware of a restless agitation behind me. Glancing around, I could see that several people were looking pensive and even slightly glum. I listened more closely to what Kuten La was saying. He was talking about details of the Kalachakra, when he leaned toward us and said quite strongly, "There will be obstacles for those attending the initiation." He looked at us intently. The room was absolutely silent. Then he laughed and relaxed again. "You've come a long way, and there will be obstacles," he repeated, "but keep persisting and you will get there."

With that, the discussion ended, and we headed upstairs to get ready for dinner. Carolyn still looked thoughtful, so I asked her what had happened.

"He was talking about all the rules Buddhists had to follow to realize God. It sounded just like the church," she said, with a sigh.

"Well, what do *you* believe?" I asked her.

She hesitated a moment. "I believe we'd best get some dinner," she replied.

Excellent, I thought, *more rice and dahl is just what I need.*

Several hours later the five of us met in our room and once again shuffled beds around to make ourselves comfortable. Tomorrow, after our meeting with Bartholomew, we would be leaving for Kalpa. It had been an active day and everyone was tired.

Chapter 15

Shimla to Kalpa–the Spiritual Pyramid and a Lively Discussion about Rules and Regulations

The group arranged itself in the sitting room early the next morning. We were already packed and ready to leave. Outside, the lawn sparkled with dew. The air was crisp and aromatic. The sky was clear, blue, and friendly looking. It was altogether a good day to travel. We settled down as Mary-Margaret adjusted the microphone. She sat back and closed her eyes.

"All right then, my friends," Bartholomew began briskly, "do you have any questions at all that we might deal with before moving on to something else?"

Ellen answered immediately. "I do," she said. "I know you've spent whole workshops on this, but would you talk for just a moment on how to turn from a seeker to a finder?"

"Yes, always a good question," Bartholomew replied, settling himself deeper into the chair. "To move from seeker to finder you must stop 'searching' and finally acknowledge the 'something' you have been looking for is already totally present. The *concepts* of seeking and finding both rest on what you have been taught to believe. For centuries, the life of a spiritual aspirant has been defined by the belief in a separate God, and a search for ways to heal that separation.

"Every major religious teaching has to account for both ends of the spiritual spectrum. It has to be able to help the beginner who is just coming out of spiritual darkness, as well as those who feel they have been getting lighter and freer as they go along. And, finally, the teaching must point the aspirant toward the 'pathless path.' Not many religions or bodies of teaching allow you to leap directly into full awareness.

"Therefore, the idea of spiritual guidance at different levels has evolved over the centuries. The bottom level appeals to those beginning 'seekers' who are looking for a comforting spiritual direction. Most people jump onto the spiritual path to get away from fear, and they welcome religious rules that suggest they breathe a certain way to find peace, eat specific foods to find love, or pray a particular set of prayers to find God. This creates a 'spiritual belief pyramid,' reflecting the idea that you get clearer and clearer, purer and purer, as you make your way to the top.

"Many religious rules are based on realistic observations and do give helpful suggestions. For instance, it is better to eat some kinds of food rather than others simply because some lodge in the body and make you heavier— not fatter—while others make you lighter and more light-filled. You can look at a dead piece of meat and a live head of lettuce, and you don't have to be a scientist to realize there is more life-force in the lettuce than there is in the meat. Now, having said that, there *are* people at the top of this 'pyramid' who have found the light within and have eaten everything! What they ate didn't matter, because they knew, in the end, that there was a balance between who was eating and what was being eaten. The body was not important. Your *belief* about what you eat is what matters a great deal.

"Look back at your own spiritual journey, and you will probably find a time when rules and regulations were essential. In fact, they may have kept you going because you felt you were 'getting somewhere.' Maybe you began to feel lighter or healthier or more peaceful, and you believed that 'following the rules' had given you what you wanted. Then somewhere along the way something happened, and you no longer believed that simply following rules would get you there.

"Rules are based on doing what someone else thinks will work. At some point in your spiritual unfoldment, you must move deeper than that. Perhaps you have already experienced enough different energies to know that some of them have nothing to do with rules. You may have also experimented with drugs and seen the reality of 'altered states.' This certainly does not follow the rules. With different experiences comes the desire to know what the deepest *reality* is, and a greater trust in what that reality can truly reveal. With this desire, you will become impatient and begin to question the religious and spiritual rules and regulations. You will want to know and feel the love of God, or experience the Light within *directly*. You will begin to feel that, if you stay locked within the belief structure of spiritual rules, the consciousness you are looking for will take forever. Somehow, following the rules has not given you the awareness you were seeking.

"You are like the boy standing in the middle of a barn filled with horse manure, shoveling away with a great smile on his face. 'Why are you smiling?' his friend asks. 'With all this manure, you know there has to be a pony here somewhere,' he replied. Where is the pony? What is the pony? You don't know, but you can see the results of its having been there. You experience moments of happiness and clear awareness that keep you going. You are motivated by a very different drive, and with that comes a spiritual maturity. You are no longer the child seeking something else to hold you up. You can stand by yourself and meet this force directly.

"This is a totally different inner stance. Now, you must face yourself with honesty. What is your motive for seeking enlightenment? It cannot be to feed your ego by showing yourself and others how wonderful you are. Nor can it be to end discomfort or pain for yourself and others, or to solve the world's problems. You want to help, because you perceive much unhappiness, but you cannot because you are also unhappy. You cannot give something you do not have yourself. Yes, a part of you is tired of being confused, isolated, and ignorant, not knowing what's *really* going on in your own life. But I ask you to look deeper. Your motive is an essential factor in moving you from seeker to finder. You must love God simply for the joy of loving the Creator who gave you the gift of existence, not for what you can 'get' or what can be done for you."

Is There Really a Separate You?

Bartholomew stopped and looked around before continuing. "Most of you spent some time last evening with the State Oracle," he said. "The Nachung was manifesting his 'teacher-self' as he answered your questions. But in another moment he is able to manifest something far more vast. He becomes the Divine Power Itself. When he wears his helmet of office, he is no longer the sweet man you talked with. Under a crown, the weight of which would break an average man's neck, he is one who has transcended the limits of body and small self. He is free to move from one reality to another, from the 'seen' to the 'unseen.' He is not stuck in the limited self. This movement is called freedom.

"*You* are not the one continuous person you think you are, forever forced to experience just what you can see, touch, hear, or think. You are *not*! When you decide to awaken to your True Nature, you will find the path turns pathless. No longer do rules or guidelines tell you how to awaken. All you can do is stay in the moment and become aware of the mysterious 'I' of yourself that is *always* present. In being present, observing the moment exactly as it is, you will awaken to the truth that there is no continuous *separate* 'you' at all! There is the vast immensity of some no-thing ever present, in which experiences come and go. On close examination, you will find that no matter how hard you try, you cannot find a 'you' separate from this 'I.' Why? Because *there is no separate small 'you.'*

"The 'I' of you who is seeking to return to God does not exist as a separate form." He looked at our puzzled faces. "Are you confused? Good. Let the words confuse the mind. In order to know who you really are, it is essential to allow yourself feel the doubt and confusion around the question of 'Is there really a separate me?' Keep on asking yourself the basic questions that arise from it. *Who is this 'I'?* Who has this body? Who is hungry? Who is frightened? Who feels good? The main question is always, *Who is this 'I'?* Keep looking for the deep inner Source from which all ideas of 'me' arise."

Mary-Margaret took another sip of water. Bartholomew continued quietly. "Before you were born, the instant you were born, and continuing on after your birth you are aware. At age *7, 27,* or *87,* this mysterious awareness, this something that sees, feels, and thinks, continues within you, through endless changes, yet always the same. You can ask an older person if they have changed, and they will say, 'No. My body has, and some of my beliefs may have, but I have not changed.' Another way of saying it: You don't wake up in the morning and ask yourself, 'Am I still here?' You have just spent part of the night in deep sleep, gone you know not where, yet you do not ask yourself if you are the same person who went to sleep the night before. Why? Because you can touch the same essential awareness of yourself in the morning that you could before going to sleep. It is that *essential sense,* that *awareness*, you are looking for." Bartholomew leaned back and sighed.

"Do you understand?" he asked, as he looked around. "When you pay close attention to what is going on inside your consciousness, you will realize that, in the midst of the most incredible physical, mental, or emotional pain or pleasure, a very familiar part of you is *aware of it all*. All change happens within this awareness. Whether it's pain, anger, guilt, fear, or joy, the question is always: Who or what is the never-changing Self in which *all* these things come and go?

"I am sorry," he said. "This is where words cannot do it for you, but we have to keep on talking until it moves from talking to a knowing in your heart." Taking a deep breath, he continued. "There is some little 'you,' a persona you identify with and call by your name *who isn't really who you are.* You have *mis*identified it. The continuous, ongoing you is *something else.* Emotions come and go, ever-changing events happen to this little 'you,' but you never question whether the essential you is there, because it is always present.

"I get very excited," he smiled, "because in the end, this understanding is the only gift I can give you. The words and ideas we share are just forms that rise and fall. All I can do is keep pointing the way. As magnificent as all these things are, they are not *it.* Forms rise and fall in *something*, and are you ever *not* aware of that 'something'? The ever-changing drama of your lives is not what you are looking for. Whatever has the capacity to change is *not it.* What you are looking for is something so immediate, so ever-present, so immense, that you have missed it. I repeat, the immediacy of the vast 'I,' the God-Self, the Light, is so ever-present that *you miss it!*

"You seek everywhere else for this thing that has been inside you all the time. It is so obvious that you do not pay attention to it. Instead, your interest is caught up in all the many-changing forms of your world. You grab at them and say, 'That's me. No, that's me.' You can play this game for lifetimes, but the essence of who you are stays with you throughout it all. Finding God is so *simple* that you have missed it."

Bartholomew sat forward, resting his arms on Mary-Margaret's knees. "Who sees?" he asked. "Just stick with that question all day. Who hears? Stick with that! Who breathes? Examine the questions directly. It is *awareness.* This awareness is aware of all other things rising and falling within it. *It* is what you are looking for. It is this *awareness* we ask you to be willing to experience fully. *This* is what you discover within who you imagine yourself to be." He paused for a long moment. "That's when you totally and utterly relax into the Light with no effort whatsoever. And then you do what you have done before. You see, you hear, you breathe, and you go about your life. It's all the same, but it's all totally different.

"So, when I say you have to move from seeker to finder, I mean you finally stop searching and acknowledge what you are seeking is already totally present. Try to find it outside yourself and you will fail. Simply sit in every moment, aware, alert, like a hawk on a mesa, and what you have been seeking for so long will begin to reveal itself.

"Your mind does not want to believe what I have just said, but what else can you do? How many more books can you read? How many more austerities can you go through? The austerities work beautifully at the bottom of the pyramid, but they are useless at the top because they indicate that what you are looking for is in the future. They suggest you have to be different than you are in order to become God-realized. That is nonsense. How can God not always be aware of Itself?

"So what do you do?" He smiled. "I don't think it hurts to hear it again. You simply sit around in your life, aware of your life. *Do* all the things you always do, and remember what we have talked about this morning. An immense 'something' inside you is aware of the ever-passing parade of your life and world. That 'something' is the essential, ever-present essence of awareness of being, which you have called 'I,' and then misidentified as the small 'I' of your limited self. So the question is: What 'I' is listening to all this? What 'I' is saying all this?" He laughed. "Don't answer, just experience."

Pointing to the Pathless Path

Bartholomew smiled and sat back. We all relaxed, mulling over what we had just heard. After a few moments, Lin took a sip of tea and raised her hand. "Could you please talk a bit about the Kalachakra initiation? What is its purpose, and how can we use it for our awakening?"

"The Kalachakra vow is one of the powerful building blocks of the vast pyramid of consciousness we have been talking about. For those of you who delight and believe in following rules, the Kalachakra vow is a wonderful outpicturing of one of the highest forms of that approach. Following rules can take you to a certain point of focus, of calmness, of openness. It cannot take you to the place of total awakening, but to the very edge of the abyss. Then you have to jump into the void, the place where there are no rules, no paths to follow. Leave all rules behind, and jump into the moment fully, with no ideas or imaginings or preconceived knowings. Jump into the unknown.

"At the deepest level, the enlightened teachers are aware of this need to leave it all behind, but they are the embodiment of a process. As such, they have to teach and practice the rules, while at the same time be aware of the impossibility of trying to put rules on the formless. Their job is to bring others to the abyss, and the Kalachakra is one way to do this. I am hoping you will allow yourselves to be flooded with, and submerged in, the immensity of power that will undoubtedly be present on that mountain. And for those of you who want to channel that power through the Kalachakra initiation and follow the vows, be assured that this is appropriate for you to do. You see, we have no rules about rules!"

Emmy looked up and said, "I am beginning to feel physically sick, and I wonder why. I have a feeling there is a possibility of my understanding what I am doing, but I can't get a sense of what that understanding might be."

"If you cannot come to this understanding within the next few days, we will go into it again. Don't stop your investigation, because you have uncovered something very important. All of you run from things you do not want to face. One of the major ways of doing that is by diverting your attention through illness. Illness can take up much of your time and energy and most of your thoughts. No blame, but please have some humor about not wanting to sit down in the middle of your life as it's being created this moment and find out who you are.

"Do not pretend that what you are diverting yourself to or from is important. Whatever it is simply doesn't matter. It's just one more action, one more thought, one more response, one more ego creation. You need to know *why* you are doing it. You create diversions to keep yourself from the terror of facing the possibility that the moment does not hold what you are really looking for. You are afraid there is no God, no Bliss, no Eternal Self. I want to tell you again, *there is!* Each moment holds all of it, and more than you could possibly grasp in your wildest imaginings."

Stumbling Over the Rules and Regulations

Darcy, tension visible in the angle of her body, blurted out, "I'm feeling pain and confusion and anger at probably having spent lifetimes going pitter-patter up the ladder, and you say this state is already *mine*, is totally available, and there aren't any rules." Hardly pausing, she raced on. "Then I run smack into Tibetan Buddhism, which has the entire pyramid in it, and all of a sudden I'm up against rules that bring me confusion and anger, and I'm getting diverted because now I'm lost in the confusion and the anger." She stopped for breath. "Can you help me at all?" she asked.

Bartholomew responded immediately. "That's why I presented the pyramid," he said. "The rules and regulations are at the bottom of the pyramid, *and they are absolutely valid!* Look at Buddhism. Remember what Buddha himself said? You can take seven lifetimes, seven years, seven hours, seven minutes, or get it now. Why would the Buddha lie? Why would he say it were available now if it weren't? At the same time, for all people at certain stages, the rules are absolutely necessary."

He leaned toward Darcy. "You have already done the rules, dear one; let's not go back and re-create that wheel," he said gently. "Stay with the possibility of freedom now." Breaking into a broad smile, he added, "And remember that the Enlightened Buddhas are giggling inside themselves as they give the rules, because they know the truth. But it is not their job to giggle in public. When these teachers have students come in, thundering like Kali, saying, 'Look, I want it now. None of this lifetime after lifetime business,' they say, 'All right, sit down, and let's see what reveals itself.' These teachers are two different people, one public, one private. They do the job that is theirs to do. When you hear a teaching that reflects both the top and the bottom of the pyramid, please know it to be a vast teaching because it can hold everyone within it. *Everything and everyone* has a place within this Vastness of Self."

He leaned back. "Look," he said, "the Dalai Lama has many different roles. At the initiation, he is not the teacher, he *is* the manifestation of the Divine Energy of the Kalachakra itself. He *is* it, and you will feel and *love* it. *You will love it*—if you don't think it—but Be it. It is the essence of Consciousness manifesting as Power!"

The silence that followed was filled with intensity. "Just get your mind out of the way," Bartholomew added, breaking the tension. Everyone laughed and relaxed. "Are there any questions?" he asked. More silence. He looked at us closely, "Any answers?" he joked.

"It's interesting for me to hear about rules and regulations, because from my side, when I read all the Buddhist teachings, I don't read it as rules and regulations," Chai spoke calmly. "I find them to be symbols and metaphors, affirming something that is already there."

"Give them an example, lovely one," Bartholomew prompted.

"If I'm conditioned through my childhood and my education to eat rice bubbles every day, and then somebody says mangos taste really nice, the person must insist, 'To experience the taste, you really must eat mangos. There's something inside of me that really wants to eat a mango, so when I hear it's okay, it's an affirmation of that feeling, and I can let go of the rice bubbles and go for the mangos," Chai laughed. "Okay? So when I read those rules you're talking about, you know, like loving kindness and positive thoughts—"

Bartholomew held up a hand and interjected quickly, "I don't think those are the rules they are objecting to, lovely one." An immediate chorus of agreement came from part of the group. "This is an important point. We have to clarify this because I don't think there is anyone in this room who would not agree that loving kindness is an absolute essential for consciousness. I think what they're referring to are the rules that say you have to give up your individual outer life, you have to regiment yourself into a monastic situation, and you have to take on many austerities. That approach is not going to work for most of this group. They are not arguing with the basic truth of what you're saying. They are in pain over hearing that in order to embody this teaching, you have to follow many physical and mental rules."

He turned to Carolyn, who had been nodding her head in agreement. "Is that what you were thinking?" he asked.

"Yes," she replied. "It's saying you have to be someone else, that the essence of who you are isn't good enough. Anything that says that in any way is painful to me."

"I think it's a misinterpretation," said Chai.

"I do, too," added Rishi, another Australian.

Bartholomew cut in quickly. "I don't think we need to get into a discussion," he said. "You are all going to come at this from totally different points of view, and if we keep discussing it, you will miss it.

"The fact remains, some people have been so disappointed and deceived by other people's rules that when yet *another* person in authority says they must follow the rules to know who they already are, they become frightened and deny their own knowing." He spread his arms wide to include us all. "Each one of you has as stringent a set of rules for yourself as the ones you thought you heard last night." He gestured toward Carolyn. "One of your rules goes something like this, 'With all my being I will present myself in a loving, centered way for the children I teach at Vista Grande School.' You have another which says, 'Every time I open my mouth, I will do my best to speak truth as I understand it.' You have an incredible set of rules, Miss Lake, and you live them out of the essence of your being as best you can. They are wonderful, *and* they are just as strict in their own way as Tibetan Buddhism." He laughed. "They are perhaps stricter than eating rice, being celibate, and meditating when the gong rings. Do you understand?" Carolyn nodded and leaned back.

He turned to the rest of us. "I want you all to understand this," he said. "You have developed your own set of rules that are impeccably perfect for *you*. If you haven't, may we suggest that you proceed to quickly get your rules together—*your rules*. My dears, there is no way to approach God power without following your own rules. These rules need to reflect a state in which you can be open-minded and open-hearted, open to Grace, to God, to Truth. The enlightened ones made only a few simple rules, but those who followed them made the rules more complicated. And over the centuries, things have become very complicated indeed.

"The top of the pyramid has a basic, essential simplicity and clarity to it. There is a lot of space there. It gets heavier and denser and more and more ponderous the farther down you go. Don't forget, the bottom of the pyramid reflects more than 2,500 years of people making rules about other people's rules. If you are at the top of the pyramid, you are someone who has gone through all the given rules and yearns to develop the rules that take you to the place where only God is, no matter what else is happening. That is the awareness you are looking for."

Bartholomew's voice softened. "So I do not think there is any real conflict, my friends. I think there is union, a knowing, and a wonder and gratitude that this pyramid has so many parts. There is always room for everything, because all these rules arise in the Vast Self, and the Self holds it all. Make no mistake, over the centuries, you have not only jumped into one part of the pyramid, but into many. One lifetime you are a Muslim. You go partway through that, jump out, come back a Buddhist or a Christian, and go on a little more. You haven't come in to any one sect, staying in it, and going straight up the ladder. This 'pyramid' holds it all. So know where you are now.

"Be clear about your own rules, and follow them wholeheartedly, with as much rigor and discipline as any one of those monks, *and* with as much joy. They follow their rules because they want to. These rules are going to get them their heart's desire, so they are very excited about them. But they are not you. You are moving to a different rhythm. Be absolutely grateful that all these creations are valid and useful."

Clare's hand shot up. "If you discover you have personal rules, I thought the idea was to identify them and then stretch them."

"I think you're talking about a limited rule," Bartholomew replied. "Give me an example of one."

Clare thought for a moment. "I think I have rules about sexuality," she said, finally.

Bartholomew and the group burst into laughter. "Of course you do! Absolutely," he agreed. "I hope no one in this room thinks they are immune from sexual rules. If any of you do, you're not paying attention."

"Listen," he said. "I have often told you that there is no area that has more rules than the sexual. The sexual chakra is the most confused center in the entire body. Why? On the one hand, you hear it will take you to heaven. On the other hand, you hear it will lead you to hell. You do something with this person and it's perfect; you do the same thing with a different person and you are damned forever. You do it in this position and everybody says that's fine; you do it in that position and they call you a pervert. *Those are conflicting rules.*

"The rules around sexuality start at a very early age, ladies and gentlemen," he continued seriously. "And they are confusing and frightening. Because of this, many of you try and turn away from sexuality, but because it moves through you so powerfully, this is almost impossible to do. The resulting confusion is caused by conflicting beliefs. In spite of this, each of you has one very sweet, basic rule about sexuality that is your own truth about sex at its highest. It is a point of truth *you* hold—not that society gave you—but that *your* heart and *your* mind and *your* awareness tell you is totally appropriate for you in relationship to sexuality. And *that* is a rule you can follow. Do you understand what I am saying?" he asked. Clare nodded.

Bartholomew looked back at us. "One of the clearest, most helpful rules of sexuality has harmlessness as its basis. As you mature, you will come to understand harmlessness in all its aspects, because ultimately harmlessness must operate in all phases of your life. The outside world may say your actions are inappropriate, but if you are closely aligned with your own truth, *you* will know when you are acting harmlessly. *If it's harmless, then enjoy it!* You have many very deep, strong knowings, and *those* are the beliefs I am talking about. They are the basic rules that guide your life, how you treat others, how you speak and think, and even the kind of work you do. All others are contrived, placed on you to keep you from doing things others don't want you to, or are *afraid* to do themselves. If you are living the rules that come deeply out of your commitment to the integrity of *your* life as you know it to be *in this moment,* you embody that integrity and act out of it. Does that help?" Bartholomew asked Clare.

"Yes," she replied.

He looked around at the rest of us. "Have we clarified this confusion about rules?" he asked. "I do not want anything left but openness. Is everyone clear?" He waited to see if any hands went up. "Good. Let us not allow the mind to create separations in this vast, amazing Oneness."

Darcy raised her hand again and spoke up through a scattering of good-natured laughter. "I'm not quite clear," she began. "As I see things now, to see such a being of light as the State Oracle, I would find it very hard to be enlightened and know the Light, then come into a room of people and share a limited teaching. Am I missing something here?"

"Yes!" responded Bartholomew.

"Good, what is it?"

"Look at the sutras of the Buddha.[19] Buddha was a total, full, Enlightened Being, and let me tell you something, lovely ones; if the Buddha were to talk from the place of his deepest knowing, he would say nothing." Bartholomew threw up his hands. "He would sit around smiling and be deeply silent. After his Awakening, the Buddha spent weeks in silence. Then he realized that some people did not understand his silence. 'Perhaps I'll have to put this teaching into words,' says Buddha. So he speaks a few sutras, and some people get totally excited. Others don't understand his silence or his words. 'Perhaps I ought to say it a little differently,' he says. So he does, and a few more people understand and go away with new hope.

"Do you see? It's all just a pyramid. You can come in anywhere you want. The Buddha climbed all over it, speaking from less than absolute silence, trying to help people who desperately needed guideposts to freedom. He knew, in his infinite wisdom, if they followed those guideposts, they would someday stand ready to leap into the unknown. Be grateful to those enlightened ones, when they have looked down and said, 'Hmm, it's a little lofty up here. I think we better build some stairs.' So they pitter-patter down the ladder. These great ones do it with the knowing that one day the ladders and steps will all dissolve, and there will only be the One."

The Maharajah's staff, in starched white coats, silently glided in and began picking up empty cups and glasses.

"All right, then," Bartholomew nodded in their direction, "let's conclude. The gentlemen in the kitchen are upset with my long sessions, which seem to get longer every day. My thanks to you all, and I'll see you in Kalpa. Have a magnificent journey . . . and don't forget to breathe."

"There will be obstacles . . ." said the Oracle.

Eleven minivans and their drivers waited in the courtyard. They had come to replace one of the buses that was returning to Delhi. The other bus would accompany us, reserved for cooks, supplies, luggage, and transportation beyond Kalpa. The vans could hold three people each but had little room for anything else. I threw my backpack behind the seat and climbed into a van with Greta and Barbara. The drivers all gunned their engines and jockeyed for position as the vans left in single file.

Once we were outside Shimla, the road narrowed and began to snake its way around and up into the mountains. It had been painstakingly hand-carved from rock, one side solid cliff face and the other dropping hundreds of feet straight down. This was officially known as the Hindustan-Tibet Highway. Sharp turns and bends made it impossible to see past the corners. Our driver would race up to them and lean on his horn, which emitted a small, rasping bleat. Then, hardly slowing at all, he would whip us around the bend. This driving technique caught our full attention, and any attempts at light conversation were quickly forgotten.

It was inevitable that there would be times when an approaching car would reach the corner at the same time we did. When that happened, the three of us would stop breathing as our driver squeezed the van against the rocky wall, and the passing vehicle veered abruptly toward the edge. When we met someone on the rare straightaway, he would pull over slightly without slowing and grudgingly allow the oncoming vehicle enough room to get by. He did this with a huge grin and loud exclamations. It made me occasionally wonder if our terror added incentive to his driving. Suddenly we heard a sharp, explosive noise, and a cloud of dust rose from the van in front of us. A front tire had blown, and the van careened madly toward the waiting abyss. Our driver didn't even pause, but swept past the now-halted vehicle and its pale passengers. The van's driver stepped out smiling and shrugged, his hands spread wide. "That's fate," he seemed to say.

When we finally stopped, it was because the road resembled the bottom of a dry creek bed. A crew was rebuilding a section that had been swept away by a landslide. Barbara, Greta, and I joined others in the group and watched as the vans very carefully picked their way over the boulders and smaller rocks. Following on foot, not one of us complained about walking. The road crew, made up of people from the nearest villages, silently watched us.

Men squatted, breaking up bits of rock with metal hammers and chipping away at larger pieces to make the rough, strong bricks that formed the retaining walls supporting the road. Piles of brick and shattered rock were lined up neatly beside them. Women worked in pairs to clear away the rubble. One held a large square shovel, while the other pulled on a heavy rope attached to the scoop. Together they managed to move a shovelful neither could have lifted alone.

Small children moved among them, keeping the men supplied with pieces of granite. Here and there, small fires kept pots of water boiling for tea.

It took me a few moments to realize that no mechanical equipment was present, and another few to grasp the significance of that. This must be how roads were maintained in the Himalayas. We smiled and waved at the workers, who laughed and clapped their hands, smiling in return. How else could we acknowledge our admiration for taking on such a task?

The vans were bunched together, back on the road. Our driver was just emerging from underneath the dashboard. He slid behind the wheel and pressed on the horn. Finding the loud results satisfactory, he motioned us back to the van, and we were off and headed for the next blind curve. From behind it came the now-familiar sound of a loud horn indicating the approach of another vehicle. The rules in this game were becoming increasingly clear. With horns blaring, whoever made it to the turn first was the winner and got to round the bend without stopping. We realized that the large horns we saw painted on the rock walls were not sacred objects but rather signs, saying: "Blind curve, sound your horn."

When I could tear my eyes from the road ahead and look around, I found the scenery breathtakingly dramatic. We were now above timberline, and the sides of the road dropped vertically beneath the jagged peaks. The air was crisp and clear, the sun shining brightly. There was no escaping the dizzying heights and sheer drops of the land we were passing through.

Rounding another curve, the driver braked suddenly. Up ahead was a long line of parked vehicles. With undisguised relief, the three of us left the van and started walking. We caught up with some of the others, as Russell and Chai went off to investigate. Our bus pulled up and joined the procession. It looked as though people had been there awhile. Some lay stretched out on pads beneath makeshift covers. Others had made themselves comfortable on mats and were sipping tea. Chai came back and joined the group.

"There's been a landslide," she said.

"Oh no!" exclaimed Mary-Margaret. "Will it take long to clear?"

"Don't know." Chai squinted into the distance and pointed. "Do you see that ridge up there?" she asked. We all looked up. "Do you hear those noises, like explosions?" she added.

"Yes." We could all hear them.

"All right, here's what's happened," she said, looking around. "They had a landslide yesterday, and it's completely covered the road. They've a bunch of guys up there now, laying explosives to make sure everything's come down. When it has, they'll begin to clear the mess."

"What are the chances of getting through to Kalpa in time for the beginning of the Kalachakra tomorrow?" asked Mary-Margaret.

"Not good," replied Chai. "His Holiness came through just before it gave way."

"... but keep persisting ..."

Everyone started talking at once. This was a *serious* obstacle. Just then, a man dressed neatly in khaki trousers and white shirt approached the group. "Pardon me," he said. Then he began speaking in Hindu. Chai, Russell, Neima, and Jumpa gathered around him and listened intently. He pointed ahead. The road made a sweeping curve where it was buried under the debris. We could see a small crowd of people and vehicles clustered together on the other side.

After conferring for several minutes, Chai returned. "He told us he has vans for hire that we could rent to take us to Kalpa," she said. "It would mean walking across the landslide and leaving most everything behind."

"Does he know when the road would be clear again?" asked Justin.

"No telling," said Russell. "They will be blasting for the rest of the day. That's for sure."

An animated discussion broke out, as we debated what to do. "What about food and our luggage?" asked Ellen.

"We can only take what we can carry," replied Chai.

The man suddenly returned and began talking to her again. The conversation grew quite lively. She broke off and came up to Mary-Margaret, a frown on her face. "That tears it; the vans are gone," she said. "Someone else got to them while we've been talking."

"What shall we do?" exclaimed Mary-Margaret.

Chai looked at the man, who was shrugging and nodding at us. "He says there's one bus left and that it can hold all of us plus one bag apiece," she answered. Chai and Mary-Margaret looked at one another. Around them, small groups of people discussed various possibilities. Drivers were coming and going. Horns honked as more vehicles joined the long line of stalled cars, trucks, and buses. We waited.

"Do we go forward or not?" Mary Margaret mused. Chai was silent. Then, with a determined look in her eye, Mary-Margaret exclaimed, " Let's go for it!"

Chai laughed. "Let's go for it," she echoed.

A decision had been reached. We would persist in the face of obstacles. Orders were given: "Take what you need and leave the rest." Neima and

Jumpa climbed up to the roof of the bus and started throwing the luggage down. Men appeared and began hauling it away as their owners chased after them trying to identify their bags. The cooks wrestled with supplies, searching for enough available food and water to last until the bus could get through. The milling became movement, as people grabbed their personal belongings and started to leave. Mary-Margaret asked Judith and Carolyn to go first to make sure the bus stayed put. They dropped what they were doing and went off with shouts of encouragement. Soon, a ragged line of Americans and Australians picked their way across the landslide.

I grabbed my backpack and took off after Eleanor. She had been to India before and had not planned on returning. Only the temptation of being with Bartholomew and the Dalai Lama in the Himalayas had lured her back. Now she flashed me a brave smile as she gingerly made her way across the rocks. The side of the mountain had slid down completely, covering the road with large boulders and rocky debris. Loose dirt made the footing treacherous. Frequent explosions erupted from the ridge above, dislodging rocks that bounced all around us. *This* is *dangerous,* I thought as I passed an official who was urging me on. I paused and looked around. The mountains towered above; the space opened below. I was standing on the edge of the world, and a wave of ecstasy washed over me as I connected with the moment in all its power and splendor.

"Move along; move along," called an insistent voice behind me. I turned to see Mary-Margaret standing next to the official, who was patting his head and gesturing at hers. As she heaved her backpack onto her head, he glanced upward. "Run, run!" he exclaimed.

"Protect your heads!" she shouted to those behind as small rocks showered down around us. We ran.

Out of breath, I reached the other side where Carolyn and Judith were slowly walking around the bus, muttering to each other. Curious, I joined Judith in her examinations.

"Just look at it," she said frowning. "There's no tread on the tires." I bent down and examined them closely. Sure enough, there was very little tread on the tires. "All the windows are broken," she continued. Standing on my tiptoes, I checked the windows. Sure enough, some of the windows were broken. Judith leaned down. "I can see through the sides, for heaven's sake!" she exclaimed. I poked my finger through a hole the size of my fist. Sure enough, some of the panels had rusted away.

"You can't even tell what color it is," added Carolyn, who had come up behind us. I stood back and examined the bus critically. Sure enough, the color could hardly be seen through the dents and scrapes in the body.

"I'm not getting on *that* bus!" declared Judith, as Justin strolled by.

He was smoking a cigarette, and calmly inspected the bus before replying. "Do you see any other way to get to Kalpa?" he asked, motioning to the empty road ahead. Carolyn and Judith looked around, then at each other.

Judith laughed. "Let's help with the luggage. I lost control of this trip a long time ago."

Carolyn agreed, and they began to add more bags to the growing pile.

By the time everything had been stuffed into the bus, there was no room to spare, and dusk had fallen. I was sitting right behind the driver and a local passenger. Loren, a British photographer who had come with the Australians, was last on. He squeezed himself and his cameras onto the engine cover. When the driver started the bus, a haze of blue smoke drifted up from the floor. I looked down. There beneath me was the ground. I stared at the back of the driver's head, willing him to get the bus moving.

We began the final leg of our journey without the benefit of headlights. Ten minutes later, in what appeared to be the middle of nowhere, under a pale moon in an otherwise dark night sky, the driver stopped the bus, and another man climbed in. He announced that before going any further, we had to pay an additional fare. Russell, who had made the original agreement, came charging from the back of the bus. He and the man were immediately embroiled in a heated discussion. We were to pay an additional 6,000 rupees, and Russell was having none of it.

After several minutes of flying accusations, a shout came from the rear. "Give him the 6,000 rupees, and let's get out of here!" yelled Mary-Margaret.

An immediate chorus of agreement greeted this suggestion. Russell gave up, and the driver rammed the bus into first gear. He drove like the devil, with a great gnashing of gears and sudden unexpected bursts of acceleration. The road unwound in the ghostly light of the moon, revealing sheer embankments with an occasional wrecked car or truck lying at the bottom. Suddenly, he slowed abruptly and switched on his headlights, illuminating a hairpin turn that ended in a narrow metal bridge spanning a raging torrent of water. The bus refused to maneuver through the turn, so the driver threw it into reverse, stopping only inches from the precipice. Fear raced up and down the aisle, touching everyone. Except for the grinding of gears and the driver's angry mutter, it was dead silent.

He rammed the bus into first gear and popped the clutch. With a loud crunch, the side of the bus hit the post of the bridge. I looked over Carolyn's shoulder out the window. The river was a silver flood in the moonlight, rushing over boulders with a careless roar of power before passing under the bridge and sweeping down the canyon. The air was thick with moisture and the smell of icy water. I finally relaxed. What else was there to do?

Once more the driver backed up and jerked the bus into first gear. With a scraping squeal of metal against metal, we were on the bridge and over it. A ragged cheer went up. The driver, in better spirits, left the headlights on, and we continued our journey at a slower pace.

A light in the blackness ahead grew brighter as we approached. It illuminated a small concrete hut, throwing the figure of a soldier into sharp relief. This was our last checkpoint before Kalpa. The bus pulled up. Chai and Russell jumped down. Armed with 32 passports, they headed for the entrance. The rest of us followed more slowly. People moved up and down the road in evident relief at being safely off the bus. Some of them scouted the area, searching for the inevitable bush or tree to crouch behind. Others settled themselves on the boulders lining the road and began to softly chant. I walked to the edge and looked down. Larry and Roberta were just disappearing into the darkness below, barely visible in the glow of a single light. Minutes later they surfaced, Larry holding a large bottle of beer and Roberta munching on crackers. To my question, she mumbled, "Store," pointing at the light.

I headed down, following a narrow path that led me to a small stone structure with an open front. Inside, the weak light of a bare bulb revealed a low ceiling and dirt floor. Wooden planks served as a countertop, behind which the almost empty shelves held a few bottles and boxes. Several small tables and chairs stood in the shadows against the wall. One was occupied by two men. A third stood behind the counter and looked up as I walked in. I hesitated, unsure of what to do next. Gathering my courage, I pointed at the dusty bottles, and said, "Beer?" With a grin, he grabbed one and thrust it at me. In response, I pulled some bills from my pocket and made bottle-opening motions. He took the bottle and some money and returned the open beer. With a smile and a wave, I was gone, wondering what they thought of our sudden appearance so late at night in an area that hadn't seen foreign travelers for 40 years.

Back on the road, several of us shared the warm beer and settled down to wait. Thirty minutes later, Russell and Chai returned, waving the newly stamped permits in triumph.

"We're all set. Let's go, let's go," said Chai.

Everyone promptly returned to the bus, and the soldier waved us through. The driver was almost cheerful as we left the river and began to climb a series of switchbacks through the trees. Now and then, a tent or hut would pop out of the darkness and quickly fall behind. Nothing was left but the sound of our engine and this constant repetitive flashing of objects appearing and disappearing in the night. By now, it was past midnight, and people were quiet. I was lightly dozing when the bus stopped abruptly. I could just make out the shape of an even more battered bus parked beside us, and beyond it, stone walls rose out of sight. Our Indian passenger got out and disappeared into the darkness. The bus started up again and pulled away. People began shifting in their seats, stretching and moving around in anticipation of the end of a long day's journey.

This was not to be. We arrived back at the same battered bus after 20 minutes of sudden stops and reverses, narrow roads, and heated exchanges between the driver and his remaining companion. Russell and Chai came up front and entered into the discussion.

". . . and you will get there."

"We're slightly lost," announced Russell to a chorus of catcalls and loud groans. "But don't worry," he said soothingly, "we have a plan." Suggestions came at him from all directions. Chai joined him. "We're going back to the main road and start again," she declared. "The lights of the quarters where we'll be staying should be full on, and maybe we can rouse someone and ask them the way. If not, we'll just follow the light," she said cheerfully.

Off we went again, finally finding a narrow road that led us higher and higher. Keeping the brightest lights in view, we finally arrived at a dead end about 200 feet below them.

"I think this is it," Chai sang out.

"And how do we get everything from here to there?" We all knew the answer.

Loren got up from the engine cover and wiped the sweat from his face. "Walk," he said, "and be grateful to get off this bloody bus." I could feel the heat of the engine from where I sat.

We followed him out and began pulling bags through the windows and off the roof. Aside from exhaustion, the group was in good spirits. Since we had no way to sort out the luggage in the dark, we grabbed whatever was closest and started up the steep path. Lee had her flashlight out and lit the way over the uneven ground. Grunting with exertion and tripping over unseen rocks, we felt our way to the top. Our destination was a two-story, concrete rectangle with verandas running the length of both floors. In the harsh light of a bare bulb, we saw that it was a rustic refuge. The pile of luggage grew as more flashlights were uncovered, allowing us to make the trip back and forth in greater safety. The last things to come up were several heavy cartons of bottled water. They held four liter bottles each, our entire supply of drinking water until our bus could reach us, whenever that might be.

Chai and Mary-Margaret bustled in and out of rooms, trying to find a place for everyone to sleep. Carolyn and I investigated the first room we came to. It was bare concrete with built-in concrete cupboards and a concrete storage room with a concrete wash tub and wooden shelves lining one wall. The concrete bathroom held a very small sink, a squat toilet, and an indentation in the concrete floor with a drain in the middle. A low, outdoor water fixture protruded from the wall, and a bright-red plastic five-gallon bucket with a large measuring cup hanging carefully from the rim stood beside it. It didn't take long to figure out how the toilet worked or where the shower was.

The beds were single metal cots covered with plywood and a thin mattress and blanket. The mats and sleeping bags we had hauled around with us in Japan would be indispensable here. Neatly folded on each bed was a small white towel, and in each cupboard two new glasses sat alone. These, the brand-new water fixtures, the electricity, and the plastic bucket bore eloquent testimony to the efforts of Dev Raj Negi and the local inhabitants. I felt a rush of gratitude at the thoughtfulness of our unseen hosts. Each room would have to hold four to six people, but after a day of relentless physical and emotional tension, nobody was complaining.

Luckily, we had all our camping gear with us, so Carolyn and I looked around for a place to pitch our tent. We found a flat area in front of the building, bordered by a low stone wall. It was close enough to be part of the group, yet far enough away so we wouldn't get trampled. Sharon and Darcy decided to join us, and we pitched our tents side by side.

It was almost two A.M. when I crawled wearily into my sleeping bag and zipped it up. I lay there, momentarily listening to the laughter and comments around me, before sinking into a warm, dark slumber.

Chapter 16

Kalpa: Day One—the Kalachakra Begins, and Bartholomew Comments on the Teaching

I half awoke to the sound of dripping water. *Rain*, I thought groggily, burrowing deeper into my sleeping bag. Drip, drip, drip. The slow but inexorable sound wormed its way to the edge of my awareness and fell plop into the middle of my consciousness. Drip? Not pitter-patter? I uncovered my head and experimentally opened one eye. I could see that the day had barely begun. Drip, splash. I sighed, the mystery solved. It was raining *inside* the tent. Fat drops of condensed water hung batlike from the dome. Drip, splat on the wet bag and now on my upturned face.

Outside I heard the sound of muted voices and the nearby rattling of pans. I poked my head out and looked around. There wasn't much to see. Visibility extended maybe 25 feet in all directions. My breath came out in small puffs of white vapor. Yesterday we were soaked in sweat; today we were freezing.

Suddenly, a man materialized from the mist, carrying a tray of glasses. He set it down, and with a grin in my direction, held up a steaming glass of chai.[20] Like Pavlov's dog, I was out of the tent in a flash, reaching for my reward. People slowly gathered, drawn by the siren smell of chai. We stood around in our winter clothes sipping the hot liquid, wondering what came next. Our Kinnauri host and his assistant reappeared, carrying large, metal containers leaking fragrant wisps of steam. These they carefully placed on a rough wooden bench. Instantly surrounded by a ring of hungry spectators, they whipped off the covers with a flourish, releasing the aromatic smell of scrambled eggs and spices. Spontaneous applause broke out as we all pressed forward. Chai, egg, large flat muffins, jam, and oatmeal made up our first meal in Kalpa. Food had never tasted better!

Thus fortified, we gathered supplies for the day and carefully picked our way among the rocks, down the steep path. Meticulously tended apple orchards and small cultivated fields lined our way to the Kalachakra. The sun burned off the mist as we descended. We came out of the trees single file to find ourselves on the edge of a group of monks, who waved us in the direction of the place reserved for foreigners. Rounding a low stone wall, we found ourselves on a small plateau overlooking a bowl-like space filled with thousands of people. The sharp, jagged profile of the Himalayas formed a backdrop that was thrown into sharp relief against a clear, blue sky. It was vast and overwhelming.

All foreigners occupied a small area to the left of and not far from the Dalai Lama. It was already crowded when we arrived. There were deep rose- and saffron-robed monks to the right and slightly above us. A 30-foot-high golden Buddha wrapped in strings of small Christmas-tree lights stood in front of them. Monks below us of both sexes and all ages sat on blankets chatting with each other or silently reading the Sanskrit text. Young monks perched in the trees to the left of us, and old monks huddled under umbrellas beneath them. Masses of saffron and deep rose flowed down the hillside, diluting the mixture of local finery and the scattering of Western clothes.

His Holiness sat cross-legged on a raised dais in front of an orange-and-gold gompa.[21] It contained the complex ritual sand mandala his monks had been constructing for many days. Large, colorful tarpaulins, held in place by thick ropes and sturdy poles, had been spread to shield him from sun and rain. Armed soldiers were strategically scattered throughout the area, calmly watchful and highly visible. The crowd spread out before him as the Dalai Lama sat quietly meditating. He looked up slowly, unclasped his hands, and the Kalachakra began.

We made ourselves as comfortable as possible on the rocky ground and gave him our full attention. Umbrellas popped open everywhere, shading people from the sun and protecting them from passing showers. He addressed the multitude of people in Sanskrit and Tibetan, with long pauses in between while his words were translated into Hindu and English. We had lots of time to watch him. He smiled often and laughed occasionally, relaxed, yet totally present to everything around him. It was easy to see that his monks adored him and that he loved them in return. His peaceful presence was reflected by his audience. We relaxed with him, open to whatever was to happen.

Three hours later, we had been soaked by the rain, scorched by the sun, and exposed to basic Buddhism. Were we any wiser? That remained to be seen, but without question, it felt good to be with the Dalai Lama. It was time to end our first day at the Kalachakra, and we started toward the exit. Suddenly, the sound of Tibetan bells and gongs was heard, and we were startled by the sudden appearance of a line of monks, weighted down with huge buckets of steamed rice and chai, running *up* the steep hillside. They scattered at the top and began filling the empty bowls and cups that were held out to them. It looked impossible for these scurrying monks to so defy gravity. They were feeding hundreds of people, and we stood transfixed by the ease and laughter with which they undertook the task.

Finally reaching the exit, we followed a rough, rocky path bordered by hastily pitched, open-fronted tents. Wooden tables and benches indicated that food would soon be available. After a quick stop for dahl and chapatis, Carolyn and I rejoined the moving stream of people picking their way down the mountain. The lack of bathroom facilities became a problem, with every bush or tree a highly visible island in the midst of a pressing mass of moving humanity. Should we or shouldn't we? In the end, we followed the local example.

The path ended abruptly at the edge of town. We thought it must be Kalpa, but it turned out to be Peo. The street was lined with more open-fronted canvas tents and wooden structures. Tibetan bells, incense, and silver jewelry were displayed alongside colorful polyester clothing and plastic boots. Beautiful handmade shawls shared space with cooking pots and lanterns. Smiling people followed us from booth to booth, commenting to each other and pointing to everything we looked at. It was easy to see what a novelty we were, and we did our best to let them know how much we admired their lovely things.

It was late afternoon when Emmy and Lin appeared with good news. A line of taxis waited at the other end of town to take weary shoppers back up the mountain. We gratefully collapsed into one and arrived back in time to join the others who were gathering on the veranda. George was the last to appear, arms full of parcels and a satisfied grin on his face. Mary-Margaret pulled up a blanket and sat down. Miraculously, we were all present when she began.

"Well, then, my friends, good afternoon, and what a time you have had," declared Bartholomew. "You went through a very intense experience yesterday. Was it at all useful?" He leaned forward and looked around. "Would anyone like to share their responses?" he asked with a smile. Everyone laughed.

"It certainly fits in with what the Dalai Lama said today about practicing patience, if that means taking things as they come," said Laurel dryly.

"Yes, a good observation," replied Bartholomew. "It was a practice in patience. And *patience* is a word His Holiness uses for accepting the moment as it is. Any time you feel impatient, it is because you don't like what is happening now, and you wish to escape to a moment you hope will be more comfortable. There were certainly some of those moments present yesterday. To stay in the moment, you *must* be patient. The reward is the discovery that each moment, when accepted and not judged, is no better or worse than any other moment." He laughed. "As you found out, your job is not to find a better moment; your job is to be aware of the present moment and be attentive to it without judgment. When you did this, you were amazed at what was revealed, were you not?"

He leaned back and folded his arms. "Do not be surprised when you begin to experience an increase in the power present here as the days go by. In spite of the difficulties you have faced, you should be feeling a little more relaxed, a little more at home in your bodies than you were before arriving. In spite of the great differences between your world and this one, you can relax into an appreciation of it. I think, in view of yesterday, some of you have found much to appreciate already," he said with a smile.

You Are Not Alone

"All right," he continued briskly, "I would like to make a few comments about the Dalai Lama's presentation this morning. One of the interesting things he pointed out was the delight in doing what the Buddha wants. What does the Buddha want? For you to experience your True Nature as Emptiness, and, in addition, to help you become totally loving and totally kind. In speaking of this, the Dalai Lama was indicating that the helpfulness of the Great Ones is ever alive and available in Buddhism, as it is in the other major religions. The same awareness the Buddha awakened to 2,500 years ago is present now. The Buddha's energy is also here to help, so please remember that help is present. Not only the Buddha, but all the Bodhisattvas stand ready to guide you.[22]

"The reason I bring this forward is to point out that the living Buddhist tradition as embodied by the Dalai Lama constantly draws on the support of the Great Ones. Buddhists turn their awareness to the Buddha or to their favorite Bodhisattva for help all the time. The difference between you is that they believe when they say, 'Help!' help will come, whereas many of you don't really expect to be answered. Therefore, when help comes, you have already moved on. So one of the ongoing assignments I would like to present while you are here is to choose any of the Great Ones and ask for assistance in awakening. You can even choose something less personal, such as the Light or the 'I' of your Being. But pick something, and stay with it.

"For some of you, it will be a time of testing this theory. After all, you've asked for help at other times, and it didn't seem to work. The way to find out if help is indeed available is to be aware of your need and be aware of *your desire for guidance.* Then pay attention, and be open to the possibility of positive results. Ask for love, compassion, peace of heart, clarity of mind, and the desire to live life just as it presents itself in the midst of all the confusion and pain. These are the easiest gifts to receive because they are now, and always, a part of each moment. It is as if you have a brand-new automobile in your garage and continue to take a hot, overcrowded bus to work every day. Go ahead if you want, but you might consider using your Mercedes.

"Answering a call for assistance is one of the things Buddha does best. It is what the Christos does best, and it is what 'I' do best. All the verbalizing between us is secondary because it has to do with the ideas and beliefs in your mind. Ideas and beliefs are fine, but they are limited. They do not have the same intensity that direct, experiential awakening has." Bartholomew smiled briefly. "So I would like to talk about how this awakening works, using the Buddha as an example, since we are in Buddhist country.

"The idea of a vast Buddha residing in the Himalayas, listening with big ears and watching with wide eyes to see if any of you are always looking, isn't true. What is true is that the Buddha awakened to the awareness of an energy source far vaster than what he identified as himself. He experienced the moment as limitless, endless, unbound in any way. He turned to the unseen world, and what he found was a formless power that guided him to his awakening. That same power is still available to assist in your awakening through an *ongoing* unfoldment. There is no separation in awareness. The Buddha was grateful for the help he received and delighted at the prospect of helping others. And so it goes, in one continuous flow."

What Does It Mean to Have a Teacher?

"The Dalai Lama said today that 'you cannot awaken without a teacher.' This can mean different things to different people. So, what does it mean to 'have a teacher'? It means you have surrendered the part of yourself that thinks it can awaken by itself and have asked for assistance. You have acknowledged your helplessness and put out the call. One of the reasons this tour is working so well is that Chai doesn't mind saying, 'Please help us' when things seem about to go wrong. People recognize her beautiful being through her open-hearted plea and are happy to help. Without that expansive 'Please help us,' things would be much more difficult. Asking for help when it's needed is one of the most mature actions a human can take. Pretending you can do it alone leads to unnecessary suffering.

"What do each of you need in the way of a teacher? It will vary. Some of you consider this 'Bartholomew' to be your teacher," he said, patting Mary-Margaret's shoulder. "We would prefer to use the word *helper* instead, as one who stands willing to help rather than to simply teach concepts. One of the main reasons we are withdrawing this 'Bartholomew' energy from this partic-ular approach through Mary-Margaret is to remove any idea that this help is in any way limited to her physical body. You do not need to have *anyone* physi-cally present other than your own self. If you approach 'Bartholomew' know-ing that only your willingness and openness is needed, it can be used in the same way as others are using the Buddha or the Christos to help them.

"Some of you have tremendous reluctance to align yourself with *any* teacher, having had some unpleasant experiences with human teachers in the past. I understand that. Please do not use the suggestion to ask the Great Ones for help to create yet another problem for yourselves. If you feel this approach isn't for you because you already have a sense of Oneness or you do not trust form, then by all means remain with that Oneness, Emptiness, the Unmanifest. You do not need a match, when the fire is already burning.

"Please think seriously about this. In the end, these energies are just friends. Buddha, Christ, Ramana, and, indeed, even Bartholomew, are just friends, willing to help. Just like-hearted awarenesses that enjoy sharing from the depths of Consciousness. Nothing fancy. No traps, no hidden agendas. The fancier you make us, the more distant we become. I hope this assignment will not be just another idea to be considered these few moments, then forgotten. I hope you will spend these days willing to trust that something unseen is pres-ent and available here and everywhere to help you come to full awareness."

Barbara raised her hand. "I like using the Vastness," she said. "And I can identify with it. I like many of the Great Ones, too. I feel they're friends, just dear friends—sometimes better friends than people. Meeting the State Oracle the other night seemed like meeting an old friend again. As he talked, it was as if he generated so much love that I asked myself, *Why not open and take in as much as you can?* But when I am open, I also end up feeling the egos of the people surrounding me."

"Ah," sighed Bartholomew, "if by *ego* you mean only the egos of the people surrounding you and not your own, then you haven't understood. What you feel is your *own* ego, not other people's. You experience it as 'them,' but it is really your own ego other people are mirroring back to you." He laughed. "You see, only one big, fat ego appears in consciousness as many tiny little separate egos," he said, as he leaned forward. "Please, this is a very important point to understand. If you react to what you think is someone else's ego, you must realize and be willing to accept that it, too, is part of you. It is not a separate alien energy, unconnected to you."

"Yet, I feel their egos bump into mine," Barbara answered thoughtfully. "As a child, I felt I experienced love and wanted to share it, but I felt it was safer to close it off," she said.

"I know exactly what you are saying," Bartholomew told her quietly. "You have often experienced the world as painful, and being open and aware of other people can sometimes cause difficulties, until you understand what is really happening." He turned to the rest of us. "Perhaps I can say a few things that will help clarify this issue. The first thing to remember if someone says something that is painful to you is that it can often reveal more about that person than it does about you. They are feeling their own resistance to accepting the part of themselves you are mirroring for them. Unfortunately, they often tell you that you are doing something that makes them feel this way. But that is not true. Remember, all of you, if you are mirrors for each other, the only way to stop the pain is to understand that it is just another part of you, a part that is frightened and defending itself. I could even go so far as to suggest that you not take such attacks personally! They will go on until you awaken to the Truth of who you are.

"None of you are eager to face the fact that it is your resistance to this mirrored reflection that is causing your dis-ease. You try to fill your world with people who will not mirror your darker selves. But eventually you must see that if it is happening *to* you, it is *of* you. This is also true in those wonderful moments when your love and beauty are mirrored back. So, what to do? To awaken to peace, you must be open to and aware of all that happens in and around you. In being quietly present, you will hear the truth of what is being spoken, not your ego's defensive interpretation of it. Then you will see clearly, and peace will be present."

Deb's hand shot up. "In that case, do I look at what they're saying, or do I look at the feelings it brings up?" she asked.

"You have to look at it all, or perhaps we could say you have to observe it all with quiet attention," Bartholomew responded. "For example, if someone says you are being too noisy, and if you have no problem with that, you may not respond. Either you don't care what they think, or you don't mind being seen as noisy. On the other hand, if someone says you are doing something wrong, you may react because you have experienced other people telling you that you were wrong, inappropriate, stupid, uncaring, or somehow didn't fit. In this case, they are making a statement that mirrors back pain, because the pain was already there, waiting to be activated yet again. It is an old, familiar feeling they simply remind you of. They do not create it. In that moment, you can acknowledge both the pain and the awareness that they did not do it to you. This kind of large, responsive, and open observation keeps you from the tendency to overreact or fall into drama."

A Surefire Formula for Happiness

Bartholomew continued. "One way to lessen the potential drama is to remember you are also capable of practicing loving kindness. When an ego speaks, it oftentimes doesn't care about loving kindness. It wants to say what it wants to say, period. The Dalai Lama addressed this beautifully today with a gentle reminder that loving kindness and a loving approach simply happen to work better for you. He did not say to be kind because you are bad if you are not. He wants you to be kind because, if you are kind, you will be happier. You will have a succession of happy, exciting, dynamic, open moments *because* you are being kind. Drop the drama, and open to loving kindness. Even if it is momentary and the resentment rises again, the results will be worth it."

Bartholomew settled back, warming to the subject. "The Dalai Lama also talked about loving kindness as being something other than performing kind deeds. Loving kindness is a feeling of gentle helpfulness that rises up out of your being and gives rise to loving action. You perform loving actions because they *feel* good, not because they *are* good. Be kind because *you* want to be happy, and you will find that your happiness increases as you increase your loving kindness."

"So if I show compassion, I realize I am compassion?" Deb asked.

"Absolutely," agreed Bartholomew. "Not only that you are compassion, but that compassion is spontaneously natural in the most ordinary sense and not hard to feel. It is part of your true nature, so what could be more natural? It is not something you create; it is already there. It is what you are, not what you become."

Lin raised her hand. "What about a situation where something comes at you, and you find yourself in total reaction? Is it possible when you're full of emotions to somehow slip out of them and get back into loving kindness? Or is it better to feel the feelings?" she asked.

"You must understand that this 'one moment' you are referring to is not all that is present in this reaction. It is the sum total response to all similar material your body has not processed. The cells hold the images you are now reacting to. When something unpleasant comes at you, your mind hears it as an 'attack' and sends that message to the cells. You feel a physical, mental, cellular tightening, because the present event plus all the other events that make up that memory trace come together in that moment. The mental images trigger the cellular response, which is one of tightening up, pulling in, cutting off."

Bartholomew smiled. "My lovely one, I wish I could say that you could all simply slip out of it, but I can't. Not yet. As you practice loving kindness toward others, practice loving kindness toward yourself. Remember that more is present in your reaction than what is coming at you in the moment with a particular person. When you realize that, you can depersonalize the incident to such an extent that you will begin to realize that understanding is indeed *your* business, not theirs. They may deliver the punch, but you have to deal with receiving it. To become aware that every event you participate in is your responsibility takes both practice and willingness.

"So feel the pressure, the tensions, as your body responds. Be aware of the heat that builds when you get angry or frustrated. Be aware of how cold you feel when you get depressed or fearful. Notice what is going on *in the body.* By paying attention to the physical, you stay out of your mind. Get out of your mind, and there is a chance that all of the computerlike automatic processing your mind runs will be short-circuited, and something new will arise. Become excited about learning the fine art of taking difficult moments and processing them with love, compassion, and healing. In the end, it is much easier to take this responsibility than it is to try to make everyone in your universe be kind and loving toward you. You may contrive the perfect life, surrounding yourself with smiling people who love and adore you, but someday you will be at the supermarket, and someone will knock your smiling pieces right off the chessboard."

"How can I be kind and not be a doormat?" asked Chai.

"If someone delivers a statement that is difficult, you do not need to collapse into a small child. You can feel your strength and be centered, even in the midst of the most incredible moments of negativity. One of the strongest statements you can make to others is to tell them you will give close attention to what they have said. When you respond this way, it is a reminder that it is really you talking to you. It also shows your willingness to examine what has been presented. It immediately makes the situation bigger. No doormat says, 'I will work with what you have said and get back to you. Then we can talk it over.' That kind of response reveals a mature integrity. No one is a victim, no one superior or inferior, just two equals dealing with a situation both have created for their own understanding.

"You can also choose not to strike back at them. Remember, you are equal on all levels, and your egos are all equally insidious." He laughed, looking around. "Individual egos think they are just a little bit better than everyone else's. Maybe not a lot better, but just a little better. So, your ego tells you this gives you the right to tell other people what to do because *it* knows best. *People make comments on other people's lives because they honestly think they know better.* It is a very interesting game you are playing, and you are playing it together. Why? So you can mirror back each other's egos and see the *uselessness* of such games. There is no permanent peace in playing this way. When you see clearly, you will stop. Then you will awaken to what is always there, past the chaos."

Bartholomew suddenly fell silent and turned around. The jagged top of Mount Kinnaur Kailash had just pierced the soft underbelly of white clouds and broken through the mist. Pale streamers, like torn veils, were flung from the towering peak, as the mountain revealed itself to us for the first time.

"Ah," he breathed, "beautiful."

"Beautiful," we echoed.

A long moment of stillness prevailed as we sat and inhaled the air coming from this powerful mountain.

Bartholomew turned toward us. Softly, with great emphasis, he spoke. "I want you to stay in the moment because something *exciting* is *always* happening there. Participate consciously. Wake up! Become aware of *your ever-present creative power.* Every moment of your life you are creating, whether actively or passively. Your reality exists as it does because you are constantly generating it."

He leaned forward again. "Be aware of your intentions. Stop expecting your friends to be perfect. Look carefully at yourselves, at *your* motives. Why are you burning to speak, to deliver that knockout statement? In the end, whatever you deliver to someone else comes back to you. Because *you* are its creator, it remains a part of you, as a child is always part of its parent. You cannot be separated from the offspring of your ego.

"When you make a judgment against someone else, your ego also experiences it as a judgment against yourself. It knows that whatever you believe about others, you believe about yourself. You will receive what you send out. If your intention is to give loving kindness, that is what you will get back. You haven't yet allowed yourselves to believe you *are* a part of the Christ, you *are* a part of the Buddha, and you *are* a part of God and Light and Love. You still pretend to be limited, driven by your egos, rather than choosing to be driven by a vaster power. But you can choose the vaster over the lesser. These are the choices you make constantly. As always, it is up to you." Bartholomew paused and looked around.

"Are there other questions or comments?" he inquired.

"How do you become aware of awareness?" asked Jim.

"Becoming aware of awareness is already one step removed from awareness," replied Bartholomew. "It means you have two things: awareness, and that which is aware of it. I want something even more direct. Drop; be still; drop deeper; become aware. Thoughts, emotions, and actions will arise. You must go back to the silence again and again, until awareness is in the foreground of your consciousness, and you see that everything else takes place within it. Right now you are living the opposite of this reality. The limited, impermanent creations of your life are in the foreground, and awareness is hidden somewhere in the background. It is possible to become so aware of the screen the images of thought play upon, that although you see these images clearly, they are no longer compelling. Nor can they push you around, because you will be resting in something permanent, peaceful, endless, deathless. Keep practicing. It is neither a thought nor a feeling. There are no words for the unspeakable."

"What about bliss?" asked Emmy from the back of the porch. "Isn't that always present?"

"When the bliss of awareness is present, it isn't a feeling; it is an immersion into the experience. If you can feel bliss, you can feel no bliss. Feelings are of the dual world. They come and go. What I am pointing to transcends the duality of the world. The difficulty, as always, is in the words. You see, *awareness is what is constantly experiencing everything.* All I am asking is for you to allow awareness to experience awareness. Allow awareness the bliss of experiencing awareness rather than something within awareness, like thoughts, beliefs, and emotions. I know it sounds confusing, but just stay with it, and, as they say, 'All will be revealed'!"

The Current Prince of Peace

"How do you like being here with the Dalai Lama?" I asked, suddenly curious.

Bartholomew laughed. "I love it. I love him, and he's very big!" He looked at me, a mischievous gleam in his eye. "Would it help to say we are old friends? I may say this in jest, but it does bring up an interesting point. On the deepest level, we are talking nonsense because the awareness of the Dalai Lama is in no way separate from the awareness you call Bartholomew. There is just One. His job is more difficult because he has chosen to take a body. And with all due respect," Bartholomew said, as he laughed again, "as you know, the body carries with it certain difficulties. As you have all done, he has taken his vastness and chosen to appear limited.

"His knowing, however, is a lot vaster and more open than yours at the present time. He has tremendous areas of beautiful nonattachment and can allow all kinds of people, ideas, events, and beliefs to move through him and around him with wonderful humor and a peaceful smile. He lets the opposites of his world rise and fall. He doesn't prefer one over the other, and yet, I think one of the reasons he travels is to be able to take as much of the world into his vastness as he can. You could say he blesses the world just by moving through it.

"In his willingness to expose himself to a world that often does not agree with him or understand him, he brings great potential for peace. He is the current Prince of Peace. He is to be honored because his job is not always easy. You are seeing him in the place where he is most loved. But in some of the places he visits, people make fun of him or greet him with hostility and judgment. They have even spit at him and thrown rocks at his entourage. In spite of this, he continues to bring peaceful blessings to all those he visits."

Rishi waved to get Bartholomew's attention. "Does the same incarnation of the Dalai Lama come back lifetime after lifetime?" she asked.

"That is a concept that fits very comfortably with the belief structure of millions of Buddhists. It means a very loving, dependable power source keeps coming back. That's one way to look at it. In the vastest sense, it's an impossibility. The Buddha himself said that there was no soul migrating through different lives. Perhaps it is truer to say that a fragment of the last Dalai Lama chooses to manifest in this lifetime as a limited being called the 14th Dalai Lama, while his vastness is, at the same time, present in other realities. Do you understand?

"To say that the same little fellow goes from lifetime to lifetime is a very limited concept. We are talking about something much more wondrous. The sliver of the Dalai Lama who returns carries the teaching, the power of his leadership, and an awareness of the role he is to play. But much more of 'him' is going on. Much more of each of you is also going on, by the way—a fact you keep forgetting. You are abundantly 'going on' in other realities, creating through other magnificent and wondrous potentialities. He happens to know this vast potentiality; you have chosen to forget it."

Bartholomew leaned back and took a sip of water. "You have been marvelous," he concluded. "Thank you for your questions. Congratulations on sharing your love and good humor under some very difficult circumstances, and I will see you again tomorrow."

Never Mind the Buses, Where Are the Cooks?

Chai stood and announced her plan for dinner. Meet in an hour, hike halfway down the trail we had used this morning, and dine in Kalpa. Since no one else knew where there was any food, this suggestion met with instant approval. Getting ready didn't take long. Various high-pitched vocal responses revealed who was brave enough to bathe from their bucket of icy-cold water. We gathered, pink of cheek, wet of hair, hiking boots on our feet, ready for dinner.

Chai led the way, more slowly now, back down the path. We had time to observe the pale stone houses, capped with roofs of blue-gray slate. Now and then a brightly painted door or window stood out in colorful contrast to the otherwise monochromatic landscape. We reached town and its one intersection. An open storefront caught my attention. Burlap sacks filled with potatoes and chiles slouched beside the doors. Inside the dim interior, I could just make out the shallow shelves sparsely stacked with tins. Small cardboard cartons stood together on either end of a dusty display counter. Behind it, the smiling proprietor waved briefly.

We returned his greeting, turned down a narrow side street, and entered a low-ceilinged room. Tables had been pushed together to form a large U. Chairs scraped against the uneven dirt floor, as we found seats in what must be Kalpa's only restaurant. Several Kinnauri men appeared immediately with trays of chai and juice. It wasn't long before the inevitable rice, dahl, and chapatis followed. I sighed, tightened my belt another notch, and grabbed two cartons of juice from a passing tray.

I was suddenly very tired. It had been an emotionally exciting, physically exhausting day. The thought of my waiting sleeping bag was irresistible. By the time we left the restaurant, it was dark. The few lights in town did not detract from the crystalline brilliance of icy stars in the deep night sky. Single file, flashlights in hand, we made our way back up the mountain toward home.

Long after the only sound to be heard was the quiet breath of the wind, a single light cast a glimmer into the darkness. It came from the window of Mary-Margaret's bathroom. Inside, she sat on her duffel bag, leaning against the concrete wall. Her eyes were closed, her open journal resting on her lap. Several moments later, she looked down and began to write.

Full of different responses tonite. Feeling so much gratitude for it all, yet the body is really ready for a jacuzzi. Fat chance! What an amazing day — what a feeling of "all things are possible" in the presence of His Holiness. Just looking at his laughing face as he greeted our straggling group made me feel Awake, Alive, and Expectant. In some strange way it feels good for the body to be feeling discomfort, hot, tired, hungry. It makes it all seem so very REAL, so foreign. I love this feeling of being foreign, as it makes me lose my usual point-of-reference that usually keeps me safe. As I begin to experience the huge energy that rolls from His Holiness to all of us, I start to cry — tears of gratitude to whatever forces brought me to this moment, to this hot, dusty land in this valley of wonder.

What good for teene — what incredible, unbelievable good for teene.

Since I can't really understand all the many intricate levels and meanings of this initiation, I decide that all I can do is to stay open, to listen from the inside, not with my ears. To listen not to the words, but to the inner silence. In the midst of all this noise of the 17,000 or so of us (150 "Westerners," which includes the Asians!), there seems to be a silence underneath it all. I feel it in His Holiness. Words come from him, yet he feels quiet, still.

The mountains — how
to describe THEIR silence.
As I understand it, this
initiation was given to
the world from this summit,
Mount Kinnaur Kailash.
That must mean that
the doorway to the vast
power that stands be-
hind this teaching is
open wide here in the
snow-capped peaks. And
as I sense their huge-
ness behind the clouds
covering their face, I feel
afraid of that snowy power.
They are so immense, so
THERE, so full of SOMETHING.
And this something doesn't
have anything to do with
words, ideas, philosophies.

It just IS. A part of me is surprised that I'm afraid, yet another part of me remembers how often I have felt this same fear when I saw calendars of the Himalaya. Just past life stuff? Just a coward? Just a puny human whose logical response in the face of such power should be fear? Who knows. One thing is clear — I will understand it better in a few days, because there is no escape. I bow with weak knees to the powers that nailed my "back door" shut. Short of running, I'm committed to this dance. Shiva, His

Holiness, and me. Breathe,
Mary-Margaret, just BREATHE.

❦

Chapter 17

Kalpa: Day Two—Trying to Describe the Indescribable

B artholomew took a deep breath. "Well, then, my friends, good afternoon," he said. "I would like to begin with some comments about today's teaching. The Dalai Lama spoke beautifully about the use of visualization." Bartholomew placed his fingers together and looked around. "It is very common in the scientifically based Western world to believe that visualization is a fantasy, nonsense—only dream creations that have nothing to do with reality. One of the statements His Holiness made was that Tantra [23] is directly involved with using visualization as a totally legitimate, bona fide path to full consciousness. He pointed out the ways to apply the latent capacity for visualization that lies dormant in everyone.

"It is a skill not often utilized because your mind, conditioned by science, tends to consider it a secondary path. However, I honestly feel that visualization can be very helpful in moments of stress, when you are feeling fear, self-pity, resentment, anger, or any other pain. If you truly wish to move out of a so-called negative state, it is possible to do so by visualizing some source of aware and awakened power outside yourself. Focusing on this image totally, with *all* your awareness, takes you out of the limited 'me-ness' of your interpretation of the moment. You have friends in High Places who know things that your small self does not.

"Some of you have already experienced the power of visualization. Children, for instance, are very familiar with this process. They visualize so well they often cannot tell the difference between what you would call reality (a questionable term) and what they are perceiving to be real." He gestured toward Clare. "The story about your lovely son, who not only saw angels, but commented that there were so many of them, is a good example. You may have had similar spontaneous visions when you were small. Any of you can return to the part of yourself that believes in such things and is willing to receive help and comfort once again."

Bartholomew swung around to face the mountains. "Look at all of the powerful deities you are surrounded by here," he said with a wave of his hand. "They are beautifully represented by the Tibetan thankas[24] displayed in the local shops. The figures in them are filled with symbology, and the arms of these deities are one of the most symbolically important parts of the paintings. These celestial beings are sometimes depicted as having hundreds or even a thousand arms. Why? Because one of the gifts the hands symbolize is the willingness to give unconditionally to those struggling to awaken to full consciousness. In most traditions, the hands do the nurturing, the giving, the healing, and the loving. It is possible to visualize these forms in their magnificent, unending bounty and to be open to the endless possibilities of being nurtured, guided, and loved by their compassionate grace. These representations are true doorways, and you can use them to find your way through to the consciousness you are looking for."

He paused a moment before continuing. "The second aspect of today's teaching I would like to discuss was the Dalai Lama's statement that it is necessary to have a spiritual path to awaken. The minute you step on a path, the path itself comes alive to help you break through the illusion of separation, the glamour surrounding the false self, and the confusion about who you really are. I wish to address this because I realize it may be difficult to accept for those of you who do not see yourselves as having an exclusive spiritual path. He leaned forward. "I would like you to get as big as you possibly can around the word *path*. I do understand that in today's teachings the Dalai Lama was referring to the Buddhist path, but that is because it is his job to do so. He would be very quick, however, to acknowledge other religions as completely legitimate paths for those drawn to them."

He leaned back and smiled. "In a group like this, most of you have experienced many different paths. One could say that either you don't have a path or that you have assimilated the truth of many paths." His smile grew. "Please don't say that you're on the Bartholomew path, because Bartholomew is only a source of information, a finger pointing to the Truth. It is not a path with rules and a price to pay if you don't follow them. So, where, then, do you go for that sense of having a strong spiritual path? What kind of teaching makes a path? It can be something as simple as the strong desire to awaken. That would create an *immense* path—one that could take you to the end of separation. The more familiar paths have rules, regulations, and forms to follow. Make no mistake—this type of approach works! But when you have a group that has had real, dynamic openings of consciousness through various paths, it becomes the *desire* to be in a state of total, open Love that is the teaching. The yearning, then, *is* the path. It is an *inner* search, a path that finally demands one to awaken here and now to one's True, God-Filled Self." He stopped and waited expectantly.

Russell raised a hand, and Bartholomew nodded to him. "During this afternoon's teachings, His Holiness was talking about selflessness and dependent arising—meaning, as I understand it, that all phenomena arise from some cause. I left the teaching early, so I don't know if this came up, but what was the first cause to begin that chain of cause and effect?

"A good question, but a difficult one to answer in words. All I can do is present you with one possible picture of this occurrence so you can 'feel,' not 'think' your way to this Truth. Look around you at these immense mountains, endless skies, and plunging valleys. It is all so vast. Then close your eyes, and see if you can get a sense of the same kind of vastness, of unending awareness as an inner void, a still emptiness within that is at the same time full. All potential is contained within this empty, still, unending fullness. It is a beginning—a source.

"At some point in what you call 'time,' a motion arose out of the stillness of that emptiness. This motion could be called 'first cause.' Then by its very nature of being first, out of it came a second and a third, and so on. The words do not make sense because there is really no way to talk about the unspeakable, but since we are, try to simply 'feel' the sense of it all."

"Did consciousness exist before that?" asked Russell.

"In the first primordial state before any motion, what 'existed' was *awareness Itself,* pure awareness, unformed, unnamed, known only to Itself. Then as first cause arose, as form arose, there was pure, *conscious* awareness, awareness now conscious of itself as form and motion. Out of that form came all of creation."

He looked around. "Do you understand?" he asked. "Pure awareness has no name, no shape or form. It is an *emptiness* that is absolutely pulsating with *fullness.* It is stillness that is totally alive and aware of itself. This is what you are experiencing constantly, although you are not consciously aware of it. It is that awareness I keep pointing to, that I keep asking you to be willing to go back to experiencing as the Source again and again. All the thoughts, ideas, and actions you experience are consciousness and awareness in motion. Behind that, and always present, is the awareness out of which all consciousness arises."

"Would that first movement then be the sense of consciousness, of 'I Am'?" asked Judith.

"Yes, awareness becoming consciously aware of the sense of 'I Am,' the Source, not the 'I' as experienced in 'me,' but the 'I' as experienced in 'I am that I am.' The 'me' came later, a personal, temporary identification with what is called 'the ego.'"

"Then out of the pure awareness would come . . .?"

"Consciousness," responded Bartholomew.

"A sense of, 'I am conscious'?" she asked.

"More like, 'I am aware of something.' Words can never describe the indescribable, but let us try. We are asking you to be aware of the awareness of that first unspecified, unnamed, unconscious but totally aware space, out of which consciousness arises. We are not looking for the sense of 'I' as in 'I am a separate being,' but the 'I' before any separation."

He burst into laughter. "Such words sound silly, confusing, and they may scramble your brains as you try to make sense of them. Good! Let the mind confuse itself, and perhaps it will fall silent in its own confusion. Then the Truth surrounding all of this can reveal itself without words. It is possible because you have never left, you *cannot* leave the Source of what you are. So why should it be difficult to be what you already are?"

From the One Come the Ten Thousand Things

"In that first movement of consciousness, that first separation, *everything* began to arise. Awareness moved into consciousness and began to create in many different realms. But that natural awareness out of which it all arose *is still ever present in you,* and the Dalai Lama is trying to point you to that. You are it. No life would exist without it! No creation would exist without it! And all creation is filled with 'it,' in all *its* forms."

Wow! My brain ached with the struggle to expand around a very big concept. I had just heard Bartholomew say the awareness I was experiencing *now* was the same awareness present *at the beginning of creation.*

"So the awareness you are talking about now is *original* awareness?" I exclaimed.

"Yes, absolutely! This is what I keep pointing to. The magnificence of the original awareness, before any 'thing' arose, *is still ever-present and available to you.* That is what I have been screaming at you about for 15 years." He stopped and took a deep breath. "You are on a long journey," he said, with a sweep of his hand. "Just like the prodigal son, you left home and wandered for eons, *pretending* to leave so you could journey and return. Simple. That's it. Now it is time to re-realize, to make *real* once again the knowing that you have *never* left the Source; you *cannot* leave the Source, because *It is what you are!* All of the deepest spiritual teachings point to the same thing; you have never left, *so you do not need to struggle to return.* In fact, the very act of struggling postpones the quiet knowing of this ever-present Truth."

Chai raised her hand, and Bartholomew leaned toward her.

"Yes, lovely one," he said.

"You know, they say in the Bible that the first movement was sound."

"The Word," replied Bartholomew.

"The Word," repeated Chai. "And from The Word came form. So is sound an appropriate tool to use in going back to pure awareness?" she asked.

"Absolutely," responded Bartholomew immediately. "It is a legitimate path of consciousness—whatever 'The Word' or sound means to you. When the wonder of sound fills you, if you stay open and relaxed, it has the power to make you aware of its Source. In fact, many teachings are based on the aspect of creating a union of awareness and a mantra of sound to bring you home. In the simple act of being fully present with sound, through hearing it or creating it, the Source of all sound is revealed."

Guy spoke up. "Today the Dalai Lama talked of the ten things that one should try to live by. They sound very similiar to the Ten Commandments. Do they come from the same source?" he asked.

Bartholomew nodded. "They are both reflections of the deep knowing that if you do certain things, you are going to be happier than if you do certain other things. I think the people who put those teachings together had observed human nature very closely. They saw what happened when one was in a state of peace and relaxation as compared to what happened when one was in a state of agitation and strife. Peaceful people tend to be happier than those at war with life or themselves. The results of those observations are the guidelines or 'commandments' you are referring to.

"The value of any of these paths is to be able to take from it to fill you with what *you* need. Here at the Kalachakra, take what works for you. Be openhearted and open-minded. Be grateful. Again, the idea is not for you all to become Buddhists, but to present you with one of the great spiritual paths of the world. You can make use of its power to help yourselves move closer to what you seek. Power is power, and can be used in many ways. Don't miss the amazing power and feeling generated here in this valley."

Bartholomew straightened up. "Are there any questions?" he asked.

Eleanor raised a hand. "Would one way to become more aware of the Source be to observe whatever you are thinking or feeling or doing, and become aware of what it's rising out of?"

"Yes!" he agreed. "Wonderful, thank you. In Ramana's words, be aware of the deeper questions: '*Who* is thinking? *Who* is upset? *Who* is afraid?' Where do these thoughts come from? And if these words get in the way, just relax into the *awareness* of all that is present, including thinking."

"I was thinking of the beauty of these mountains," Eleanor added, "and then I realized that they rise and fall, too. What do they rise out of?"

Bartholomew responded, "Everything rises out of awareness and returns to awareness. Let's go back to today's teaching. First is the original awareness, and out of that awareness arises thinking, form, action, remembrances, worlds, and universes. Your job is to relax further into the moment into what is present every moment, as all of it comes and goes." He waved a hand. "All of this—your body, your mind, this entire amazing world—has arisen out of *one* thing. What is that one thing? *That* is the question all seekers are seeking to answer, not as an exercise but as a reality. That which you seek is nameless, formless, and it is totally aware. It is *your* awareness— *yours!*" he exploded.

He sighed and leaned back again. "You are, this moment, totally and completely aware. That is why Ramana could say that everyone is already enlightened. What did he mean? That you *are* that Light, the Light of Awareness, of God. You have *never* been anything else. So realize this and be free."

"Is this awareness aware of itself?" interjected Emmy.

Bartholomew laughed. "You'll have to tell *me* when you find out," he said.

"I would say 'no'!" she replied quickly.

"Let's play with that a moment. If awareness is aware of awareness, it would seem that we have two things present. In fact, when you *try* to become aware of awareness, you end up becoming frustrated. You will keep forgetting to try, and the struggle to be aware will become the obstacle. Ultimately, all you can do is relax and observe what is always there. That is why the path is simple but not easy. You must simply be aware of what is present, with no idea of what to expect. No translation into like or dislike. Whatever you see isn't it. Whatever you think isn't it. Whatever you do isn't it. Yet it is present in all of these. So what is it? If everything you know or can ever imagine is not it, then what is?" he questioned. "You know *something* is always present, in doubt and seeking, thinking, and action, in remembering and forgetting. *Something* created all this. What?"

He relaxed. "It is foolish not to believe in a creative principle. Look at all the amazing creations," he said, gesturing for us to take in our surroundings. "Don't limit it by saying, 'God created all this' and assume you have found the answer. How do you know? You must investigate by the relaxed observation of what is present."

He leaned forward and looked at us intently. "Your mind tells you that you are separate from God, from the Creator. Look around, and you will *see* that everything is one. No separation exists. Is anything really *separate* from anything else? Is your body separate from the ground, the ground from the sky, the sky from the universe, you from all of it? Well, can the something that created this world of 'no separation' be separate from what it has created? It is an *impossibility!* It's just as impossible for you to be separated from your Creator as it is for a mother and father to be cellularly separate from the child they created. The child may forget who created it, but that does not change the source of its creation." He leaned back. "It is impossible," he repeated.

"Why was it created?" asked Rishi.

Bartholomew threw up his hands. "For creative enjoyment! For creative delight! For creative fun! To experience the robustness of the diversity of the Createdness. And it *has* been fun. This mountain," he said, pointing at Kinnaur Kailash, "is having a marvelous time being this mountain; make no mistake about it."

I glanced at the beauty surrounding me, closing down, feeling somehow cheated. I wouldn't describe the thrust of my life as having fun. It sounded like much more fun to remember I was not separate. *"Why* did we forget?" I asked impulsively.

You Know the Ten Thousand; Now Know the One

He looked at me calmly. "Basically, forgetfulness happened when you got too entranced by the diversity of creation." He smiled. "You have created a very exciting little world, and your awareness simply got more and more involved with it. Now what you are saying is that you wish to continue exploring the diversity while knowing the part of your being that always has been deeply and completely Itself. That's what the path is all about." He continued softly. "You don't want to give up the ten thousand things; you simply want to add the remembrance of the Bliss, the Source of it all.

"Why give it up? This creation of infinite diversity and separation is, in its way, also wondrous," he exclaimed. "But now know the fullness of all of it, the many *and* the One. It's your birthright. The awareness of the Deep Self, your True Nature, that which everything sprang from, is not something you have to earn, and it is not something you have to pursue or strive for. It is simply something *you have to become aware of.* You know the basic rule. What you put your awareness on, you become aware of. Obvious, isn't it?" He turned to Emmy with a smile. "At this stage, Miss Cheney, awareness seems to be becoming aware of awareness, but there is an even deeper awareness than that. Stay with it and you will understand."

Russell caught Bartholomew's eye. "Okay," he said. "A lot of us have had experiences of Oneness. How do we stay with it?" he asked, as the rest of us loudly agreed.

"If you will just begin to do the smallest amount of relaxing into any of the observations we have been sharing these last few days," Bartholomew said, looking from one of us to another, "you would experience what you are looking for. The difficulty with a legitimate 'path' is that you can be trapped into thinking that if you *do* follow it, you will automatically become enlightened. That isn't necessarily true. You may be following the formula when all of a sudden doubt creeps in, and you begin to feel something is missing. That is where many of you are now. You need to realize you are on a pathless path. Continue to live your life aware there is a vibrant, silent, creative principle everywhere, ever-present, and in everything. Be *willing* to become aware of it. Be *willing* to let it guide *you* rather than you following set ideas and rules. Trust the moment to reveal the Truth of that moment. Just relax and allow it to happen.

"Relax and allow it to happen again and again until you *know* what each moment *really* contains, past any idea, thought, or form. As the Dalai Lama has explained, first cause is empty, and *empty* means 'without form.' It also means without disturbance—absolute stillness, even in action."

"It's forgetting the directive for seven hours," Emmy interjected sadly.

"I know, dear one," Bartholomew replied gently, leaning toward her.

"And then it's like trying to swim to the surface from under very deep water," she continued. "It's like trying to awaken from a very heavy sleep, just trying to get in the moment, just for a second sometimes, and other times it happens fast, and then it's gone." She stopped. "Is it just constant practice?" she asked.

"My dear one, all you can do is *do* it, not *practice* it. My prayer is that soon you will become aware that you *do not have to practice*. Listen," he said clapping his hands together to emphasize each word. *"You don't have to practice being because you are always being."* He stood up and began marching in place. "Got it?" he asked. Peering at Mary-Margaret's feet moving up and down, he said, "This is practicing. I'm practicing awareness. Practice, practice. But is there a separation from awareness while I'm practicing awareness? When I stop practicing awareness, does it cease to exist?

"Where can awareness go? It is here, now, always, in the midst of your remembering and your forgetting." He sighed and sat down again. "You see where we are once again? This is it. If I am practicing awareness, then I am *practicing* awareness, but *awareness* is doing everything, *including* practicing awareness and forgetting awareness. It is the practicing, the forgetting, having the guilt about not practicing, and the delight of remembering awareness. *Awareness* is doing it all!"

"What's the difference between that awareness and mine?" I blurted out in confusion.

"There *is* no difference," he said, looking me straight in the eye. "But *you* need to know that, firsthand. Until that time, the words mean nothing."

"Then why am I doing all this?" I asked, feeling hopeless.

"You are concentrating on trying to *find* something. I want you to move back one step. Instead of trying to *find* awareness, stick with the knowing that *the desire itself* is the awareness you imagine to be separate, a thing to be found. Everything is awareness! Even when you are totally asleep, you are aware. Just keep on." He leaned closer. "Let me ask you something," he said. "Right now, are you aware of frustration?"

Choking with laughter and frustration both, I burst out, "You had better believe it! It is certainly *one* of the things I am aware of right now."

"So who is aware of this frustration? What is the feeling of the 'I' in the 'I am frustrated'? Is it also there when you say, 'I am peaceful'? Something in you never changes, never rises and falls, and is totally aware of what is happening. Something observes it all, feels it all, responds to it all. Stay with it."

He looked around. "All right, stop, drop everything, and just be empty for a minute. Everyone, just be empty, hear, breathe, and sit. Just be." We sat silently.

"You are the vast, limitless space," he said quietly. "The 'I' that I am pointing to is the space in which all of this arises, including your body, including your mind, including your pain, your frustration—all of it. Just relax into it."

We were silent. Then Larry spoke up. "As soon as I relax, I feel an energy start pulsating. For the last few months, it's convulsed, but in the last few days it's started to smooth out. When I was in the Kalachakra today, it almost felt like I could ride that energy back to where I want to go. I wanted to surrender and go with it. Is that it?"

"Yes," Bartholomew agreed. "That's the same energy as the sound Chai was talking about. It will take you to the silence." He looked around.

"Look, all of you. Whenever awakenings take place, or when openings in consciousness begin to happen, the body experiences them in different ways. Sometimes it feels like you've plugged a 220 power line into a 110 wiring system. The power is jolting. Do whatever you can to stay with it and allow it to happen, even for a short time. Fall into that feeling of discomfort, as difficult as it is. If you don't divert it, the energy will make new pathways through the cellular structure of your body. It will run through your physical body and release blocked power. The cells will relax in a new way. Is it difficult? It can be. But please, don't forget, a lot of help is available, and a lot of willingness to help. You have to ride it out, but don't forget the wave you are riding on!"

Laurel laughed ruefully. "Sometimes I think this must be incredibly simple," she said.

"My friend, I keep telling you, *it is so simple you miss it!*" Bartholomew shouted in enthusiastic acknowledgment of the truth. "It is so obvious, it is so *what you are,* it is so constantly happening that you miss it! And when you say, 'I have to become aware of my awareness,' it is a joke!"

"If it's so simple," interjected Darcy, "if it's our birthright, why aren't there more enlightened people?"

"My dear," he responded, "that is an intellectual question and entirely understandable. You are getting ready to pop your illusory bubble. Before you do, you will choose to go through a lot of mental games, including asking more questions and having more doubts." He looked around. "I want you all to watch for this. When you finally maneuver yourself into a situation where you are forced to drop your limited beliefs, your ego will come up with a lot of mental chatter in the form of questions and doubts and 'Yes, buts . . .' The part of the ego that does not want the quest to end begins to ask unanswerable questions in an effort to distract you. When you wake up, you will realize that you are in a sea of enlightened ones, which includes everyone here. There are many enlightened ones, because *everyone* is enlightened. So please don't worry. You all have as much awareness as any one of God's creations has ever had or ever will have. You have as much potential as anyone, so do not let hopelessness overwhelm you.

"Great things are happening on your planet at this time. It is always humorous to hear people say 'nothing is happening' when so very much is happening. Just stay with the process. Don't worry. Nobody is getting away from anybody until *everyone* knows there is only *One*."

Bartholomew let his hands fall and leaned back. "All right," he said. "This is enough for today. Thank you, thank you, thank you," he said, bowing slightly to us, "and let us meet here again early tomorrow morning," he concluded.

Feathers One Day, Chicken the Next

I couldn't move. "Blown away" seemed an accurate description of what I was feeling—blown away, tired, angry, depressed, confused—and I didn't even know why! I moved myself from the veranda to a chair overlooking the valley. I propped my feet on the low stone wall and looked out with unseeing eyes. No one approached me. My mind nagged at me to remember what had been said, as though that was the solution to everything. Voices inside my head kept giving me different commands. Go farther into it! Let it go! Feel it! Work with it! Get it together! *Give it a rest,* I thought.

Gradually, amid a swarm of thoughts and feelings, I experienced a few simple moments of awareness. The warmth of a late afternoon sun on my skin, the sound of murmured voices, the bell on a donkey, the coolness of moving air. I could see again. The clouds were below me rushing through the valley. The tip of Mount Kinnaur Kailash poked its snowy crown into a pure blue sky. And I was hungry. *Enough of this,* I said to myself, and heaved myself up to search for dinner.

The meal turned out to be another gastronomic adventure. The group hiked all the way down to Peo since the taxis only came up from there. We crammed ourselves into an oversized tent. A cooking fire was burning in one corner, and several of us squeezed onto the bench nearest it to escape from the cold and damp of recent rains. The bench end promptly sank into the mud, resisting every effort to restore it to equilibrium. In desperation, we gathered nearby stumps and wooden crates to sit on. The menu was simple—a choice of chicken soup or fried lo mein. Hope surged through me. Lo mein meant noodles! Without hesitation I ordered, and sat hunched over the wooden table drinking chai, waiting to see what would appear.

The sharp pungent smell of garlic preceded the plate of dark, steaming noodles set down before me. I loaded my fork and took a bite. Every taste bud in my mouth collided in a mad scramble to be first to experience the sensation of pasta, fried in oil, swimming in soy sauce, and covered with bits of red chili and garlic. I dug in, finally leaning back when my plate was empty. Deeply satisfied, I was very willing to let myself be led to a waiting taxi. I was asleep before we reached home.

It was later the next day that I asked Mary-Margaret if she had written any more in her journal. With a sigh of weary patience, she rummaged through her backpack and handed me several small sheets of folded paper. I opened them and read.

Still no food, no cooks, no luggage. But what a wonderful bunch of Warriors this group is! They may gripe, but there is laughter in their tone. I sense very little self-pity. There even is laughter as we hurl ourselves down the mountain, slipping and sliding as we struggle through open

sewers that the grass has
disguised. "Dorothy, we're
not in Kansas anymore!"
YM got that right.

I'm in love with His
Holiness, with his voice
and laugh and total concentration. What a beautiful
way he has of Being Himself.
I find that the very
best way for me to sit
still for those long hours
in the ever-changing weather
is to rock front-to-back,
following his rhythm.
I can see him through
the sea of open umbrellas,
and I follow. Then it's
so easy. Movement, yet
not twitching and shifting

and poking out people's
eyeballs with my "brolly".

He talked today about
visualization, and what a
great aid it is in the
Tibetan Buddhist path. It
is so much a way for
the Tibetan Buddhists, and
seems to be extremely help-
full, totally necessary. Yet I
feel so distanced from it for
myself. Even trying to
visualize something "good"
ends by boring me. I can
remember the years when
I loved doing mantras and
visualizations, but it has
all fallen off. Since Bartholomew's arrival on the
scene, plus the years of
Ramana, I have begun

to realize that because
"doing Bartholomew" is
so effortless, I want
"doing Awakening" to also
be effortless. I can see
the mountains from my
bed if I really stretch,
and I don't feel them "doing"
themselves. Whatever they
are doing, if anything, it
seems to be effortless, yet
look at their immensity,
and beauty and wonder.

   Am I trying too hard?
Is "doing Bartholomew" my
teaching to be fearless
enough to just stop doing,
and to see what happens?
Whenever I tried to "do
Bartholomew", as I did in
the first months of the

work, it ended up a
mess. Somehow the
thinking mind and this
Bartholomew Space just
don't go together. It feels
like I have to choose one
or the other, to move around
in my mind or drop into
Bartholomew. I realize that
I have been learning, all
these years, what these
mountains seem to already
know — Bartholomew happens
when I just relax and
stop imagining, thinking,
desiring, trying, reaching.
It happens when I am
still, still deep inside.
And that is so simple,
this being still inside.
Is the inside always still

and I just don't notice? Yes, it seems like a resiful thing to start noticing!

Chapter 18

Kalpa: Day Three–
Bartholomew Answers
Personal Questions

T wang. *Twaang*, thud. Sharon had tripped over the staked lines holding our tent down in front of the physicians' residence. The sound of smothered laughter came from next door. Carolyn was still asleep. I dug out my flashlight and looked at the time. *It's morning,* I thought, poking my head outside.

The first strokes of light revealed an opalescent mist threading its way among the slate roofs of the town beneath us. In a long layer above it, a string of clouds was parked bumper to bumper over the valley, and the mountain thrust a snowy peak into the clear vault of sky, deep in conversation with the approaching sun.

Today we would have our audience with the Dalai Lama, whose private physician George had already seen. He had received medicine and instructions to go to Dharamsala when His Holiness returned there.

Our hosts rounded the corner of the building, carrying stacked trays of glasses and our stockpot filled with chai. I ducked inside and pulled on the same pants, shoes, and jacket I had been wearing since we left the bus at the landslide, and grabbed a glass of chai as I headed for Jim and Ellen's bathroom. When I returned, I could hear the gasps and groans of people bathing in the ice-cold mountain water. Guy, Clare, Rishi, and Deb emerged, appearing damp and cheerful.

After breakfast, we all settled down on the veranda, enjoying the drama of unfolding clouds below. Mary-Margaret came out, sat on her blanket, and closed her eyes. Justin, his wet hair slicked down, joined her and unpacked the small tape recorder. He carefully checked the tape and connections before handing her the microphone.

She opened her eyes. "So then, my friends, good morning," Bartholomew began, rubbing his hands together in anticipation. "Let us have a question-and-answer session today. I have had various people ask for one, and when the Kalachakra begins in a few hours, we will have other things to deal with. This is a good time for it."

Laurel took immediate advantage of the opportunity. "Yesterday you told us that when we wanted to ask for help, we should hold a picture in our minds. I've had trouble visualizing. In the last year, when I close my eyes there is great space." She could not contain her tears as she continued. "And I want to ask *you* for help, but I don't know how to visualize you, and I don't know if you are in the space."

"Yes!" Bartholomew responded joyfully. "Yes, I am, if the space is empty."

"It's empty!" she exclaimed.

"Then, yes, absolutely," he assured her. "My dear, not only what you call Bartholomew but also so much more is in that space that you can't miss the help. It's *all* totally and completely there, so, yes. You see, lovely one, when you begin to risk falling into that empty inner space, no idea or preconception can precede it. I mean, how much can you say about space? Very little. That makes it the perfect vessel for total awareness to move in. Therefore, instead of *you* putting rules on *it,* awareness can begin to reveal itself to you, past any ideas you have. It's perfect."

Laurel sniffed. "Will it reveal itself?" she asked.

"Try it and see," answered Bartholomew. Then, looking at her closely, he said, "Of course it will."

"Promise?" she asked, laughing.

"You have my word," he said quietly. "You do your job, and I'll do mine. Remember, we are in this together."

"I know," she said, smiling, "but I get real mad at you sometimes."

He laughed gleefully. "Most intensely involved people do. Oh, the number of obscenities I've heard!" he exclaimed. "It is very difficult when you are being spiritual to come up with a spiritual obscenity, but people manage." He smiled. "I have told you again and again that I welcome the arguments, the resistances, the volatile give and take. The person most difficult to reach is the one who is so unaware of the excitement of the process, or so uninterested that they have no response.

"As you begin to move with love toward this energy called Bartholomew, resentment will also arise. After all, they often arise together. They are polarities. You are going to have deep moments of caring when you say, 'Bartholomew, whoever you are, I love you,' and other moments when you say, 'Bartholomew, whoever you are, you are a pain.' One comes with the other in the world of duality. It is totally acceptable. Do I want your love? Yes, but I want your attention just as much! I don't care if your face is smiling or frowning. I will take either extreme at any time. Another way of saying it—I am big enough to take it all. And so are you. All of you." He looked at her intently. "I love you," he said simply.

"I would like to share an experience I had yesterday afternoon when we were chanting," Guy said. "I went into a meditative space, and it was such an uplifting feeling. My body was just stretching up and felt like a rushing sound, but without the sound. Is this the space?" he asked.

"Yes," Bartholomew agreed. "You are getting there. The rushing sound without the sound is the entrance. As they say in your country, 'Good on you, mate!' That's wonderful, beautiful. Well done!"

Roberta raised her hand. "I keep re-creating similar difficult situations in my life, where sometimes the players are different and sometimes the same players come back in. When I think I have worked through something, it shows up again maybe a year down the road. What am I failing to see in these situations?" she asked.

Bartholomew leaned back. "We can say various things about that," he mused. "You all learn your lessons in different ways, but we can make some general comments about the process. For example, men often learn their lessons differently than women. That is why it is sometimes difficult for men and women to learn together. The whole male/female situation begins with two different frames of reference, so when the two want to play together in a vaster sense, oftentimes you have to create a third kind of framework together."

He straightened up and leaned forward. "The masculine often learns through jobs, power, or logic in the physical world. The feminine takes a different stance. They are often more concerned with relationships and their intuitive world. So we have a very interesting situation when men and women get together. Men are reluctant to jump in and start playing in the emotional world, and women hesitate to jump out and play in the linear, logical world. It helps to create a third area of growth that is not *just* the emotional and is not *just* the logical. This can help keep you from going down the same old road of separation and loneliness. Right now you really think if you continue down those same old roads, you will keep learning new things. But there is the possibility that, as a woman, you have learned all you need to know about the emotional side of relationship, and what you need now is to create a place where you can meet the logical 'other' side and build a new way of being together. It can also be the opposite, with men willing to expand out of the logical into a new interconnected space that incorporates the intuitive."

A New Way of Growing

"Let me give you an example." Bartholomew made a circle with the thumb and forefinger of each hand and held them up. "Let's say one of these spheres represents the inner world of the feminine. The other represents the external world of the masculine." He moved the circles together until they overlapped. "When you bring the two together, you create a third area of integration larger than either of the other two. To do this, you must be willing to let the other person's reality into your belief structures. You have to be willing to allow in something that, at first, may seem foreign or dangerous to you. Allowing the new, perhaps uncomfortable, frame of reference to come in creates a willingness out of which a new way of learning emerges."

He dropped his hands. "It is necessary to bring these two parts together because, in reality, they are both parts of who you all are. Every woman needs to be more involved with the logical, linear world to be able to balance the checkbook and to explore a career. The inclusion of the opposite frame of reference brings growth. At the same time, men need to take risks in their emotional relationships, with all the spontaneous, nonmental interactions that process involves. Both may use relationships to begin this blending. You may say you are doing it 'for your love life,' but in reality you are doing something far more important. You are balancing your own psyche. You are trying to develop both parts of your being—for the masculine, to also be that soft, open, nourishing awareness; for the feminine, to develop power and skill in the world."

Bartholomew addressed Roberta directly. "So, my friend, when you consciously decide to create this new way of growing into your wholeness, it will happen. If you don't, you will go back down the same road of one-sided response in your relationships again and again. You are fortunate in your situation because you have a friend who is also working on his consciousness," he said, nodding to Larry. "It is more difficult for those who are in relationships with people who do not share such an interest. Those of you who do not have a motivated partner must forge ahead and have the courage to do this on your own."

He turned toward the rest of us. "There are many ways to grow. If you are tired of having no money, tired of the drama you are constantly creating in your life, be willing to create something else. People are always banging on their relationships to give them what they want and are then surprised when their relationships do not improve. The only thing happening is that everybody gets bruised and everybody gets bored. The old way is not working. *What* to do?

"We suggest you turn to another part of your life, and put your energy into that. The resulting feeling of self-esteem, delight, and enjoyment will blend back into the relationship. If you feel disempowered in any area of your life, concentrate on empowering a different one. Every time you empower any part of your world, *all* parts of your life benefit, and the power of your exciting creation will spill over into other people's lives as well."

Ellen caught Bartholomew's attention. "I know how to try very hard at my teaching job and feel that I do my best in the world. But I don't know how to do it with this path of Realization," she said. "I feel as if I don't try hard enough."

"My friend, that is almost a universal statement," he responded. "It is because most of you set very high standards for yourselves. You have an idea that you have to be an expert at what you do, never failing and never making mistakes. This is also true of your journey to awakening.

"I would like to relate an experience of Mary-Margaret's that I think applies to all of you," he said, leaning back. "This was many years ago, when we were just beginning our work together. She was often filled with terror for fear she would not do the work perfectly. She was afraid she would make some error in the delivery and that her mistakes would end up being dangerous and harmful to others. One day, as she was relaxing, we pushed through and gave her a message that was very clear and simple. I give it to you now: *If you wait to do whatever you are moved to do for God and humanity until you can do it perfectly, you never will! You must be willing to do the best you can and realize it is the best. Do not stop because you cannot do it perfectly.* In Mary-Margaret's case, and I'm sure she would not mind my stating this, she knew it was her ego telling her she had to be perfect in order to do the work. Had she listened, none of this would have happened.

"It is impossible for you to do 'spiritual things' perfectly. Simply be human, relax, and do your best. You can either look at all the things you have accomplished and say, 'Ah, good!' or look at all the things you haven't accomplished and say, 'Oh, bad.' It's entirely up to you. But be assured, the 'Oh, bads' do not help you generate a feeling of well-being inside yourself. If you listen to them, you are never going to experience peace. Even if you did your spiritual practices six or twelve hours a day, the need to be perfect would ensure your feeling badly about the hours you missed. If you make a plan that includes a realistic amount of time per day for your path and stick to it, you will find that you become more and more pleased with yourself." He smiled at her.

"You can't win if you have an idea that you have to stay aware 24 hours a day. That might be your final goal, but you are going to fall right on your face if you hold yourself to that now. You may have definite ideas about designated times or rituals necessary for you to have a sense of well-being in relationship to your path. But please be realistic about them. You may decide to meditate once a day, or decide that once every hour you are going to stop and drop into awareness. Maybe you wish to spend 20 minutes of your lunch break doing this. Know your limits, and make sure these short-term goals can be met. If you start punishing yourselves by doing things you don't want to just because you think you *should*, you are going to leave the path. It will be too difficult and will not give you a sense of well-being. A spiritual path is not taken to increase your sense of worthlessness.

"The Dalai Lama has talked about this from a slightly different point of view. He said that when you follow your path and throw yourself into it, obstacles begin to disappear. The illusion begins to dissolve, and you build the spiritual power to awaken. Every time you do your spiritual practice, you build a little more self-confidence. You accumulate a feeling of well-being, which is constantly there for you to call on. If you say, 'Maybe I'll meditate, and maybe I won't,' you will not build an awakened view of yourself. You will always be filled with guilt and restlessness over what you haven't done. If your focus is vague, as in, 'I'll just walk around being loving all day,' all you will notice is how many times you forget! It is easy to fall into robotlike living. It takes focus and desire to awaken.

"The smallest commitment to focus on 'what is now' helps you build your spiritual power. You can say, 'Well done,' because you do not feel remorseful or guilty. With that added increment of power, it will become easier to be more aware of each moment, thereby adding even more power to your desire to awaken. Every successful person, no matter in what area, knows they must spend a certain number of hours a day pursuing whatever goal they are focused on. You may think that this basic lesson doesn't apply to a spiritual path, but it does.

"If you have a partner, join with him or her, and work out a plan together. It is not loving to make important spiritual decisions that affect your relationship all by yourself. For example, and this happens a lot, one of the partners gets on a spiritual path and says, 'In order to be enlightened, I have to give up sex.' That is a unilateral decision that can end up being very harmful. So, if you have a partner of any kind, including children, make sure when you lay out your spiritual plans that you take everyone into consideration. There are always ways to do this with love and humor, if you will just look for them. Set realistic goals, be clear about them, and follow them. Then you will have a sense of well-being about yourself."

Patricia raised her hand and asked Bartholomew to talk about what we need to understand about emotional pain.

"Many of you have a belief that pain is some overwhelmingly terrifying monster that swoops down, or up, from some hidden place to overwhelm you and bury you in its depths. You have the idea that you somehow sink to the bottom of pain and then push off the bottom and make your way to the surface for air. But the truth is, emotional pain is a response of the cells to a thought that in the past has been painful. The cells 'remember' and respond by contracting, causing you pain. Instead of thinking about the pain, or making up ways to get away from it, simply allow that feeling to fully enter you. No resistance, no thoughts about it, just feel it fully—really experience it with full gusto. Welcome it with interest, and you will find on close observation what the true nature of pain is. And when you discover that, you will no longer fear it. At the center of emotional pain is the very same mysterious life that is at the center of all energy, all form, all formlessness."

After a moment's silence, Judith spoke up. "How do we get our cells and our bodies to feel safe and at home in this really unsafe world?" she asked.

"Excellent question," replied Bartholomew. "The cells, if allowed to relax, would feel very much at home in the world. The Earth plane is their natural environment, and your cells are aware of this 'at-homeness.' But they take directives from the mind, which often creates fear by using past events and future worries. If you continually churn fear thoughts through your system, the cells will respond by contracting. This increases the fear, which cycles into yet more contraction.

"So what is recommended? Allow yourself to fully feel *whatever* is present without trying to push it away. Get out of your mind and into your body.

Breathe it, feel it, and be aware of it. You will start to feel 'at home' and alive in your body. Create thoughts about the magnificence of the body. Allow yourself to love and cherish your body, again and again. This will make it a safe place in which to live."

Changing Your Sexual Dialogue

Clare's hand shot up. "I have a question about sexuality," she said. "I have this partner whom I love so much, but I just keep shutting down sexually. What am I doing wrong?"

Bartholomew looked at her closely. "What a brave woman for bringing this up!" he exclaimed. "You are not doing anything 'wrong,' but let us go into it more fully." He turned and addressed us all. "One of the greatest misunderstandings is the statement that sex is simple. I think without question that sex and sexuality are two of the hardest physical expressions to experience with joy and a sense of well-being. The insidious idea that all you have to do is jump into bed and something called 'sex' takes over is a mockery of the truth. What really takes over is not some storybook creation, but all of the incredible conflicting sexual messages you have ever heard. No chakra in the entire system is given as many contradictory messages as your sexual center. For the most part, you are totally confused about it, and when you love someone, you run right up against all that confusion. You try to push it away and find you can't. Then comes the guilt, sorrow, and withdrawal.

"There *are* solutions. Those messages the mind has given to the physical body about sexuality have come from many places. The number-one solution is to take your notebook and write down all the ongoing, nauseatingly familiar dialogue you are constantly giving yourselves about sexuality and sex. Do not limit it to the negative, because the positive can be just as frightening. Allow the lid of your underground world to open, and be willing to really see what is there."

He spoke to Clare directly. "Let us postulate a situation from childhood. You, as a lovely young lady of 13, are entering puberty. I do not imagine your parents gave you a lot of positive encouragement about your sexuality at that time. In fact, they might have even suggested that you were too young to have such feelings or that such feelings were unnatural. You were undergoing the physical change from child to adult, and they may have even advised you not to think about it," he said wryly. "Do you understand what mixed messages you were getting? Your mind says no while your body is saying yes." Many of us nodded in agreement. "So get the confusing messages out. You might end up laughing because there are so many contradictory, funny ones. Embedded in this mess, you will discover all kinds of conflicting feelings about the good, bad, and indifferent information you have received. By uncovering it, you will begin to hear the programming more clearly."

He turned to us, grinning openly. "I never thought of myself as a sex counselor, but here we go. Number two—and the Buddha would love this— just as one of the basic approaches to finding your True Nature and the bliss of God-Consciousness is through visualization, so the same can be true with sexuality. Frankly, the people who are most sexually successful will tell you that much of the reason for their success comes from a combination of visualization and staying fully focused in the moment. Using this combination, they create a feeling of beauty and openness.

"Partners can build this sense of beauty through visualization. The thought-form you create together becomes real and begins to emit the feeling of love. This feeling blends back into the cells of the body. The body listens, because the body has been trained to listen. Give your body a wonderful vision of the two of you, and share it with your partner. Together you can build a thought-form that feels beauty-full and safe. These visualizations can transform your experience. Remember, what you focus on becomes more alive, whether it be positive or negative. You have been focusing on negative sexual thought-forms. Now is the time to focus on positive ones.

"Sex is a very difficult arena to play in. It can be very painful, and yet it is claimed to be the opposite. Your cells follow your beliefs. They resist the experience of sexual sharing when all those past experiences and your responses to them have created fearful pictures in your mind. Create a picture that will flood your cells with delight at the excitement of fulfilling the new sexual awareness you have created." Bartholomew paused. "And that is my answer," he concluded.

"What if you're not *in* a relationship?" asked someone from the back of the porch.

He looked at us steadily. "That is more difficult," he conceded. "To create a dynamic sexual visualization for yourself without someone else present can create physical and emotional frustration. Sometimes you simply have to acknowledge that, at this time and in this place, given your present situation, sex is not in your karmic picture. This is not to say that it cannot be at a later time, but this will not be helpful to you right now. I will also say that if you have created a life where a sexual relationship is absent, it hasn't been created by mistake. It was not that the 'karma committee' withheld something you needed when you weren't looking. The lack of this opportunity in your life is not there as punishment, but to give you the space to learn something different, something that may be necessary for your awakening."

He took a slow sip of water. "Let me explain what I mean," he said. "You can program a period of time or an entire life where sexual activity is not present for the very basic reason that you need to awaken to other aspects of your life. You may not like that on the conscious or physical level, but you can't fight your destiny. You *can* fill your cells with the willingness to radiate power, love, and openness without an emphasis on sex. You can radiate it to yourself, to others, and to everything equally. Power attracts power. Building your power sets up a silent sound, and the sound resonates back to you and increases.

"If you believe you don't have what you consider a 'successful' sexual life, whether it's nonexistent or just in a mess, you set up a very different sort of sound. This also becomes a subliminal part of your cellular and emotional response. The resonation cannot bring you what you want, because you're sending out the wrong message. When you are sending out messages such as, 'I am not very good at this,' or 'I won't get what I want,' or 'I'm not able to give,' that is what comes back to you.

"So, again, a suggestion. All you can do is be responsible for filling your cells with the message that you have a magnificent physical body, radiant with power, love, and energy, freely given, and leave the rest to karma. Then, if it is in your grid for someone to experience that sexual aspect with you, so be it. If it isn't, you won't have that lonely sense of deprivation, of not having what you need, because you will have received what you needed from yourself. If that isn't irresistible, I don't know what is.

"Some of your sexual frustration is not sexual at all, but a frustration because the body has not received enough attention. You feel that the attention has to come from someone outside yourself. Well, if that someone outside is not there, and *you* do not do something to help the cells feel nourished, they are going to feel deprived. The feeling may or may not be sexual, but you may interpret the feeling as very sexual. So see what is real, and respond accordingly." He leaned back, relaxing.

Emmy looked up and addressed Bartholomew in a low voice. "I still have a tremendous sadness that I have hurt my son. He never should have been hurt or belittled in any way or made to feel less than the wonderful person he is." She stopped and swallowed hard. "I think you get the idea."

He peered at her. "Are you stating that no woman should give birth to a child unless she is going to be the perfect mother? If this were true, do you know how many children would be on this planet? None!" he said ruefully. "Because the enlightened ones usually aren't interested in having children, and the rest of you are pretending to be imperfect. You say you have damaged your son, and, at the same time, you say he is wonderful. So I ask you, if he is so badly damaged, how does it happen that he is so wonderful?" He paused briefly. "I am asking you to stop scolding yourself for being human," he added gently.

"I would love to," she agreed.

"Dear one, it is your ego speaking, not your love. Love says to him, 'Sweetheart, I made some mistakes, and you made some mistakes. That's the way it goes and I love you.' It is your ego creating the pain. Love understands itself. Love admits that imperfect events are created, yet love still remains present. Does your son know you love him to death? Yes he does!" he said emphatically. "All of this agony is coming from *you*. It is not coming from *him*. If I could be blunt with you, my friend, you are suffering from a torqued ego. It's the ego that's pushing you in the wrong direction, away from awakening to all the love you have shared and toward areas of guilt, sorrow, and doubt."

Bartholomew turned to the rest of us and explained. "She raised this child alone for many years. Did she make some mistakes? Yes, why not? Why would she be the exception? And he has made mistakes, too, and will continue to. That is the way of it." He looked at Emmy. "Lovely one, please realize, when this feeling of guilt comes up, it is your ego. It is destroying the joy, delight, and love you feel for your son. You can either fall into guilt or stay with the love."

"I would like to get out of guilt," she said quickly.

"All right, simply remember each time it comes up that it is your ego screaming accusations at you, just to keep a curtain between you and the love you feel for this young man. Because, my friend, as long as you feel the guilt, you cannot feel the love, and that can end up, in your terms, being damaging. So just stop it! Begin to respect yourself as a dynamic, supportive, loving mother, and remember the infinite number of times you *were* that. Guilt is keeping you separate from the beauty of that realization, and I ask you to just let it go!"

He looked at us silently, a small smile turning up the corners of Mary-Margaret's mouth. "All of the difficulties you have presented today are absolutely legitimate concerns of consciousness. At the same time, I would like you to remember, this child you are worried about, this deficiency you think you have, whatever pain, guilt, or loss you are feeling; all of it is totally *temporary*. It is just phenomena rising and falling in a vast sea of God-Light and Power. Eventually you will know that whatever you are experiencing is *not at all important; nor is it real*. Reality is that vast awareness in which all of this takes place. Yes, be aware of the drama; play your part with gusto, but never lose sight of what is Real. Reality is the awareness ever-present in both pain and pleasure, winning and losing, having and not having. Don't overlook the obvious. Bliss is here and now."

He gestured toward Emmy as he spoke to the rest of us. "You would have done your son a terrible disservice if you had always been 'perfect,' whatever that means. How painful it would have been for him to walk out into an imperfect world and out of your paradise. You are all human beings. You do the best you can with what you have. That is the way of it, and, at the same time, *it is not who you are*. It is a temporary situation, and the job is *always the same*—to awaken to that ever-living, abundant awareness that thunders through all of these many-changing facets of consciousness. You will all find it, because it never left you. Your job is not to be happy; *it is to become aware*. Never forget that, and, at the same time, play the drama with as much delight and openness as you can." Bartholomew dropped his hands and leaned back.

"All right, that's enough for today. You need to get ready for the audience with His Holiness this afternoon. If you'd like to ask him a question, write it down and give it to Chai. She and Mary-Margaret will go over them and remove any duplicates before the meeting. Make sure it's the deepest question you can think of. Being close to His Holiness is a wonderful opportunity. You will be together, eye to eye, heart to heart, the Self with the Self—only One. Thank you all, and I'll see you tomorrow."

A Precious Audience with His Holiness

Before the group could disperse, a commotion broke out from the side of the building. Around the corner came Neima and Jumpa, heavy cartons of water balanced on their shoulders and huge grins across their faces. Guy and Larry jumped to grab the water as we surrounded the two Tibetans, laughing, shaking hands, and pounding their backs. Chai extracted herself from the crowd and called for order.

"The buses have arrived!" she shouted to mad applause. "*With* the missing luggage," she added above the noise. "A quick lunch will be ready soon, and we'll have dinner here tonight," she concluded triumphantly.

We scattered, everyone in a hurry to get ready. I headed down the hill to the parking area to collect my bag and some clean clothes. Others moved purposefully toward bathrooms and their red plastic buckets. A few people pressed folded questions into Chai's hand as they left to get ready. Carolyn backed carefully out of the tent holding a long, white box. It contained the prayer stick[25] we had brought from the mountains of Taos as a gift for His Holiness here in the mountains of the Himalayas. No one had seen it yet, and we planned to open it right before we left.

Jumpa reappeared with a tray piled high with stacks of sandwiches. Neima was close behind, lugging our big pot full of chai. Everyone grabbed a sandwich and a drink as they passed. Multicolored shirts, skirts, vests, scarves, jewelry, and sashes appeared like magic. Just like kids, we wanted to look our best for a beloved teacher. At last we were ready. Carolyn unpacked the prayer stick, and I held it aloft. There were murmurs of approval and exclamations of delight as the wind set the feathers dancing and the sun struck rays of colored light from the crystals. The stick passed from hand to hand, so everyone could place a prayer in it. Chai also gave out the white prayer scarves she and Russell had managed to obtain for the ceremony. They showed us how to fold them so the scarf would fall between our hands when we opened them. It was the way the Dalai Lama would bless us.

Then, very carefully, we picked our way down the familiar rock-strewn path to our seats. Everyone was nervous. We straightened each others' clothing and tried to keep ourselves clean on the dusty ground. Our neighbors turned to stare at the fine clothes and fidgety bodies. We shushed and elbowed each other until Chai came and beckoned us to follow her. In single file, we all quickly marched behind the dais and around to the far side of the gompa. There, we removed our shoes, and a small monk bowed us in.

Inside, everything vibrated with strong, bright colors, and the energy hummed around us. We had no time to stare at the intricacies of the giant sand mandala that had been so painstakingly created for this ceremony. The monks quickly seated us on the carpeted floor, and His Holiness came in, smiling and nodding. He sat on a platform and greeted us in English.

His secretary approached with our questions in hand. His Holiness briefly answered several about meditation and the Buddhist way. Then he picked up another folded paper and read, "I work in a healing profession and have discovered that I have a serious physical problem. I'm concerned that I won't be able to help others because of it. Can you help me?" It was George's question! The Dalai Lama held the piece of paper in his hand a moment, then smiled.

"Help *yourself* first," he said, "or you won't be able to help anyone else. Do not worry about it being a problem. We all have problems." He burst into gleeful laughter. "Even *I* have problems. We do what we can in the face of them and trust it will be enough."

The Dalai Lama's expression became thoughtful as he read another slip of paper. "You ask how you may help the Tibetan people who are suffering from Chinese atrocities," he said.

There was a common concern among the group about the fate of the Tibetans remaining in Tibet under the Chinese occupation. We knew about the 70,000-plus Tibetans killed since the Chinese invasion, and we also knew that a great majority of them had been monks and nuns. Many of us had seen news photos of the destruction of their monasteries and had heard about the sacred objects that had been systematically stolen by the Chinese. What, we wondered, could we do about it?

The Dalai Lama's answer was simple and direct. "Whenever the opportunity to help presents itself," he said, "no matter how small it may seem, please act on it. Whether it is political or economic, directly or through prayer, please act on it."

Then he picked up the last question and read, "On the final day of the Kalachakra, there will be an opportunity to participate in the Initiation. How can we take these vows that we know we cannot possibly fulfill given our different lifestyles?"

The vows included renunciation of a large array of foods, colorful clothing, and sexual relationships; along with the commitment to adhere to certain prayers and rituals, among other things.

The Dalai Lama remained silent for a moment. With supreme compassion, he gave a slight bow and replied, "Simply take it as a blessing." Then he signaled to his monks and got to his feet.

"Come," said his secretary. "His Holiness wants to take a picture with you." We jumped up and immediately arranged ourselves around him. He held Chai and Mary-Margaret's hands as one of the monks scooped up a camera from the floor and took the picture.

"No, no," said His Holiness. "The flash wasn't working. Try again." The monk chose another camera and tried again.

"Wait," said His Holiness. "No flash. Try one more time." The monk laughed and picked up a third camera. When we were ready, he pressed the button and the flash went off. Then, one by one, the Dalai Lama took our scarf-draped hands between his and blessed us. I gave him our prayer stick and told him where it was from. "Very beautiful," he said, passing it to his secretary. Then he was gone. Carolyn nudged me. "That was *my* camera that finally took the picture," she whispered. We filed back out of the gompa in a daze and took our places as the Kalachakra began.

The next morning, Mary-Margaret handed over her previous day's journal without my even asking.

This day felt like we were really transported to another World, another culture, another wonder. Our private meeting with His Holiness was so much more than I had expected. Sitting there in front of him, surrounded by ancient thankas that covered the walls from floor to ceiling, and before us the incredible sand mandala it just wasn't any reality I had ever experienced before or had ever dreamed I would be able to. Power, focused and full, yet bright and light everywhere! His Holiness' laughter as he said "Even the Dalai Lama has problems! Many problems! Everybody has problems!" His plea for us to work for world peace, to do what we could to bring harmlessness into our lives and into the world and to do what we could to help his people — all this modern-world down-to-earth practicality in the midst of the most ancient setting. Wonder-full. Short, but oh so sweet. A time to treasure for a lifetime. I feel such gratitude, and

realize I want everyone I
know to share this moment
with me. So I think of
everyone I know, all in
one bundle of energy, and
bring them into this
moment with me. It feels like
all of us here, this small
group, are really here for
so many others. The
group seems to be full
to overflowing.

Afterwards, too full to
sit quietly, I walked along
the road that meandered
through the hills above the
village. I keep feeling "This
is really real. I am here!
This is really happening.
I'm walking along an ancient
path in the most sacred

mountain range in the world.
The presence of such
holiness, such wonder!"
Yet it all still seems so
dream-like, giving me the
feeling that I sometimes
get of watching things
happen to Mary-Margaret,
watching intently so that
it can be recalled again
and again—savored and
held close.

I had been concerned
about whether to actually
take the final initiation,
because there was absolutely
no way that I would ever
be able to keep all the vows
of renunciation that the
initiation requires. I don't
even want to! So how to

reconcile? His Holiness made it so easy. When asked, his response was simply "Take it as a blessing." How simple how perfect, how easy to do. I can do that with the deepest gratitude and respect.

❧ ✻ ☙

Chapter 19

Kalpa: Day Four—Space and a Meditation on Emptiness

Bartholomew cleared his throat and opened his eyes. "Well, my friends, good morning," he said. "I would like to begin today's discussion by pointing out some similarities between the silence of the inner path, which we could call 'our way,' and what we have been so delightfully observing during the Kalachakra these last few days. It is easy to notice the surface differences of things and ignore the deeper similarities. There is but one Truth, and the one Truth is gloriously free of all dogma." Mary-Margaret settled herself more comfortably as Bartholomew continued.

"If you were listening carefully to what His Holiness said yesterday, you may have observed that he was talking about the same spiritual pyramid of consciousness we discussed in Shimla. He gave instructions for following the Sutras, as well as the path of Tantra. As he talked about Tantra, he revealed two approaches—one for those who felt they could follow the higher path, and one for those who did not feel they could reach such lofty heights. He told those who chose the less rigorous path not to worry, but to absorb as much of the teachings as they could accept. He is a marvelous 'father' in the way he encourages all his 'children,' is he not? It was a masterful presentation, giving comfort and encouragement to everyone, no matter where they were on the pyramid.

"When he spoke about the highest part of the Tantric path, he was talking about a meditation on emptiness. As he discussed the meditation, he presented the concept of visualization as the way to achieve it. He also made it clear that anyone who wished to, had the ability to meditate on any form of the Buddha. He further stated that the Buddha had assisted many of his disciples in their meditations, helping to inspire magnificent visions of himself and the Bodhisattvas. These visions of Buddhas and the great Bodhisattvas differ from each other. Why? His Holiness stated it clearly: Everyone needs something different. As the benevolent father, he doesn't tell you which form to meditate on. He allows you to make that inner decision for yourself.

"He went on to discuss two different but related approaches to the meditation on emptiness. One is to envision the deity as outside yourself, then meditate on the emptiness *within* the deity. The other is to see *yourself* as that deity and meditate on the emptiness within. This meditation on deities is truly brilliant, as it encourages meditation on vast beings, not on what we would call 'lesser' images. In the work we do together, we have simply sidestepped the necessity to envision the form of an enlightened being or deity. We ask you to acknowledge that everything inside and outside yourself already contains spacious awareness or emptiness. That way, every time you open your eyes, you are looking at emptiness, because emptiness is at the core of everything. And every time you close your eyes and look 'within,' there, too, is emptiness.

"There is nothing purer than the space around you. I don't care if you are in Los Angeles in the middle of the worst degree of air pollution—the space itself cannot be tainted. Space *cannot* be tainted. Just as you can take a piece of gold and create the ugliest, most 'evil,' most harmful form with it, the distorted image does not change the nature of the gold. It is the nature of space to be absolutely pure in essence, and whatever is in it cannot affect that essence. So you can forget thinking that there is good space or bad space, higher space or lower space. It's *all* one space.

"Medical research has come up with the statement that your body is 99 percent space. That is a lot of space! When you turn your awareness to that mystery, dropping all conceptions about the space, you will find that it is pure awareness without form, words, or boundaries. It, too, is the vastness of Life itself, without any limits. It does not need anything added to it or taken from it. It doesn't have to seek anything. It doesn't have to be purified or let go of. It simply is what it is. In this respect, the Buddhist path and our path are similar, if you stick to the basic, essential teaching of emptiness.

"The Dalai Lama speaks to and touches the hearts and souls of the 17,000 people who are here, some of whom are attending the Kalachakra without the slightest idea of what it's all about. They come simply to be in his presence. At the same time, many of the most exalted monks in his order are also here, ready for this high initiation in the Tantric path. You have two diverse needs, and both are being met. When you listen to the Dalai Lama, please appreciate the magnificence of what he is doing and how he does it with the most incredible humor, charm, power, and delight possible. When His Holiness speaks, the power is present. It is a beautiful thing. So may we suggest that you just relax, be still, and become aware." Bartholomew leaned back again.

"There is a lot of discussion in the West as to whether or not His Holiness is an enlightened being. That is because many people have very different ideas about how an enlightened one lives his or her life in the world. They usually expect the enlightened one to stay in one place, drawing people to him or her for teaching and silence. This is true, but there are many ways to move in enlightenment. There are no rules on how one should act. His Holiness stated categorically that no one can teach the Dharma who is not enlightened." He leaned toward us. "And what was he doing? He was teaching the Dharma! So let us put the question of his enlightenment to rest. Out of his own mouth came the answer to the question.

"The Dalai Lama is a man who is also politically adept, able to maneuver in and out of all the nonsense that goes on in those circles. He keeps his balance and his humor in the midst of some tremendous difficulties. Imagine the amount of pressure exerted psychically on him by the many thousands of people looking to him as their spiritual leader. Then add to it their intense pain, rage, and fear over what has happened to their country. He acts as a sponge, absorbing all of this, because he is the father to those people. It is an incredibly difficult job, and, in the midst of it, what do you see? A marvelously alive, capricious, laughing entity. The person you had an audience with yesterday in the gompa was not the same one you saw the day before. The intensity of the man was much stronger because he is increasing his power each day. It was a highly charged interview. He was manifesting more than what your eyes could see. He spends many hours each night preparing for the next phase of the initiation. Then he channels that energy into the rituals you observe. The intensity will continue to increase as the days progress.

"Having said all that, I would also like to remind you that a tremendous amount of latent power is in these mountains called the Himalayas. Whether you choose to go to the initiation, walk on the mountain road, or take the day off and stay right here, I want you to be open to it all. The impact of what you are experiencing has caused many of you to close down on the cellular level because personal physical fears around the 'foreignness' of this place are rising up in you. Your cells are following the messages of fear buried deeply in your minds.

"Many of you are finding yourselves on an emotional seesaw. One moment you're happy; the next you're afraid. You are often moving between agony and ecstasy. It's all part of that delightful creation known as the human condition, which is duality itself. And that is absolutely all right. Nothing needs to change. All will be well if you can just watch the different responses as you would an interesting play where the actors and plot shift and change. If you try to be consistently happy and to make the people around you consistently happy, you are missing the point. The point is to go through *all of it,* to be aware of the ever-changing faces of your experiences, and to learn that you really can get to the place where you do not prefer one aspect over another.

"If someone is miserable, it is not your job to tell them they should be happy. Your job is to admire their unhappiness, just as you would admire their happiness. Your job is to remember that they are manifesting a part of you that *you* are not manifesting at the moment but *could* at any time. Follow it all with awareness. One morning you will wake up frowning, and the next you will wake up smiling. None of it matters. What matters is the observation of each other and your very self, because that's what reveals the ever-changing face of human consciousness. You *must* learn to accept it all and quit demanding that your world always smile at you. If you are not always smiling, why do you expect it to? Sometimes it does, and sometimes it doesn't. One is not preferable over the other, unless you hold to the doctrine that your purpose in life is to live happily ever after." Bartholomew leaned forward. "Ladies and gentlemen," he said lightly, "that is the ending line of many fairy tales, not the end purpose of Life." He smiled.

"One of the most important things His Holiness said to you in your private session with him yesterday was 'Sometimes I have problems.' The enlightened one says this with a smile on his face and a twinkle in his eye. No self-pity, no needing not to have problems. There is no escape from the rise and fall of the human cycle for you or for him, and there is no necessity to escape. He knows this.

"Did you notice that wonderful moment in the midst of yesterday's formal ritual when one of his monks was presenting him with something, and he playfully smacks him over the head! Everyone is being so serious, and His Holiness smiles and goes whack, right over the head. Wake up! What a gift that smack was. It was amazing that the young monk didn't drop what he was holding. It was a marvelous moment, filled with humor and lightheartedness. People all over the world will see it on film, and it may begin to change their ideas of what is holy. In that moment of authenticity, the Dalai Lama weakened the false beliefs about how a wise one moves in the world. In him we have a very human awareness just being himself, and, at the same time, pulsating with amazing power." Bartholomew dropped his hands and took a sip of water.

"I bring this to your attention because many people are less than enthusiastic about awakening to their enlightenment. They are afraid it is going to be boring. Look at His Holiness. Does he look bored? This man is having a wonderful time traveling around the world, praying and meditating, talking and laughing with people, and spreading peace and unity wherever he goes. He deeply knows that all of it is an illusory play that rises and falls in the whole of what he would call Buddha-Mind, what I call the space of Awareness. It rises and falls, containing within it what the Dalai Lama referred to as the Clear Light, and what I call the Essence.

"The Clear Light is without personification, without preference, without judgment. After all, how much can you say about Clear Light? It has no form, shape, or color and is always simply, presently clear. That is the highest teaching in the spiritual pyramid, and the Dalai Lama revealed it. We are back to where we began. The Essence, that which was present before form and consciousness arose, was the Clear Light. If you can go about your day looking for the Clear Light within yourself, in everyone else, and in everything around you, you *will* awaken to its reality.

"This is what all of these great ones are saying," He gestured toward Kailash again. "There will be a time when these magnificent mountains move into another kind of formation, just as you will move into another kind of formation. The form does not matter, because it is the Clear Light doing it all. Buddhism is a magnificent teaching and worthy of your admiration. At the highest, it carries *the* truth of consciousness, and, at the very bottom, it carries hope, structure, and organization for people who need those things to enable them to begin their journey on the path of consciousness. Does that mean you all need to become Buddhists? Of course not. But please leave here with gratitude for having spent these days immersed in one of the greatest paths that has ever come to this planet. And its teaching, at its essence, is no different from the one we present. Are there questions?"

Laurel straightened up. "Is enlightenment the end of the path?" she asked.

Bartholomew looked at her in amusement. "Do you think the Dalai Lama is finished?" he replied. "He has just arrived at a stage where, when he chooses to go on, he will be ready to create a model of consciousness that is even vaster than what he is creating now. The paths you are all on keep changing all the time. As each one of the enlightened ones goes on, each presents new information for whoever will listen. All of this is an ongoing, endless, flexible expansion and deepening."

Laurel shrugged. "It's like, if you reach it . . ." she stopped and started again. "There's always this war going on inside me. I want to reach it, but if I do, I worry maybe it's over."

"Now you know just by the observation of His Holiness that it's not," responded Bartholomew. "What a gift. I keep telling you, enlightenment is ever-exciting, ever-playful, ever-extending. Do you think I, whatever 'I' am, is finished? That would mean an end to consciousness." He glanced around. "Do you think I am going back to sit in the void like this?" Mary-Margaret slumped over, her eyes glazed. "Full of voidness? No, how boring," he added, straightening up. "Submerge yourselves in the excitement and robustness of life in whatever way it unfolds. The ways are endless."

The Power of Chi

"Many of you fall out of awareness as the day goes on. True?" We agreed. "As the outer world gets more frantic, you get more distracted. Distraction bleeds away your focus, your awareness of the power within. That's all the path is about, focusing on the moment enough to break through the illusion into Reality. There are various ways to do this, so let's talk about some." He paused and took a sip of water.

"Yesterday the Dalai Lama spoke about building your *chi*. The word *chi* has several meanings, so let us just call it your 'personal' energy or life force. You cannot focus this energy simply by thinking about it, because thinking is only a mental process. But it's a good place to start. Let us say, for example, you are building a home and have a structural problem you have been worrying about. As you focus more and more on the situation, seeing it in your mind's eye, you begin to sense the shape of an answer. Something in your heart rises up to meet it, accept it, and agree with it. Your entire body joins with the mental idea to produce some action.

"We can use other examples. Let us say you are wondering about whether to move, buy a car, start a new job, have a child, marry, or partake in any of the exhilarating choices you humans have. When you focus in quiet observation on your choices, things begin to clarify, and if you are paying attention, you will notice that energy begins to move in the body as well. What makes action happen in not strictly a mental process, but the motion of the mind plus the fullness of the body." He laughed. "You would not be here in India if your heart and body had not followed your mind.

"You have had many mental inspirations you have not focused on and put into action. Therefore, you have not gathered your power or chi in those areas. When you gather power in one area of your life, it expresses itself in other areas. You gather power upon power, from all parts of your being. In one sense, we could say that the whole purpose of life is to gather enough chi to break through the illusion of separation to the Truth.

"What gathers chi? When you focus on your thoughts and inspirations, discover what is true for you, and then act on them. Follow through. Stay awake. That gathers chi." He leaned forward and looked at us closely. "Congratulations to all of you for gathering enough chi to get here," he said. "And to be accepting and loving toward each other and those others you have met along the way. Well done." He smiled. "It has taken a lot of chi, perhaps more than you thought you had at times." He leaned back. "Stay totally focused. Stop your mind from drifting. *Focusing* gathers chi.

"Here is another thing that builds chi," Bartholomew continued. "In the midst of resentment and anger, when you so badly want to withdraw from or attack another person, do not follow through. That gathers chi," he said simply. "Every time you follow the impulse to strike out or withdraw through fear, chi disperses. All of a sudden you have lost something, and you can feel it as a loss of energy in the body. Contrast this feeling of loss with what happens in the body when you move toward someone in love. You receive something for yourself as well as for them. It's like the difference between taking your hands and pushing something away, which disperses power, and pulling it to you, which brings it in. You gather your chi when you recognize that you would like to scream, stomp, or otherwise act out what you are feeling to the person in front of you, and instead choose to silently join with them in love in whatever way you can."

Bartholomew rested an arm on Mary-Margaret's knee. "I will tell you another way you lose chi," he said, leaning toward us. "Every minute you spend mentally gossiping about what is 'wrong' with other people, *you* lose. The relentless mental judgment of your perceived world constantly drains you of chi. Please understand, you either gather your chi, or you give it up. Those are your only choices. If you are feeling weak today, chances are that you lost chi yesterday. The physical/mental/emotional gathering of energy is a way of empowering yourself. It is very simple," he said, relaxing. "It happens when you are totally aware and present in the moment, even if you are full of the grumblies. You don't have to be smiling to stay aware. You can be furious and stay in the moment, aware of your fury, and aware of the tension and heat in your body.

"If you feel guilty about something you have done, instead of simply worrying about it and prolonging the guilt, try something different. Consciously decide to attempt not to repeat the action that has produced the guilt. The decision *not* to do something harmful builds chi. Or, if you feel you have harmed another person, consider going to them in reconciliation. Either way, deal with it and drop it. Guilt is one of the greatest depletors of chi."

Darcy raised her hand. "I understand I'm riding a phenomenal wave of power through this place, the people, and the Dalai Lama, and I feel a dread about going home," she said earnestly. "Again and again, I've had the experience of the power we all bring in together, only to lose it when I'm back home in the life I left behind. I want so much to keep it. What can I do?" she asked.

"My friend, the answer is going to be very mundane," responded Bartholomew. "You just have to stay in the moment *wherever* you are, exactly as that moment presents itself. The mind is what deflects you when you go home. It becomes very busy because of your many obligations there. Here, you don't have to think about anything. You can allow others to handle the details. You simply go along for the ride, experiencing the power. You must remember; there is no more power in the moment *here* than there is in Santa Cruz, California. It is the *idea* that certain moments are more powerful than others that deflects you."

He laughed. "Believe me, you all gathered as much chi on that bus ride coming here as you have since sitting with the Dalai Lama. Every one of you stayed in the moment. You stayed with your terror, your frustration, and your anger. You were humorous. You chanted your hearts out. You did it beautifully." Bartholomew paused. "And I want you to know," he added brightly, " that it's not going to be as bad going back." We breathed a sigh of relief.

"Remember yesterday," he continued, "when the Dalai Lama stated that only the most advanced lamas are able to teach the path of anger. Let's talk about that in relation to chi. Anger is a helpful tool if you use it as your own personal teaching technique. When anger is present, acknowledge it. Hold it to you. Do not hurl it at someone else. At its deepest level, it has *nothing* to do with the other person. Do not lose the power of your chi by attacking someone else or by thinking *about* it. It is your power. Stay with it. Become selfish about your anger. Feel it, understand it, get close to it, and find out what it has to say to *you*. Experience it in your body, fully. Watch what images come up in your mind. *No judgment!* This is the path. This is gathering your chi. When you stay with the anger without judgment, you discover what is at the very center of anger. It is the same at the center of everything—Awareness, the Self, God."

Bartholomew stood up and began pacing. "All right," he said, "let's talk about sexual chi. You have sexual desire for lots of people, whether you claim it or not. We would suggest, however, that acting out that energy with everyone you feel attracted to might create some dramatic messes in your life. So, you might consider not acting on them. Hold on to that sexual fire. Like any strong energy, it can teach you many lessons. You do not have to be in sexual relationships to use this energy. It is a part of having a body, and it can help your spiritual transformation tremendously. Do not run from or toward these feelings. Simply pull them up and into the heart, and allow them to melt it. It is not a difficult path. God certainly does not smile on people who have sexual partners and frown on those who don't, or the other way around. So use what is present in the moment. The more you pull the power up, the warmer the heart gets. This is building your sexual chi. Then one day the heart gets hot enough to burst into flame." He stopped and sat down. "Are there any questions about any of this?"

Linda answered. "What I have been working on that seems the most effective for me is opening to the love. And I'm wondering, is there something behind the love?" she asked.

Bartholomew smiled impishly at her. "I'm not going to answer that," he replied. "Keep going; keep going. You are onto it."

"You don't have any little, ah, helpful hints?" she asked with a smile.

"I wouldn't dream of interfering at this stage," Bartholomew answered, laughing. "It's as though you've been taking skiing lessons for years and are on your own for the first time. You're starting down the slope when the instructor yells, 'Wait, I have one more thing to tell you!' What would happen? You'd fall flat on your face. So keep going. You don't need any more words. All the help you'll ever need is always present."

What Is *the Ego?*

Guy raised his hand, and Bartholomew nodded to him. "I know the times I'm distracted most from being in the moment are when I'm indulging in total happiness or total sadness and I feel it's related to the ego. Yet, when I'm in the moment, I feel separated from the ego. What is the ego? Is it still part of me, or is it separate?" he asked.

Bartholomew settled back. "An excellent question that has many different answers," he said. "I will simply give you one definition. Ego is a collection of thoughts that arise when memory brings past material into the moment. There is no continuous, single, ongoing ego. Yet, you all run your lives as if there were. The ego rises and falls, starts and stops, changing constantly, moment by moment. You think this ever-changing ego is in control of your life. That is a joke! You continually recreate your identity of 'me' because you want something you can call the 'real you.' You do this rather than stay in the spontaneous moment.

"Let me ask you this. Who is looking for the ego? Who is trying to destroy it? Who is hearing sound? Who is feeling? Who is thinking? To answer these questions, you must examine the content of the moment closely. When you do, you will find an ever-changing cluster of memories that appear and disappear like the bubbles in a pot of boiling water. What does not appear and disappear is the 'I' that is continuously present watching the bubbles. *It* remains the same. On close examination, it can be seen that the ego is not a consistent, *ongoing* reality. It is something that memory recreates *imperfectly*, over and over again. A memory is not even a replica of the original event. You recall something that happened yesterday, but it doesn't reflect the totality of the event at all. It is only a flat and imperfect recollection of some of those past images.

"When you are in the deep silence of the moment, you do not feel this separate 'me.' Thinking fades, and there it is—that no-thinking awareness. The identification as 'me' drops, just for a moment, then thought rises up again. You play this same game over and over.

"You can learn to be present with others in the moment while also allowing the silence to speak for you. The greatest love between people is shared when each is in the moment, with no memory of the past and no thoughts of the future. They see each other as they are *now*. There is no, 'You did that—bad,' or 'You did that—good.' One gift you can always give is to be with anyone in the stillness of the moment. Practice this enough, and suddenly you will see someone you have known for 40 years as though they were brand new. You will be struck dumb with amazement at how beautiful and how wonderful they are. They are not who you thought them to be. It is your faulty memory that re-creates them to *your* specifications and judgments. You create each other according to what *you* want to see, to what fits for *you*. Then you either like or dislike your creation."

He peered at us closely. "Is this too hard to understand?" he asked. Heads moved in denial, and he continued. "Whatever memory is present in the moment is there simply because you have chosen to bring it in to divert yourselves from what is really going on. When you realize this, the ego can no longer trick you into believing that those chosen memories are who you really are.

"You spend a lot of time thinking about past and future because you have been running away from the power of being in the present—not just now, but throughout your lives. You juggle many things at once, having fun or being miserable, but always being very busy. Occasionally your Deep Self slams you up against the wall, so you will stop and be quiet. One of my jobs is to shake you up a little and give you tools so you don't have to slam yourselves against that wall. I am asking you to stop *now*. All you have to do is learn to be still *inside* in the midst of all thought, all action, all emotion. Look at the Dalai Lama. He has one of the most incredible schedules you can imagine, and he is still at peace. I do not mean for you to stop what you are doing— just learn to be still in whatever it is."

Sharon's hand shot up. "I've been close to this experience of being slammed up against the wall. I'm always busy or afraid that if I stop, I'll lose my continuity, my sense of self," she said.

"Lovely one, just look at His Holiness, and you will see someone who lives in silence and hasn't lost anything. In fact, he has 'gained' his Self. It is not the Dalai Lama's job to worry about his full schedule or the demands of his life. His job is to be totally present to each one of the people before him. He is concerned with their spiritual awakening. Whatever his schedule, the job is constantly to serve. His very presence makes people question themselves. 'Am I being conscious? Where is my awareness? Am I clear? Am I my ego or the Self?' He has obligated himself to be the spiritual counselor for millions of people, and that's a very big job.

"Your external life will become more expansive and creative if you, too, will stay in the present moment. Do not worry; being in a body demands that your life has continuity. Trust me, beautiful ones. Your concept of continuity comes only from memory. You still think your steaming brains are what keep things going, and it isn't true. I will say it again. The most dynamic, alive, aware, mysterious power is moving through your life every moment. Its job is to be awake and aware in every aspect of your being. And it will do its job. Your little ego is very inconsequential when viewed from the position of all the incredible potential possibilities. Do you understand? Please, stop thinking yourselves into the next moment. Trust that if you stay in this moment, the next will be there for you to experience. Does it involve risk? Yes. Is it worth it? Yes!

"You are the laboratories of consciousness, in which an experiment in a new kind of coming of the Light is taking place. It is difficult because there are very few footprints to follow for this particular kind of awakening. It is awakening in the midst of an active life. I have told you that you are the outriders, and you have to keep going. Is it hard? Yes! Trust the process. Go back to the Buddha. He said you can awaken in seven lifetimes, seven weeks, seven hours, seven minutes, or you can do it now! Believe me, he knew what he was talking about."

The Convoluted Question of Karma

Justin turned and faced Bartholomew. "If the small self really does not exist and whatever I am I created and re-created, then in truth, whatever 'I' am has no karma. Whatever I am can move into and re-create a small self for whatever reason I choose. Maybe karma, duties, and future and past problems are habits. I can choose not to re-create any of it at any time, or I can do all of them. It's my choice. So if I want to have karma, that's my business." He crossed his arms and leaned back.

"Absolutely." Bartholomew laughed. "There is no such thing as karma, except what you bring into this moment as a memory of the last moment. Buddhism tells you clearly: There is no continuous self. The Dalai Lama has also said it. Look as hard as you want, and you will not find a continuous *self*. There is only change and impermanence. What *does* continue is the Self, the Ground of Your Being, God, the Light. You are and have always been the Light. You are and have always been the Deep Self, the Source, God, and Love. Everything else rises and falls and has nothing to do with anything except the joy of creating in an impermanent reality. You create to experience, so experience fully. That is why karma is such a joke. It, too, is *impermanent*. If you wish to create karma from past actions, you will say with absolute assurance that you can, in this moment, fully create whatever state you wish. Either way you are the creator of your 'selves' every moment.

"In one moment you can decide to drop your bad mood, open to love, and be in the present. And you know you can choose to drop your happiness and be ever-present in your grumblies. What you don't know, because you haven't paid attention, is how many other things you can create in the moment. As a partner in the dance of the Divine, you create from energy fields that are not usually available to your conscious mind. Sai Baba, for example, twirls his hand and out of thin air comes all this stuff.[26] It's not really hard to do if you know you can. *You* have those powers, but, even more important, you have the power to create a total awakening to the Clear Light in *this* moment. People like Sai Baba help because they break down ideas about the limitations of physical creation. You don't need to be Sai Baba; just be yourself."

Justin leaned forward again. "What strikes me is that we have always been free to create our realities, and we are doing this to ourselves. As much as we want to play at our creations of ourselves, it's *totally* our choice, and we are *totally* free agents in doing it," he said fiercely.

Bartholomew folded his arms, a slight smile on Mary-Margaret's face. "That's right," he agreed. "That is why it is so beneficial not to complain about your life. In the deepest sense, it is you who have created it. If you think you have a terrible life, it is a mature step in consciousness when you move away from the idea that something or someone else is responsible for whatever state you happen to be in at the moment. *You* are 100 percent responsible for your life because you created it 100 percent. If you complain, you are complaining to yourself. Claiming this truth is a powerful awakening."

"I don't think I can live up to any of it," wailed a voice from the back of the group.

"Lovely one, what if I told you there was nothing to live up to? What if I told you it's your mind that is making you miserable, causing you to not believe in your Self? What if I told you it is your thinking that is destroying your inner peace? What if I told you it is your thoughts that are confusing you?" He paused. "I am telling you *all* these things!" he said explosively. "It is your thoughts, your ideas, your expectations of yourself that are false! You have come here to experience every moment, fully and completely, without preferring one moment over the other. Would you rather be in the mountains walking with His Holiness or have a nice hot shower? How could you choose between those preferences?

"Please hear this," he said intensely. "Your minds create your misery. They create your sense of separation, your sense of failure, your sense of inadequacy, your sense of unworthiness, your guilt, your drivenness! I want

227 ॐ

you to overthrow the tyranny of the mind and drop into the moment. It is the only way out! The mind will endlessly confuse you. It is the mind's job to present choices. It is your awareness in the moment that brings you to unification. Look at a tree, your beloved, or an angry face—stay with whatever is present, and the overriding magnificence of the moment will be revealed. It is full of what unifies you. The mind diversifies, confuses, and separates. The silence unifies."

Justin looked over the top of his glasses and continued his discussion with Bartholomew. "I would like to get back to this thing about the small self," he said deliberately. "I, for whatever reason and whoever 'I' is, continue to re-create a small self. This is a choice I make, and I include re-creating karma in it. When it is recognized that this is being done freely, then I will probably start choosing something else. Yet, at the same time, I will feel the most incredible compassion for all those who freely, without knowing it, re-create in every moment the most painful identities for themselves."

Bartholomew looked around and winked. "He is on to something," he said with a smile. "Exactly," he agreed. "That *is* where compassion arises."

"So if we all have the transformational impulse to be here, the initiation is inevitable," declared Chai. "The process can even be trusted to take care of those who think they are not going to get initiated."

"Not only that, you don't even have to be at the initiation," observed Bartholomew. "The beliefs you have about space and time are what give you the idea that you do. When the Kalachakra is going on in the valley, it is possible to be receiving it in other places as well. You know, the Dalai Lama is not so puny a man that he can't send his energy up the mountain. He is doing this initiation for thousands of people, and each person leaves here filled with that energy. It is an amazing magnetic event, and it will be with you in a very personal way. You cannot be separate from this initiation.

"It is a seed transmission, and I would like to stop for a few moments and explain how that works. On an energy level, the Dalai Lama is dispersing endless numbers of empowered 'seeds.' Observed psychically, they are power-packed, luminescent spheres from which electromagnetic currents emanate. As the days progress, that magnetism grows. He transmits it out into this valley, where the earth itself acts as a conduit. You are filled with the seeds of electromagnetic, enlightened awareness, and each one of you will feel it differently. When you leave here, *you* will move out with an electromagnetic field of consciousness different from the one you arrived with. You will transmit the seeds without any attachment, without any appearance of ego, and, in most cases, without any knowledge of what you are doing. Thus you will spread the seed of an incredibly powerful awareness from the Clear Light of Consciousness. This is what I mean by a seed transmission."

"There seem to be a number of different deities, a number of different flavors to the seed transmission," Paul commented. "Are the differences everywhere?" he asked.

"Yes, they are," answered Bartholomew. "For example, it would be very unfair to have a deity that was so powerful that it would overwhelm someone who had fear about beginning a spiritual path. So 'lesser' deities are more accessible to those who are at what I would call the bottom of the pyramid. They are the sweet, benevolent ones. When you get further up, you run into the heavy 'stompers.' They are the ones who shake you up. They eternally question your perceptions of reality. Finally, with the highest awareness, you find out they are all filled with emptiness.

"The flavors of the deities differ in various cultures. Buddhism is present in a great part of the world, but Buddhist deities don't all look alike. Different forms fill different needs for different times, and for different world cycles. When the world needs it, an Avatar[27] appears. At this time, new images are coming into the Earth plane because the world needs them. Wonder-full times are coming! Actually, wonderful times are already here, but you may not believe that," he said wryly.

"It is hard to see the wonderful times when we see all the poverty and difficult living conditions of so many thousands of people," interjected Patricia.

"When you see someone in a difficult situation, try making a statement in your consciousness like this: 'I deeply honor your having chosen the situation you are now in. Go well with it.' And then, from the heart where the honor for all beings lies, it will become clear that they have chosen what was perfect for them at that time. You will actually know this, not think it. Just be willing to see the Truth of the situation."

"In using persons with hard lives as a mirror, is the pity you feel for them also pity for yourself?" asked Guy.

"It could be a reflection of your fear for yourself. 'If it can happen to them, it can happen to me.' There's also the difficulty of looking at someone in pain. It's so much easier to deflect, not to look. But in honoring their choice, you are also honoring yours. Remember, the psyche cannot differentiate between what you think about others and what you think about yourself. So, when you honor the intention and choices of those you think are in difficulty, you are also honoring yourself in a very direct way. It works because ultimately there is only One."

"What can we do to help our bodies get through these difficult circumstances?" Patricia asked.

"Many of you were brought up with rigid rules about your bodies. They are the 'do's and don'ts' of the physical. Out of the resulting confusion, you have distanced yourselves from your bodies. I do not think that any of you give them the love, care, and attention they deeply need. You rely on others to do it through massage, medical attention, approval, diets, sex, etc. These help, but are secondary. There are times when your body is really looking for *your* attention. You are the beloved. It wants the one thing it doesn't have, which is your loving and approving focus on it.

"I am going to suggest something I know will be difficult for those of you who have a problem with appreciating your body. I want you to take off all your clothes, stand in front of a full-length mirror, and look at your body. Praise it until it begins to soften and look beautiful to you. Do it day after day. You will begin to see the false view you have projected on what is reflected in that mirror. The reflection will fade, and you will see who is really there. You will begin to see an amazing beauty coming back to you, a beauty not only of the body but of Life itself. The sight of it will make you weep."

Deb raised her hand. "Is anger a way of escaping yourself?" she asked. "When I get caught up in feeling irritated and angry, I know I push that onto the outside world. Sometimes I don't know why I'm so irritated."

Bartholomew looked at her sympathetically. "Oftentimes, irritation arises from not liking what's happening in the moment. You don't like what you are experiencing or thinking, or you have an idea there is someplace better to be and some better person to be with. The body responds by wanting to get you out of there. You might fall into a bigger mess when you do, but at least you are moving.

"Irritation is only the tip of a deeper fear. I suggest you stop this mental or physical running, and find out what is really going on. It is your own ego being selective. Move toward the uncomfortable moment and embrace it. There is a statement that says, 'What you resist persists,' and it is true. So stop resisting. Stop thinking about what is happening, and experience it fully."

Jim spoke up. "I have an underlying issue about self-worth. It interferes with my life in lots of ways. Could you give me any suggestions about how to work with that?"

"When self-worth is an issue, it is because memory presents you with a conglomerate view of yourself that reflects inadequacy. It is brought into the moment by past conditioning. Anyone who feels a lack of self-worth and looks to the external world for a sense of worthiness is doomed to failure. You must begin to change that view with the only thing you have—yourself. Start an ongoing mantra of love and appreciation for your body, mind, and your abilities. Give yourself the praise and acceptance you hoped to find in the outside world. With *awareness*, give yourself what you are looking for elsewhere. When you wake up feeling dynamic, alive, and loving, the people around you act loving, dynamic, and alive toward you. Conversely, when you wake up with the grumblies, it's the grumblies that come back to you. Take responsibility for making those choices.

"Be very clear about what kinds of messages you want to give yourself. Be serious about learning to love yourself. Systematically feed your cells a deep, abiding appreciation. If you will but look, all of you have things you deeply appreciate about yourselves. Find them, and give them back to yourself as gifts, over and over again. The world will reflect exactly what you have now created, a belief in the deep integrity of your own being."

Bartholomew stretched and smiled. "Tomorrow is the culmination of the Kalachakra. There will also be a full moon around 8:30 in the evening. What better way to complete your time here together than to have a full moon meditation. So, I will see you tomorrow morning for the closing," he ended.

A Lazy Afternoon

I did not go to the Kalachakra that day. I wanted to be with the mountain, so I dragged a chair to my favorite place overlooking the valley and sat down, propping my feet against the wall. Settling deeper into the chair, I made myself comfortable, hooked my hands behind my head, and waited to see what would happen.

Fat clouds piled up to the northeast. They gathered at the mouth of the valley, frustrated in their attempts to enter by a lack of altitude. As a child I had always wanted to see them from above, and I experienced a combination of amazement and expectation as I watched the drama unfold beneath me. Lazy images came to mind. Cloud marshmallows. Cotton balls. Fat angel wings. They changed their shapes with amazing speed as they collided into each other. Bump, bump, bump. Up popped one, flinging itself over the edge of the barrier and into the valley, dragging three or four recalcitrant companions behind. The others instantly followed, surmounting the immovable obstacle, and, with the speed of an express train, they swept across the valley toward the exit on the far side.

Meanwhile, Mount Kailash sat facing me, 10,000 feet higher, watching the show with predictable aplomb. The wet roofs of Kalpa looked like blue-gray fish scales in the distance below. Sporadically, people would silently appear with their chairs to line up along the wall near my front-row seat. We all watched, fascinated by the lemming-like clouds that formed a milky stream, lapping at the banks of the mountain as they followed their leaders. A faithful segment bobbed and bowed cheerfully to the midsection of Kailash, familiar but ever respectful. The omnipresent mountain held herself aloft, her twin crowns sparkling in the sunlight, choosing instead to converse with the sky.

I glanced up as Mary-Margaret approached. She pulled up a chair and sat down. Her notebook was in her hand. She made herself comfortable and sat quietly awhile before she began to write.

> I have decided to stop wasting time in wandering around in my mind. I realized that we are halfway through our Kalpa experience, and there is a necessity to really let go. To me that means stop letting my mind float, even into "uplifting" thoughts. I see my tendency to look at, say, one of

the majestic eagles that drift in the air here, and then made up stories about how their flight symbolizes the journey home, leaving the earth plane behind, lifting it-self into the Light, blah, blah, blah. All of that may be "positive thinking," but when I land back here in the moment, what have I gained?

Nothing! I'm still here. And here, in this valley time is so present, so now, so tender-your-nose now, that it feels less interesting to leave the moment, even for a moment! I feel that His Holiness is helping

in this, because there is
no question where he is. When
there are short moments of
him relating to others outside of the prescribed
presentation, he seems
to be utterly new and
now with each changing
situation — patting a
child as a father, laughing
at a Westerner with full focus
and appreciation for what
we are going through, and
then the glance of
the Guru when one of
his disciples asks what
appears to be a serious
question.

They all say it —
now is the only moment.
I understand now, really

understand. And what
is really interesting to
me is that, here in
the midst of what
could be called many possibly
boring moments, they don't
bore me when I stay with
them — stay fully, totally
bored. What fun. Because
here in this moment, no
matter what else is present,
what makes this moment
wonder-full is that the
SELF is here — and that
is what makes each
moment wondrous. It's not
what is happening, it's
the SELF that brings
the interest, the intensity,
the wonder. It's all this
"running from the moment,"

into either past or future,
that takes away the
joy, the bliss. Because
the Bliss is the Presence
of the Self Itself for
Itself.

These silent days
are revealing this to me,
clear and direct. I am
no longer afraid of the
Silence, or of this moment.
Because the Self is there—
always fully there—
as Its Very SELF. What
joy. What peace.
What a relief!

❦ ✳ ❦

Chapter 20

Kalpa: Day Five—the Time for Indulging the Small Self Is Over

Bartholomew straightened up, took a deep breath, and cleared his throat. "Well, then, good morning, my friends. This is the last time we will all be together here in Kalpa; therefore, I have several things I would like to discuss before we part." He motioned to Joanna, Chai's sister. "To begin with, would you please share what His Holiness said about foreigners yesterday."

Joanna made her way forward and took the microphone. Unfolding a small piece of paper, she glanced at us and began to read. "After a brief explanation of Shambala and a historical account of the Kalachakra initiation as being especially suited to large groups of people wishing initiation into this Tantric way, His Holiness went on to say how many people had traveled from all over the world to be here—not as tourists, but to be part of this empowerment." She examined her notes closely before continuing. "He said that the powerful, positive energy of a group of foreigners is helpful to the initiation. The environment created is one of love, openness, and positive energy. It lays a strong imprint in the minds and hearts of those here, and it is also helpful for the peace of the world as a whole." She folded the piece of paper and handed the microphone back.

Mary-Margaret, Bartholomew, or both had tears in their eyes as he addressed the group. "If you doubted why you came, now you know. It is important to understand that the only thing that will save your planet is love. That means love of all people for all people. It means the undifferentiated love that sees through the differences and beholds only the similarities. Everything you have suffered, every fear you have endured, every hardship you have faced is insignificant to what you have achieved—not only for yourself but for each of your countries, for this land, and for the planet. The brotherand sisterhood of humankind is necessary to save your world!

"As you take what you have received here and move out from that place of receiving, you will come to know what is meant by the One Heart of God. There *is* only one Heart. It is your destiny to understand the tremendous importance of being able to open your heart at any time, in any place, to anyone, in any situation that is before you, and to be a living representation of that love, compassion, and wisdom. The extent to which you spend the rest of your lives strengthening that loving power within you through your actions, speech, and thought is the extent to which you will change from a relatively limited human consciousness to a vast, pulsating energy holding the greatest power of awareness. It *is* your potential. Whether you live into it or not is up to you."

He continued with quiet urgency. "You can choose to partake of your own unending capacity to become the vehicle that transmits and transmutes the essence of Love every moment of your life. You can partake of it with each other, with your environment, with your thoughts, *with yourself.* Which brings me to the point I would like to leave you with."

Leaning back, he looked at us closely. "I find that many of you act lovingly toward other people. You do all you can to see through your differences and perceive what is good, true, and beautiful in others. But you constantly sit in judgment of yourselves. You run a dreary liturgy of the things you should have done and should not have done in your life. I am asking that you give up this kind of self-recrimination, because there is no time left for such things. The time for that kind of self-indulgence is over, and it *is* a self-indulgence— meaning an indulgence of the small self. What has been taught here these past days has given you the experience of a vast expansion of consciousness.

"Every time you belittle yourself, you decrease your power, with the result that you have less to give. In the end, it is selfish to go around scolding yourself. I am asking you to stop being selfish in the ultimate sense. In the last analysis, the comings and goings, the risings and fallings of the small self are very insignificant in comparison to the magnificent potentiality of the Vast Self. Every moment you have the opportunity to gather chi. Doing so *will* transform your life. When you gather your power, not your arrogance, nor your feelings of self-importance, you come into the awareness of the power of the present, alive and clear, and it moves into all levels of your life.

"Here is where you can use the ego to help you. Use your will to set your intention. You want to move with clarity and right action. You want to move from the Heart of Consciousness, and not from some confused state of separation. You want this for yourself and for the world. Your awareness is clear. All you need to do is decide, from this moment on, that your only job is to gather the Love itself. You will not be disappointed. It is an amazing power of consciousness—a radiant, absolutely clear light of awareness that pulsates through every moment of creation. It is yours to access at any time, should you choose to focus on it.

"Yesterday we talked about the power of anger and how it can be used to transform your understanding. Oftentimes, however, you hurl the anger at yourself or someone else, and your language accurately reflects how you give it away. You say, in the vernacular, 'I lost it,' or 'I just blew it.' So you already know about giving away your power, although you may not recognize it. Everyone loses when you do this. It isn't that you should not be angry. Anger is part of the rise and fall of consciousness. Do not stop being angry, but please understand what to do with it and how to use its power. It is a dynamic sweep of energy that can bring great clarity to your inner life. Keep it with you, and use it to release, let go, and open to your inner space. Mix the anger with some humor, and take it as your own personal experience.

"Learn from all your emotions, not just the holy and pure ones. You will always experience a rising and falling of the entire spectrum of human awareness, and it is *all* magnificent. Your responsibility is to know that it all has to do with you and not with what goes on outside. If you continue to blame the world, to scold and manipulate it, you will continue to experience a loss of power. You must decide if you are going to stand tall, motivated by the heart and mind of consciousness to do something for the rest of the planet, or if you are going to move increasingly in the orbit of your own small self. Again, the choice is yours."

You Are Responsible for What You Create

Bartholomew continued more quietly. "If this teaching should end here today with this discussion, you have been given all you need. Please know, there is nothing new to add. You, as Awareness Itself, are responsible in the deepest sense for every moment of your life, so let us talk a bit about that. However else you look at it, having come to this part of the globe has placed a responsibility on you. You have sat in the presence of an enlightened one, and you have been deeply honored. You have been in a location that is as powerful as any point on Earth. You have survived many hardships and difficulties, and I would like to congratulate you for your humor, your courage, and your acceptance of all of it.

"It has not been easy, but we know that every time you acknowledge and release the anger, the depression, the sorrow, the fear, and the self-pity, your power increases. To the extent you have ceased to complain, openly accepting the moment and everything in it, is the extent to which you have empowered yourselves. But having come to this place at this time, you do carry a responsibility. The responsibility is now, as best you can, to act on what you have heard. Act on what you have seen. Act on what you now know. This planet is in turmoil. So please act now on what you know deep in your heart.

"Your very thoughts either help or hinder. As you leave here, you will feel yourself to be different. Pay attention to the changes that have taken place since the last time you hurled yourselves up and down the mountains in your bus. What is the difference? See if the fear has been replaced by strength. Claim it. Claim the victory of all you have done. Do not throw away what you have learned."

He looked down and laced his fingers together. "It has been a privilege to share this experience with two great countries, the United States and Australia. Australia, you know your star is rising. You are going to be one of the spiritually empowered nations, and we wish you all good luck; if things continue as they are going now, a new kind of awareness will arise, and Australia will be one of the centers for it. You have a magnificent country, beautifully endowed with a brand new, yet ancient, exciting energy to be transformed into anything you want. I am happy to have been with you, and if the gods are willing, we will meet again. As for the Americans, I imagine I will see most of you another time. Our paths do seem to cross and recross. The coming together of the energy of these two countries at a power point in a third country is an important motion of consciousness, and we are extremely grateful for it. Please remember, although nations may seem separate, there is but One heart." Bartholomew straightened up.

"Many of you think your life is insignificant, that you are just one small person in a vast world. I would like to tell you that that is not so. How much responsibility you accept for being a conscious, creative awareness reflects the degree to which you fulfill your destiny in the world. Your destiny is the same no matter who you are. It is *to be responsible for every moment of your life and to create for the world the very highest possible awareness you can bring to it.* That is your job; there is no other. Know it, and your life will change. The situations you find yourself in will no longer be so intensely personal. When you drop away from the personal and move to what I call the universal, you will see that your small problems are just that—small problems that rise and fall and keep changing their faces. Dissolve the problems of today by fully experiencing them. Yesterday is forgotten, and tomorrow has not yet arisen. Live from the center inside you, realizing that every moment you have the opportunity to build the power of consciousness for yourself and all sentient beings, indeed for the entire planet.

"It isn't just humanity that is going to end if this planet is destroyed. Many other life forms depend on you and have relatively little say in the way things are being played out. You create with great speed and great power. Other life forms create more slowly. You have a tremendous responsibility to the entire planet. It starts with you, and it ends with you, and if I sound too serious, I am sorry, but it is important. *You are important.*

"I don't care who you are, whether your life seems insignificant or grand. I don't care how much or how little money you have, if you are neurotic or exotic. But I do care about one overriding thing. Are you willing to pick up your responsibility as a co-creator of consciousness, or are you going to continue pretending that something else is creating it and you are powerless? It takes maturity to acknowledge yourselves as the co-creators of consciousness. You can continue to create an environment for yourselves that is full of self-pity and self-importance, moving within it in an insular fashion, taken up with your own small, petty problems. Or you can decide that whatever your situation, another choice still remains. Are you going to be alive, dynamic, creative, loving, kind, and helpful in the midst of it, or are you not?

"Be willing to be responsible for your thinking habits. Do not sit around in the incessant, repetitive patterns of the past, allowing yourself to think 95 percent of the thoughts today that you will think tomorrow and the next day and the next. How nauseating and how boring and of what use? When you become consciously aware of your thoughts, you can align yourselves with a deeper consciousness. You are participating in a vast, amazing creation. Your thoughts become vital, and you can take control of your creations instead of allowing them to be the haphazard occurrences they are now, derived mostly from your ego's polarities.

"As you move between the poles of desire and repulsion, be aware of what you are thinking. There is no time for private thoughts that pollute your life. It is time for open forgiveness, for open letting go, for abundant love and kindness. What you have already gone through to be here this day is far more difficult than what I am asking of you. Do you want to be a conscious being as badly as you wanted to get here? It takes that same strength of motivation.

"We know that you can do this, because we know your basic nature is total, complete love, compassion, and wisdom. We also know that when you cease to play your intimate little games, you will know it, too. At the heart of *everything* is the Light. It cannot be other, but you will not find it if you continue to let your past thoughts run your life. So, shut them up. Sit down in your life; and begin to hear, see, breathe, and be aware. Fulfill your destiny. Awaken to Life Itself. Your individual lives, I am sorry to say, are relatively unimportant. Your universal life is absolutely important. Are there any questions about this?" He leaned back as Lin spoke up.

"Could you explain what you meant by co-creators?" she asked.

"Many teachings come along that say that you alone are the creator. The ego takes hold of that and uses it as proof that the limited self is the creator. The ego does not know anything about the true creative process. When I call you a *co-creator,* you can become aware of something called 'you' and also that something vaster is mysteriously present. A co-creator is 'you' plus something 'else.'"

He looked at us with a smile. "We really use the word *co-creation* in order to trick you," he said. "In the end, when you truly see what is happening, you will find but one creative principle at work, and it could never be the limited ego. We use words to reach you, but words do not reflect the depths of these realities. So then we use images that may mislead you to point you toward the Truth," he laughed with delight.

"We have to trick you. Otherwise, the mind grabs the wrong end of ideas, such as 'you are the creator.' How could your ego create the incredible depth and complexity of the life you are living? Do you really feel that your little ego has created all this," he asked, waving at the mountains, "including the Dalai Lama and all the rest of it? Do you really think your small ego, which can't even get you out of a funk when you are in it, creates all this?" he asked incredulously. "The ego would like you to think it can, so we trick you into thinking of yourselves as co-creators. But in the depths of Truth, there is only one creative principle."

There Is No Continuous You

"Does that creative principle also create the ego?" interjected Sol.

"First, remember that there is *no* continuous ego," responded Bartholomew. "We have already talked about the fact that you do not have a linear, continuous self, so there is no continuous ego. What happens is this. You bring in a memory trace from a moment ago, an hour ago, yesterday, or any other time in the past. But it is just a trace of that event, not the event itself. If the ego were real, then every moment the ego had ever lived should be able to be re-created in the present moment." We looked at him blankly.

He looked back. "Let's say it another way, as it is a difficult point to understand. *You* say you are a continuous self, a 'me.' If your ego were a continuous, ongoing reality, you should be able, in this moment, to feel the entire impact of every experience you have ever had—even ones as far away as your birth. But is that true? Can you do this? Of course not. These events are constantly dissolving, no longer 'there.' So where is the continuity? Do you understand? If the ego is a real 'thing,' a real 'form,' you should be able to access this reality. If you were a continuous self, the entire continuous self should be present in this moment. But that is not happening. You bring to this moment other fragmented, selective moments from your past, and rarely do they reflect the true reality. You select exactly what you wish to, making changes and additions to suit yourself."

He looked from one of us to another. "Where do you experience 'yesterday'?" he asked. "In *this* moment. There is *only* this moment. Yesterday is not here until you create it here, today. You choose to bring in these fragments because it makes you feel you are a continuous person. I agree that you seem to have continuous bodies, but even that isn't so. Modern science now concludes that your cells are constantly dying and creating a new body, so ask yourselves whether you have a continuous body as well. You need to realize that what is truly real can never die." He stopped abruptly. "And I've confused you utterly," he said.

"No, no," came the scattered response.

Mary-Margaret's eyebrows shot up. "Are we getting there?" asked Bartholomew.

"Yes, yes," we replied, "don't stop."

"I know it's just not the way you want to think about it. You would prefer the safety of a continuous self," he conceded. "But please do give deep consideration to this. If you were a continuous ego, this moment would be overflowing with every pulsating thought, belief, idea, experience, memory, and awareness that ever happened to all of you since you popped out of whoever you popped out of. Trying to make your continuous self a reality is keeping you from experiencing what is really continuous."

He paused, focusing on us intently. "What is really continuous has *always* been present!" he continued passionately. "It is the 'I Am' of the 'I Am.' It is the source out of which all else flows. It is before the beginning and after the end, and it is the true nature of Consciousness. *It is awareness itself!* That is what is continuous and nothing else. Anything else you choose to bring into this moment you do to convince yourselves that you indeed exist as a continuous, ongoing, limited, observable human being.

"Stop being transfixed by this view of yourself. Drop the insistence on that view of yourselves as fragmentary little things, 'Oh my God. Do people love me? Am I too fat? Will I have enough money?' All around you, thundering through every cell of your body and every particle of consciousness, is the reality of what you are. You are short-changing yourselves, and you don't need to. You *can* stop this habit by doing any one of the things we have discussed. Drop out of the mind, and sit in the moment. Listen without trying to hear anything special. See without judging what you see. Breathe with relaxed awareness. Be willing to be in the moment, without judgmental picking and choosing, accepting and rejecting. Rest in the moment, totally open, totally full, totally present, and it happens! The awareness reveals itself. Do it now, or do it later, but you will do it!"

He stopped and continued quietly. "There is but one reality pulsating through everything, and the rest is illusory. You are not who you think you are. You are not a frightened, ephemeral, ever-changing, pulsating, rudderless fragment of consciousness. You are the vast, endless magnificence of total awareness, and it is your birthright to experience that in its fullness. It is my prayer for you each moment of your existence that you come to know it, fully and completely.

"We are back to asking you yet again to simply become aware of that familiar feeling you have come to call *yourself*, a feeling you have *misnamed* and called 'me.' In reality, that feeling of *familiarity*, that feeling that is ever-present in all stages from exhilaration to depression, love to hate, fear to joy, is *who you are.* You have misnamed the 'I' and called it 'me.' The one that comes and goes is the limited 'me.' The one that is always with you, that is present from the first moment of awakening from sleep to the deepest part of your dream state is the essence of 'I.'

"You are constantly feeling the essence of the 'I.' The feeling you have felt every moment of your existence is what you are seeking. It is that upon

which everything else is reflected. Now, even as you sit here, it is that awareness that is ever-constant. You see, you are seeking what you already are. It is
so obvious, so unchanged, so strong, and so familiar that you have missed it.
Please, don't miss it."

Bartholomew relaxed with a smile. "Well," he said, "having yelled at,
bullied, and badgered you, I would like to remind you of how much I love
you. Those of you who are going on to other exciting adventures, take me
with you if you choose. I would enjoy the journey. Those of you who are
heading back to Delhi, go with my love. I thank you all for a most extraordinary experience. You have come a long way on your journey home. Please
don't forget it. And I love you."

Mary-Margaret bowed her head, and we sat silently for several minutes.
Then people began to hug one another and make plans for leaving. Those of
us going on would stay an extra day in Kalpa to renew our permits and
arrange transportation for the rest of the trip. I was looking forward to a day
of rest. Most of us were physically depleted and some on the verge of illness.
At the moment, I had nothing to do and nowhere to go, so I crawled into my
tent and took a nap.

It was late afternoon when I joined Mary-Margaret for a last interview.

In the End Is the Beginning

We sat on the low stone wall. The slate roofs of Kalpa were beneath us,
submerged like pebbles under a river of rushing air, through which the clouds
streamed like foam down the valley. The sun was still warm, the air cool.
Mount Kailash, aloof as ever, stood wrapped in colossal secrets. The tour was
almost behind us. It was a time of endings and beginnings.

I popped a tape into the recorder, prepared to participate in Mary-
Margaret's impressions of India while the experience was still fresh. We
would have plenty of time later for analysis and reflection. Right now I wanted her immediate responses. I plugged in the lapel mike and held it between
us as we sipped our hot chai in silence.

"This trip . . ." I began.

". . . has been a *trip!*" she finished.

We both sighed. "How did we get here anyway?" I asked, looking at the
mountain.

Mary-Margaret cocked her head questioningly and looked at me side-ways. "I mean, I've heard how Chai got the tour together, but what made you pick India in the first place?"

"Well," she said, "I had been unable to find a tour for this summer that felt right. Lots of possibles but no real inner yes. When I was in Australia to do some workshops, Justin and I stayed with Chai and Russell. They showed us photographs of the Himalayas taken during a tour Chai had done in the past. They were amazing! Just seeing them made me decide. It started out as a normal tour of Northern India, which included seeing the Dalai Lama in Dharamsala. Later, when it was clear he was not going to be there but was going to be in a remote mountain village in the Himalayas, we decided to try for the full adventure. It also seemed like a very exciting time to see the Dalai Lama in his natural surroundings so near to Tibet. If we were closer to the border, it seemed to me we would get more of the essence of the people and of his amazing power with the Kalachakra initiation, so here we are."

"So here we are," I echoed. "And you are finally headed back to the States after being away almost two months. How does it feel?" I asked, curious.

Mary-Margaret paused before she answered. "I have been thinking a lot about all the trips we have taken with Bartholomew these last nine years, because we are coming to the end of them soon. I had a strong feeling just last night that the purpose of our traveling all over the world is to do what we can to increase the brotherhood and sisterhood of humankind. I hoped other countries would see Americans at our best, each of us excited, open to, and intrigued by their different cultures, eager to see how other people live, think, and view their world. It may sound 'corny,' but I felt that we are carriers of the Light, as they are, and that we could share our Light with theirs. It seems to me that we have the opportunity to know we are all the same underneath our different points of view, cultures, and belief structures. Here in Kalpa, as we exchange Namaste,[28] smiles, and warm eye contact, it feels like we are coming closer to the goal. It feels good to see the same children and mothers every day. The smiles seem to get wider the longer we are here.

"I also jumped at the chance to come here because of that mountain over there," she said, gesturing fondly at Kailash. "Here we are at the foot of Shiva's home, 16,500 feet straight up. It makes me lightheaded just to look at it!" she exclaimed. "It's a spiritual point of power, without doubt. Mount Kailash is considered by some to be the most important power point in the entire Himalayan range, and here we are. Amazing! I feel that it's both a privilege and a responsibility, and I think the responsibility is where we all need to focus. We have the responsibility to take in all we have been taught by the Dalai Lama, Bartholomew, each other, and these ancient mountains, and then go out into our own lives and *do it!* I sound like a preacher pounding a pulpit, but you get what I mean, don't you?" I nodded.

"The experience of being here, for me, is about seeing kindness, peace, love, compassion, humor, understanding, and just plain humanness!" She went on with some excitement. "And increasing similarities and empowering the similarities, trying to humorously override the dissimilarities, and to make room in our hearts and our minds for everyone and everything and all those interesting differences." She paused for breath and continued quietly. "To find a place in us that sees it all as One—one great, magnificent creation—and then to just go out and live our part of that wholeness fully and rambunctiously.

"You know, I feel so strongly that it was an incredible honor to have been granted a private session with His Holiness. It meant so much to be able to give him the prayer stick you and Carolyn brought, as a symbol of the unity of the ancient way of 'our' mountainous world in Taos with the ancient way of 'their' mountain world here. I just pray that we all go back and shed more light in the world in whatever way we can."

We went back to sipping chai as I thought this over. "It seems to me this whole trip has been a process leading to the experiences you are describing," I said. "And because of the discomforts, the landslides, the fear of the narrow mountain roads, the sickness, and all the things we've been through with each other, this group of Americans and Australians has had the opportunity to practice exactly what you are talking about. I wonder if we have been successful," I mused.

"Oh, yes. I don't think there's any question of that. I think, if anything, we go back a lot more fearless, grateful, and aware of our own ego selves. Whatever the condition of the road home, the inner condition of all of us will be much different from when we started. I think many of us have come upon our fears of survival, like physical survival on the bus, especially the incredibly decrepit one we traveled on. Having faced that, I don't feel we will ever be as afraid of similar things again on the physical plane—ever. After all, we did live through it!" We laughed.

"I think we go back a stronger, certainly more grateful, group. I think many of us have felt a great deal of gratitude. I have heard people say again and again, 'My God, I am thankful for the simplest things I have always taken for granted, like food, water, safety, shelter—and insect repellent.' We have been tremendously honored by the people here who may not have enough of these simple things, yet seem content. As we walk around the villages, we see the laughter on their faces and must realize that there are all kinds of ways of being happy in the world. Some magnificently alive, joyful, empowered people are walking around this very cold and lofty, isolated place. They seem to use what we think of as hardships to empower themselves. They keep the sun in their faces, the flush in their cheeks, and the smile in their eyes through it all. It doesn't take a TV antenna or a flush toilet or radiant heat to make them happy. I guess it takes an inner willingness to blend with the world as it is being presented, and I feel tremendously honored that we have interfaced with it all. I only hope I can remember it when I get home."

"Yes," I agreed. "Even though we don't speak the same language, everyone has been incredibly kind and generous. By our standards these people have very little themselves, yet they have given us so much. It's a new feeling to be grateful for plywood-lined cots, a two-inch-thick mattress, and a few thin blankets to sleep under."

Mary-Margaret nodded. "This experience has shown all of us how little we need," she said. "The things that dictated whether I enjoyed the day had nothing to do with the weather, which could literally change every five minutes. It was cold and damp or wet and hot and everything in between, including windy. It has been very clear to me that none of this makes a real difference. Most of us would now agree that it's something inside us that dictates whether the day will be joyful, or full of griping and self-pity." She paused.

"It seems to me that, on the inner planes, we have all come a long way as far as understanding ourselves. Certainly, I have come to see my own weaknesses very clearly. And it's all to the good, because it's only through knowing myself that I can then choose to be something different from what I have been in the past. It feels to me that everyone here, to one extent or another, has had to face themselves, whether they liked it or not. Must be something in this rarefied air." She grinned.

"Yes." I laughed. "And we certainly have had plenty of opportunities to do that. The bathrooms alone have been enough to bring out the best and worst in us."

Mary-Margaret tossed her head and chuckled. "At least we never have to wait in line to take a shower," she said.

"No, we don't," I responded. "But we might have to wait in line for the bucket another person is using to flush the toilet with."

"You know, I'm getting used to those toilets built into the floor, and they are a lot better than having to stumble around the great outdoors in the middle of the night. But we do have bugs in the bathroom as well as in our sleeping bags," she said.

"And spiders that go bite in the night," I replied, enthusiastically extending the list of hardships that had been met and conquered.

"Absolutely," she replied, becoming serious again. "On this tour, we have no idea what the next moment will bring. In Hawaii, where I was raised, we have scorpions and centipedes, and I have tremendous respect for them. It's not that they will kill you, but they can cause great agony. Overcoming the fear of walking into the 'bathroom' and squatting on one in the dark has dropped away, and I can simply be totally aware of the cold, the smells, and the dark. For me, it's just the desire to be here now! Thank you, Ram Dass!

"This land is vast yet feels somehow lonely to me. You have to meet it on its own terms. I find these mountains very masculine, and at first they were frightening. In Peru, the Andes were so feminine and so nurturing that I felt it was very much 'my place,' a place for a woman. There, women were out front and empowered. Here, I see the opposite. You rarely see the women, except near their homes or at the initiation. It's a man's world, and the mountains reflect it, so I've had to come to grips with that empowering masculine energy, which I find everywhere here. For me it brings up fear. I guess that's why it's Shiva's playground. He allows His consort to play with Him, but it's still His home."

Mary-Margaret paused, gazing at the immense mountains in front of us. "All this has clarified my own path since I have been here. Whatever wisdom comes is fine, but what I want is to have compassion for all of it. I want to be able to look at each and every one I see with an equal vision of compassion and love, so I don't feel a preference for one person over another. The Dalai Lama represents my hopes for myself in his tremendously equal-hearted handling of everyone. You see it so clearly as you watch him move through the ceremonies. He laughs, and, at the same time, he has tremendous dignity. I think His Holiness is a wonderful inspiration. So my prayer is for that kind of universal compassion from me and from you, and up here, right now, I feel it's possible—if we stay aware."

The sun had dropped lower in the sky, backlighting Kailash and sending rays of gold-washed light shooting from Shiva's home. "Except for one day, you have been to all of the Kalachakra, haven't you?" I asked as I watched the changing light.

"Yes," she said.

"What was your personal experience of it?"

Mary-Margaret wrapped her Tibetan wool vest more closely around her. "Well, I loved the teaching," she began, "but I can't really understand all of it—it's not in my way of understanding. The Dalai Lama has to transmit information that will take root in the uneducated farmers as well as in the mind of a Sanskrit scholar. He has to bridge those differences in comprehension and come up with a teaching that is meaningful for both, seemingly different, awarenesses. Then he added all of us Westerners for whom he must find a way to reach, inspire, and transform. Quite a job!" She smiled.

We paused, soaking up the view. "Each day we heard many pearls of wisdom, and my gratitude goes out to Bartholomew, who gathered the pearls and presented them to us as gifts of similarities, instead of points of difference. Bartholomew used all the teachings to strengthen our own excitement and understanding of life. I feel it pushed us to the limit to be there. The site was hot, crowded, and intense. Our job was to sit there in a state of as deep a contemplation as possible, listen to the four translations, be big enough to allow the body to experience the heat, the wind, the cold, the discomfort, and yet keep the Being centered and the awareness firm in the moment, hour after hour."

"That was a very tall order," I commented.

"For me, I had only one way out, and that was to keep feeling the moment. We were crammed into a space that couldn't possibly hold us, but it did, and it was a monumental act of concentration to stay there and allow the present moment to be fully felt, instead of trying to somehow move it out of one's awareness, as in fantasy. I find it a very similar practice to what we do in the sweat lodge at home in Taos. Success depends on the ability to stay open and aware in the heat, in the dust, in the wind, or in the cold. Here, just when the teaching was about to get clear, someone started talking next to you, and you couldn't hear it. Then you had to deal with your response. Do you yell at them to shut up? It's been amazing."

A seven-cloud collision took place in the sky above us. "The combination of Bartholomew, His Holiness, and this setting has certainly been powerful. Together they generate an incredible amount of intensity," I commented, eyeing the clouds apprehensively. Mary-Margaret's response quickly brought me back to our conversation.

"I feel so strongly," she said, "that from now on, Bartholomew's teaching is going to intensify. I must say, I have no idea when he is going to end, and

I don't think we should hold May of 1995 as a firm date.[29] I have a sense of the growing urgency of the teachings. I feel that the power and simplicity are both increasing. The single-pointed message is there, and I think we must look on our time together here as his most important farewell advice to us. I don't feel that the urgency or the intensity will decrease when we return to our 'ordinary' lives. I don't think we have to come to these places to get the power for transformation. This transformation can be done anywhere. Wherever we are, we could call it the transformation of the Vastness.

"I watched in amazement as Bartholomew united two somewhat disparate groups," I remarked. "The Australians seem strongly connected to the Buddhist teachings, and the Americans, who, aside from yourself, have very little knowledge of Buddhism, must have often wondered what we were doing here. At the beginning of the trip, it looked as though we were starting to polarize. Bartholomew constructed some beautiful bridges of understanding between 'his' teachings and the structure of Buddhism as presented by the Dalai Lama."

Mary-Margaret shifted her weight on the stone wall as the first few drops of rain fell. "Well," she began, "to me, Bartholomew has always manifested the incredible ability to uncover the similarities among people, whether they be lovers who came to him in conflict, people with differences in religious beliefs, or conflicts between different ways of seeing. These are intense times we live in; we've got to get it. Bartholomew keeps pointing out that the heart is a place where we do join. I think it's because of Bartholomew's incredible love that we are able to be bound together. I think that, without his love, many things on this trip would not have come about, and the differences could have deeply separated us."

The rain came down harder. We reached for our umbrellas, snapped them open, and persevered.

Mary-Margaret turned to me and said, "It's an astonishing principle of what could be called 'love in action.' It's one of the greatest teachings I know, and I would have been stunned if Bartholomew hadn't been able to pull it together for us. I think his power is enormous. He has a way of binding us into the one hum of life instead of the ho-hum of separation. To me, that's God in action. And I marvel at it." She rested her umbrella on her shoulder.

"More and more, the feeling is growing in me what an incredible honor his partnership with all of us has been. It is an almost overwhelming privilege that we have had a hand in the Bartholomew work, and if it ended today and we never heard another word, I would never stop being grateful. I feel we have been given everything we need. It's up to us. Bartholomew has said it all. I sense the teaching is complete in many ways, and there is just the intensifying of it now, which is our personal job and our personal commitment. This experiment could end anytime."

I took a deep breath. "I think, in the end, what you are saying is that Bartholomew and the Dalai Lama are doing exactly the same thing. They bring together and disseminate spiritual information and love to people at all levels."

"Yes," she answered. "The love, the peace, and the insistence that the only separation is in the mind are shared by both. The Dalai Lama was very clear in his early presentation that all religions need to be honored deeply. It was a tremendous opening statement that set the tone for our entire time together, and yes, I find much harmony between these two beautiful teachings," she concluded.

"Well, the sun is going down, the rain is falling, dinner is ready, and we go our seemingly separate ways tomorrow," I observed. "I'm glad it's all in the mind."

Mary-Margaret looked at me. "Yes, and I'll see you again in Taos," she said with an enigmatic smile.

Full Moon Celebration

We met on the veranda that last night. The rain had stopped. Twilight turned to dusk, then to darkness. The setting sun was replaced by a distant glow behind the mountains. Stars appeared, then disappeared, as the radiance grew stronger. Paul and Carolyn stood by the wall, waiting silently behind their cameras. We sat quietly in rows facing Kailash, in that transitory moment between sunset and moonrise. Sol squeezed soft chords of music from his harmonium, humming to himself.

Then, suddenly, the glowing crescent of the rising moon emerged, throwing the mountain into sharp relief, and kindling a fire in the belly of a few loitering clouds. The moon rose as it had for millennia, unaware of its beauty. Pale rays fled from its face like liquid flung from a woman's hair. The goddess was reborn again, dazzling, full, powerful, and serene.

The music grew louder as Sol began chanting praises to the One. His voice was soon joined by others, and the power of their singing raised the hairs on the nape of my neck. I was struck dumb by the sublime beauty of the moment, as the moon ducked behind a cloud and rolled up into the sky.

It was late when Mary-Margaret pulled her bag into the bathroom for the last time. She made herself comfortable, took up her pen, and recorded her impressions of our final day at the Kalachakra.

> Today, the weather changes its face every few moments, which is a teaching in itself. You just let go, fully present with whatever presents itself. It is so easy to do that here. But the fear comes up that it will not be this easy when we return to our "other lives." The fear comes up that when life speeds up, this knowing will fall away. Having really heard the sound of silence, I yearn to stay with its fullness.

Suddenly I am aware that I have begun to create a false seperation between Silence, myself, and the moment. And then I remember the very basies of the Bartholomew teaching — "There is no seperation in Awareness. None at all. There is but One — The One. Any idea that there has been or could be such a thing comes from the mind, and is an illusion." So, no place to go, nothing to do, nothing to find, nothing to lose.

Tonite the chanting seemed particularly exquisite. His Holiness planned the end of the initiation to coincide with the full of the moon, and there we sat, chanting it up into the waiting clouds and dark sky.

We close a chapter in our lives tomorrow as some of us return home, and others journey on. A part of me feels sad that I won't be going on with the intrepid wanderers, yet so much more of me feels fully complete. What gratitude — what awe —

what peace. all now,
right here. I'm Home.

✳

Chapter 21

A Parting of the Ways

It was a subdued group that gathered on the veranda for a final morning round of muffins, jam, oatmeal, and hot chai. We murmured trivialities to each other, the way people do who are parting after sharing deep experiences and don't quite know what to say. Those staying behind helped carry luggage down the steep path and check to make sure nothing was left behind. Mary-Margaret gave her jacket to Neima and her Taos ball cap to one of the Tibetan women. Cameras clicked in a final flurry of picture-taking as the vans were loaded.

I felt sad at this parting, unable to believe we were now going off in two different directions. Six of us and the Australians would head north to the Rotung Pass and Manali, while the remaining Americans would go back to Delhi and home. I could still hear Bartholomew saying to take him with us, and I fervently hoped he could be in two places at the same time.

Finally, the last bag had been stowed, and the last person tucked into a van. We went from one to the other, hugging farewell through the open windows. The drivers started their engines and left in a cloud of dust, jockeying for positions on the one-lane road back to Shimla. We stood with our arms around each other for comfort, as the dust settled and the last van disappeared. Then we made our way down to Peo to renew our travel permits and arrange for our own transportation. It wasn't until I returned to Taos that I got to read Mary-Margaret's description of their journey back to Delhi.

We reached Shimla in
the dark hours, utterly
exhausted and yet grate-
ful that we were all
alive. Some moments we
had doubted we would make
it at all. Tires blown
out, no headlights to see
through the pea-soup fog
in the black night, vans
violently breaking down, and
piles of landslide debris
all along the return route.
It didn't seem like the
same road we travelled on
to Kalpa just days ago.
Rubble everywhere, trees down,
boulders by the side of the
road. The summer storms
have caused incredible land-

slides these last few days.

I can remember the events of today so very clearly. This morning, after goodbyes that were difficult for me, we started down the valley on our return to Delhi. We left early, so as to avoid having to drive at night on these "no-road roads." All of a sudden our van stopped. We got out and looked down the road, and what do we see? Another landslide twice as large as the one we traversed traveling into Kalpa. I stood there, trying to think. It took them three days to clear the last one, and this one was so much larger! We have planes to catch—what can we do?

George and I walked closer and stood examining the mess. Suddenly he said, "Isn't that the monk who showed us into the gompa the other day?" And there he was, this figure in a maroon robe, leaping from one part of the land-slide to another. We waited as he came closer, and I held my breath and made a fast decision. I didn't have any idea what the rules were for monks when it came to talking to distraught women, but I knew I had to try.

I identified myself and the group, reminding him of our visit in the gompa. I described our need to be in Delhi for our flight to the United States, and voiced my concern that it would take too many days for them to clear the road. What did he advise? Should we try to backtrack and take the long way around the mountain? He looked at me with his beautiful Tibetan smile and softly said, "His Holiness will be coming through here this afternoon at three o'clock." He smiled again, bowed, and left.

That was that. If His Holiness was going through, we would get through, because our cars were in front of the line.

I told the group, and it was amazing how full of peace and acceptance they were, considering what we would have to face if I had made the wrong decision. If anyone doubted, they didn't tell me. All I heard was laughter, jokes, camaraderie. Whatever was before us was "it." And, certainly, the landslide was a huge "it." But how would the new manage to get all those boulders off the road in such a short time? Easy. They had a bull-dozer brought in from one side and another from the other side, and simply pushed all the boulders over the side of the road, letting them tumble down into the valley below. It took longer for the bull-dozers to reach the site than it did for them to push them off!

I asked our Indian guide why they brought in the machinery for this slide, when they had not done so for the last one. His answer was, "India would lose face if the Dalai Lama and the Tibetans were not able to get through today. It would be an embarrassment to our fine country." Well, good enough. I'd take any reason, just as long as we got off this mountain.

Finally, they signaled that it was time to drive over the newly-cleared path. Not a road, not by a long shot! Just a "sort of a pathway." A bus was the first to try it, and we watched as it lurched from side to side at precarious

angles. They made it!
Everybody yelled. We started
across. We all made
it. What an incredible
relief!

Behind us we saw
the cars in His Holiness'
entourage. They flew
over it. They were powerful
cars and soon swept past
us on their way to
Shimla, Tibetan flags
flying from their radio
antennas. They wave,
we wave.

Suddenly a noise
reached us from the
valley behind us. It
sounded like falling
mountains. I turned

and saw the landslide cover the road. We drove on with a sense of wonder. We had been blessed yet again. But by Who or What? No matter — gratitude was everything.

Seven days later, the six remaining Americans were standing outside a hotel in Delhi waiting for transportation to the airport. Darcy disappeared and returned with a grin, waving a newspaper.

"Look!" she exclaimed, handing me an article she had torn out. "We were wondering if Mary-Margaret and the others made it back in time to catch their flight last week. Look at this!"

Carolyn read the article over my shoulder. "They had another landslide but made it back with a day to spare," she said with satisfaction.

I glanced down at the small piece of paper she had given me, and smiled at the perfection of it all.

tered a huge loss of Rs. 101 crores last year
its accumulated losses are about Rs. 700 crores

Highway reopened

SHIMLA, Aug. 23.

The Hindustan-Tibet highway, which had remained closed for the last six days, has now been thrown open and buses are plying to Kinnaru and beyond. — UNI

Endnotes

1. Edited by David Godman, *The Teachings of Sri Ramana Maharshi* (London: Arkana Books, 1985), 20. (For those of you interested in Ramana's teachings, I highly recommend this translation.)

2. Mary-Margaret Moore has been "channeling" the energy Bartholomew for 17 years. She describes the process in the introduction to *I Come as a Brother:* "I begin by sitting quietly, calming myself through breathing. Next, I set my intention for the highest outcome possible. Then I wait, relaxing into the moment, eyes closed, yet alert. In a few seconds, the power begins to build around and in my body. I seem to become more alive, alert, and aware. Tingling sensations enter through the top of my head, travel down the neck and shoulders, and lodge in my chest area. The space around me becomes silently alive. When that feeling has grown to a certain intensity, I 'know' we are ready to begin."

3. Kalachakra initiation—A four- to six-day transmission that permits Tibetans to practice the highest Tantric yoga.

4. Dalai Lama—Literally meaning "Ocean of Wisdom," the Dalai Lama is the spiritual and political ruler in exile of the Tibetan people.

5. Dhargyey, Geshe Ngawang, "An Introduction to the Kalachakra Initiation," in *Kalachakra Initiation* (Madison, WI: Deer Park, 1981), iii, v.

6. Kitaro—A New Age composer. "Ten Years," © 1988, Amuse American, Inc., Geffen Records.

7. Nara—Japan's oldest former capital.

8. Niro Markoff Asistent, *New Age* magazine, September/October 1991, pp. 38–41, 109–118.

9. Vista Grande School—A private school that Justin and Mary-Margaret Moore started in the mountains of northern New Mexico.

10. Goethe—A German poet, author, and mystic from the 18th/19th-century European Enlightenment period.

11. Shiva—A very ancient Hindu deity and destroyer of illusion.

12. *"I Come As a Brother"* was published in Japanese by Mahoroba Art, 1992, Yuko Takaki, publisher.

13. Gagaku—Literally meaning "elegant music."

14. Dharamsala—A hill station in the Himalayas of Northern India. In 1959, Prime Minister Nehru personally selected Dharamsala to be the Dalai Lama's permanent home in exile.

15. For those of you too young to remember, Tyrone Power, Clark Gable, Abbott & Costello, and Jean Harlow were all major stars in Hollywood. Their movies spanned the decades between the 1930s and the 1960s.

16. Mary-Margaret and Justin had conducted a series of workshops in Australia prior to joining us in Japan. Most Australian tour members had been to these workshops.

17. Prana—The word for "life force" from the Hindu tradition.

18. Nechung—The Nechung Oracle is held by the Tibetans to be "the spirit of the Chief of Demons from pre-Buddhist Tibet entering the monk medium. Nechung became Chief State Oracle during the Great Fifth Dalai Lama's reign. Since then, he has been consulted for all major political decision-making." The Oracles were bound to become protectors of the Buddha Dharma in the eighth century by Guru Padmasambhava. *Tibet in Exile,* text by Jane Perkins (San Francisco: Chronicle Books, 1991), 78.

19. Sutras—The teachings of the Buddha.

20. Chai—A strong, hot Tibetan tea laced with evaporated milk and spices.

21. Gompa—A Buddhist place of workshop.

22. Bodhisattva—"One who has developed such a high level of wisdom, love, and compassion that, having attained enlightenment, he elects to return to the cycle of rebirth to help other beings reach enlightenment, too." *Tibet in Exile,* Jane Perkins, 13.

23. Tantra—The later commentaries on the sutras by disciples and scholars.

24. Thanka—Sacred paintings of Buddhist deities, usually taking the form of a scroll.

25. Prayer stick—Incorporating feathers sacred to North American Indians with other symbolic objects; a stick used in ceremonial gatherings for prayer.

26. Vabuti—The ashes that Sai Baba generates out of the air with sacred hand movements.

27. Avatar—An Awakened One on the Earth plane in body form.

28. Namaste—A Hindu greeting meaning "The God in me bows to the God in you."

29. Bartholomew was scheduled to end his public work with Mary-Margaret by May of 1995.

Books by Bartholomew

"I Come As a Brother": _A Remembrance of Illusions_

As a part of the vast, amazing Source, Bartholomew comes as a brother, teacher, and friend. Fourteen transcribed meetings deal with our relationship to ourselves, each other, and the Divine. From sexuality to St. Francis, Bartholomew's wisdom, compassion, and humor point us toward a more expanded awareness.

From the Heart of a Gentle Brother

Bartholomew brings meaningful perspective to questions about relationships, money, sexuality, drugs, and AIDS. Valuable insights are offered into the world of Devas, symbols, myths, and allies. Individual and group exercises are included to help us open to the Light that surrounds us.

Reflections of an Elder Brother: _Awakening from the Dream_

Anyone seeking to reawaken their experience of Oneness will find guidance in Bartholomew's basic message. It is his contention that we only need awaken to who we really are to find that which we seek. He reveals the illusions of self-imposed limitations and reminds us constantly that we have never been separate from the Source.

Planetary Brother

Bartholomew explores the transformative opportunities inherent in personal and global conflict. He reminds us to hold a vision of harmony, and offers steps we can take to help ourselves and our planet move toward greater peace, love, and understanding. The book to read for all who are longing to increase the peace in their hearts and peace on the planet.

Journeys with a Brother: *Japan to India*

A group of ordinary people find extraordinary insights with the help of Bartholomew. On a trip that takes them from the temples of Japan to the heights of the Himalayas, they travel together to experience a sacred Initiation given by the 14th Dalai Lama. It is the story of the Self accompanying Itself, delighting in all aspects of Its journey.

Ordering information may be found at the front of this book.

❊ ❊

About
Mary-Margaret Moore

Mary-Margaret Moore spent her first 18 years growing up in Hawaii and the next 5 obtaining two degrees from Stanford University in California. She is married and has four children. She has been a seeker of clear awareness for many years, gaining clarity from the study of the Christian saints, Zen, the Sufis, Advaita, and most of all, the teachings of Ramana Maharshi.

Notes

Notes

✳ ✳

We hope you enjoyed this Hay House book.
If you would like to receive a free catalog featuring additional
Hay House books and products, or if you would like information about the
Hay Foundation, please contact:

Hay House, Inc.
P.O. Box 5100
Carlsbad, CA 92018-5100

(760) 431-7695 or **(800) 654-5126**
(760) 431-6948 (fax) or **(800) 650-5115 (fax)**

Please visit the Hay House Website at: **www.hayhouse.com**

✳ ✳